編者的話

　　「指定科目考試」是進入大學的主要管道，各大學會依照科系的需求，指定三到六科的成績，作為招生入學的標準，因此「指考」每一年度的考題，對考生而言都非常重要，都具有參考及練習的價值。

　　為了提供同學珍貴的資料，我們特別蒐集了 102 年度指考各科試題，做成「**102 年指定科目考試各科試題詳解**」，書後並附有大考中心所公佈的各科選擇題參考答案，及各科成績一覽表，同學在做完題目之後，不妨參考那些統計表，就可以知道有哪些科目需要加強。

　　這本書的完成，要感謝各科老師協助解題：

英文 / 謝靜芳老師・蔡琇瑩老師・李冠勳老師
　　　葉哲榮老師・包容任老師・廖奕涵老師
　　　劉　毅老師
　　　美籍老師 Laura E. Stewart
　　　美籍老師 Christian A. Brieske

數學 / 高　鳴老師　　　歷史 / 李　曄老師
地理 / 王念平老師　　　公民與社會 / 李　易老師
物理 / 林清華老師　　　化學 / 邱炳華老師
生物 / 游　夏老師　　　國文 / 李雅清老師

　　另外，也要感謝白雪嬌小姐設計封面，黃淑貞小姐、蘇淑玲小姐負責打字及排版，李冠勳老師協助校稿。本書編校製作過程嚴謹，但仍恐有缺失之處，尚祈各界先進不吝指正。

劉　毅

目　錄

102 年大學入學指定科目考試試題
英文考科

第壹部分：選擇題 (占 72 分)

一、詞彙 (占 10 分)

說明： 第 1 題至第 10 題，每題 4 個選項，其中只有一個是正確或最適當的選項，請畫記在答案卡之「選擇題答案區」。各題答對者，得 1 分；答錯、未作答或畫記多於一個選項者，該題以零分計算。

1. Industrial waste must be carefully handled, or it will _____ the public water supply.
   (A) contaminate　(B) facilitate　(C) legitimate　(D) manipulate

2. John's vision was direct, concrete and simple and he recorded _____ the incidents of everyday life.
   (A) universally　(B) scarcely　(C) passively　(D) faithfully

3. The government cannot find a good reason to _____ its high expenses on weapons, especially when the number of people living in poverty is so high.
   (A) abolish　(B) escort　(C) justify　(D) mingle

4. The writing teacher has found that reading fantasies such as J. K. Rowling's *Harry Potter* may inspire her students to think and write with _____.
   (A) creativity　(B) generosity　(C) superstition　(D) foundation

5. Since several child _____ cases were reported on the TV news, the public has become more aware of the issue of domestic violence.
   (A) blunder　(B) abuse　(C) essence　(D) defect

6. Helen's doctor suggested that she undergo a heart surgery. But she decided to ask for a second _____ from another doctor.
   (A) purpose　(B) statement　(C) opinion　(D) excuse

7. All candidates selected after _____ screening will be further invited
   to an interview, after which the final admission decision will be made.
   (A) preliminary   (B) affectionate   (C) controversial (D) excessive

8. To prevent terrorist attacks, the security guards at the airport check
   all luggage carefully to see if there are any _____ items or other
   dangerous objects.
   (A) dynamic   (B) identical   (C) permanent   (D) explosive

9. In the desert, a huge mall with art galleries, theaters, and museums
   will be constructed to _____ visitors from the heat outside.
   (A) convert   (B) defend   (C) shelter   (D) vacuum

10. Judge Harris always has good points to make. Her arguments are
    very _____ as they are based on logic and sound reasoning.
    (A) emphatic   (B) indifferent   (C) dominant   (D) persuasive

二、綜合測驗（占 10 分）

說明： 第 11 題至第 20 題，每題一個空格，請依文意選出最適當的一個選項，
　　　　請畫記在答案卡之「選擇題答案區」。各題答對者，得 1 分；答錯、未
　　　　作答或畫記多於一個選項者，該題以零分計算。

第 11 至 15 題為題組

　　The undersea world isn't as quiet as we thought, according to a New
Zealand researcher. Fish can "talk" to each other and make a range of
　　11　　by vibrating their swim bladder, an internal gas-filled organ
used as a resonating chamber to produce or receive sound.

　　Fish are believed to speak to each other for a number of reasons,
such as to attract mates, scare off predators, or give directions to other
fish. Damselfish, for example, have been found to make sounds to scare
off　　12　　fish and even divers. Another discovery about fish sounds
is that not all fish are　　13　　"talkative." Some species talk a lot,
while others don't. The gurnard species has a wide vocal repertoire and

keeps up a constant chatter. Codfish, ___14___, usually keep silent, except when they are laying eggs. Any goldfish lover who hopes to strike up a conversation with their pet goldfish is ___15___. Goldfish have excellent hearing, but they don't make any sound whatsoever. Their excellent hearing isn't associated with vocalization.

11. (A) choices   (B) objects   (C) accents   (D) noises
12. (A) threatened   (B) being threatened
     (C) threatening   (D) being threatening
13. (A) merely   (B) equally   (C) officially   (D) favorably
14. (A) by all means   (B) for example
     (C) as a result   (D) on the other hand
15. (A) out of luck   (B) in the dark   (C) off the record   (D) on the rise

第 16 至 20 題爲題組

     The U.S. Postal Service has been struggling financially for some time. It plans to stop delivering mail on Saturdays, ___16___ Aug. 1 this year. This decision was announced on Wednesday without congressional approval. ___17___ forbidden to do so by the Congress, the agency for the first time will deliver mail only Monday through Friday. It is expected that this ___18___ will save about $2 billion a year. In recent years, the postal service has suffered tens of billions of dollars in losses ___19___ the increasing popularity of the Internet and e-commerce. The postal service plans to continue Saturday delivery of packages, which remain a profitable and growing part of the delivery business. Post offices would remain open on Saturdays ___20___ customers can drop off mail or packages, buy postage stamps, or access their post office boxes. But hours would likely be reduced at thousands of smaller locations.

16. (A) starts   (B) started   (C) starting   (D) to start
17. (A) When   (B) Unless   (C) Once   (D) Lest

18. (A) move (B) round (C) chance (D) fact
19. (A) at (B) with (C) under (D) between
20. (A) so that (B) as soon as (C) in case (D) ever since

三、文意選填（占 10 分）

說明： 第 21 題至第 30 題，每題一個空格，請依文意在文章後所提供的 (A) 到
(L) 選項中分別選出最適當者，並將其英文字母代號畫記在答案卡之
「選擇題答案區」。各題答對者，得 1 分；答錯、未作答或畫記多於
一個選項者，該題以零分計算。

第 21 至 30 題爲題組

People who want to experience an overnight stay in arctic-like cold may try the ice hotel—a building of frozen water. Despite the seemingly unattractive prospect of sleeping in a room at minus 15 degrees Celsius, every year about 4,000 people ___21___ to an ice hotel in a town in Canada.

The only warm things at the ice hotel are the candles on the bedside tables. The air is so cold that you can see your ___22___, which turns to liquid and appears as tiny droplets at the opening of your sleeping bag. The tip of your nose feels numb—almost as though it were ___23___. Getting up for a little while—to drink a glass of water or go to the bathroom—seems ___24___ without risking death.

Since an adventurous spirit alone is not enough to ___25___ more than two hours at the icy hotel, the staff briefs guests on what to wear and how to behave. Normal winter boots and outfits ___26___ little protection from the cold. The guests also learn how to ___27___ quickly in their arctic sleeping bags and how to prevent eyeglasses from freezing.

For individuals who need to escape the cold for a brief period, there are outdoor hot tubs in the hotel courtyard. You should make sure you have stopped sweating before you go to bed, though, because any ___28___ freezes immediately. Guests who are not ___29___ can quickly get cold feet and a blocked nose.

Comfort, however, is not the ___30___ to stay in the ice hotel.
Guests want to feel like polar explorers. For them, the first hot cup of
post-expedition coffee is pure delight.

(A) breath 　　　　(B) careful 　　　　(C) check in 　　　　(D) deposit
(E) frozen 　　　　(F) impossible 　　　　(G) moisture 　　　　(H) offer
(I) purpose 　　　　(J) sufficient 　　　　(K) warm up 　　　　(L) withstand

四、篇章結構（占 10 分）

說明： 第 31 題至第 35 題，每題一個空格。請依文意在文章後所提供的 (A) 到
　　　 (F) 選項中分別選出最適當者，填入空格中，使篇章結構清晰有條理，
　　　 並將其英文字母代號畫記在答案卡之「選擇題答案區」。每題答對者，
　　　 得 2 分；答錯、未作答或畫記多於一個選項者，該題以零分計算。

第 31 至 35 題為題組

　　In the Dutch colonial town later known as Albany, New York, there
lived a baker, Van Amsterdam, who was as honest as he could be. He
took great care to give his customers exactly what they paid for—not
more and not less.

　　One Saint Nicholas Day morning, when the baker was just ready
for business, the door of his shop flew open. ___31___ She asked for a
dozen of the baker's Saint Nicholas cookies. Van Amsterdam counted
out twelve cookies. But the woman insisted that a dozen is thirteen.
Van Amsterdam was not a man to bear foolishness. He refused. The
woman turned to go without the cookies but she stopped at the door,
saying, "Van Amsterdam! However honest you may be, your heart is
small and your fist is tight." Then she was gone.

　　___32___ His bread rose too high or not at all. His pies were sour or
too sweet. His cookies were burnt or doughy. His customers soon
noticed the difference and slipped away.

A year passed. The baker grew poorer and poorer. Finally, on the day before Saint Nicholas Day, no customer came to his shop.   33

That night, the baker had a dream. He saw Saint Nicholas pulling out gifts from his baskets for a crowd of happy children. No matter how many presents Nicholas handed out, there were always more to give. Then somehow, Saint Nicholas turned into the old woman with the long black shawl!

    34   He suddenly realized that he always gave his customers exactly what they paid for, "But why not give more?"

The next morning, on Saint Nicholas Day, the baker rose early to make cookies. And to his surprise, the cookies were as fine as they could be. When he had just finished, the old woman appeared at his door again. She asked for a dozen of Van Amsterdam's Saint Nicholas cookies.   35

When people heard he counted thirteen as a dozen, he had more customers than ever and became wealthy. The practice then spread to other towns as a common custom.

(A) Van Amsterdam awoke with a start.

(B) In walked an old woman wrapped in a long black shawl.

(C) The more he took from the baskets, the more they seemed to hold.

(D) From that day, everything went wrong in Van Amsterdam's bakery.

(E) In great excitement, Van Amsterdam counted out twelve cookies—and one more.

(F) Staring at his unsold Saint Nicholas cookies, he prayed that Saint Nicholas could help him.

五、閱讀測驗（占 32 分）

說明：　第 36 題至第 51 題，每題請分別根據各篇文章之文意選出最適當的一個
　　　　選項，請畫記在答案卡之「選擇題答案區」。各題答對者，得 2 分；答
　　　　錯、未作答或畫記多於一個選項者，該題以零分計算。

第 36 至 39 題為題組

All pop artists like to say that they owe their success to their fans. In the case of British band SVM, it's indeed true. The band is currently recording songs because 358 fans contributed the £100,000 needed for the project. The arrangement came via MMC, an online record label that uses Web-based, social-network-style "crowd-funding" to finance its acts.

Here's how it works: MMC posts demos and videos of 10 artists on its website, and users are invited to invest from £10 to £1,000 in the ones they most enjoy or think are most likely to become popular. Once an act reaches £100,000, the financing process is completed, and the money is used to pay for recording and possibly a concert tour. Profits from resulting music sales, concerts, and merchandise are split three ways: investors get to divide 40%; another 40% goes to MMC; the artist pockets 20%. The payoff for investors can be big. One fan in France who contributed £4,250 got his money back 22 times over.

Crowd-funding musical acts is not new. But MMC takes the concept to another level. First of all, investors can get cash rather than just goodies like free downloads or tickets. Also, MMC is a record label. It has the means to get its music distributed around the world and to market artists effectively. "Artists need professional support," says the CEO of MMC's international division.

While digital technology and the Net have created a do-it-yourself boom among musicians, **success is still a long shot**. Out of the 20,000 records released in the U.S. in 2009, only 14 DIY acts made it to the Top 200. Also, with less revenue from recorded music, music companies have become less likely to take risks, which has led to fewer artists receiving funding. The crowd-funding model, however, allows for more records to be made by spreading risk among hundreds of backers. And the social-network aspect of the site helps expand fan bases; that is, investors become a promotional army.

36. Which of the following titles best expresses the main idea of the passage?
    (A) Web-based Music Production
    (B) Fundraising for Music Companies
    (C) Music Fans Profiting from Investments
    (D) Crowd-funding in the Music Industry

37. How much money does a band have to raise via MMC to have their music recorded?
    (A) £10.　　　(B) £1,000.　　　(C) £4,250.　　　(D) £100,000.

38. Which of the following statements is true about MMC?
    (A) It has helped many do-it-yourself musicians get to the Top 200.
    (B) There are works of fourteen artists posted at a time on its website.
    (C) It allows fans to provide financial support to the musicians they like.
    (D) The biggest share of its profits from a crowd-funding project goes to the musician.

39. What does the author mean by **success is still a long shot** in the fourth paragraph?
    (A) Success is everlasting in effect.
    (B) Success is not easy to achieve.
    (C) Success often starts with one big shot.
    (D) Success should be every musician's long-term goal.

第 40 至 43 題爲題組

　　In science fiction TV programs such as Star Trek, tractor beams are used to tow spaceships and move objects. For years, scientists have labored to replicate this feat. In 2013, they succeeded. A team of British and Czech scientists, led by Dr. Tomas Cizmar, say they have created a real-life "tractor beam," like the kind from Star Trek, which uses a beam of light to attract objects, at least at a microscopic level.

　　Light manipulation techniques have existed since the 1970s, but this is thought to be the first time a light beam has been used to draw objects towards a light source. Usually when microscopic objects are hit by a beam of light, they are forced along the direction of the beam. After many years' research, Dr. Cizmar's team discovered a technique that allows for the radiant force of light to be reversed and to use the negative force to draw out certain particles.

　　Dr. Cizmar says that even though it is a few years away from practical use, the technology has huge potential for medical research. In particular, the tractor beam is highly selective in the particles it can attract, so it can pick up particles that have specific properties, such as size or composition, in a mixture. "Eventually, this could be used to separate white blood cells, for example," Dr. Cizmar told BBC News.

　　It has been a primary plot device in science fiction TV programs and movies to allow objects like spaceships to be trapped in a beam of light. But Dr. Cizmar said this particular technique would not eventually lead to **that**. A transfer of energy happens in the process. On a microscopic scale that is OK, but on a large scale it would cause huge problems. A large object could be destroyed by the heating, which results from the massive amount of energy necessary to pull it.

40. What is this passage mainly about?
    (A) The application of lighting technology in modern society.
    (B) The uses and limitations of a scientific invention by a research team.
    (C) The adoption of light manipulation techniques in medical treatment.
    (D) The influences and effects of scientific developments on science fiction.

41. Which of the following is true about Dr. Cizmar's tractor beam?
    (A) It moves big objects as the tractor beam did in Star Trek.
    (B) It is the first light beam device that pushes objects forward.
    (C) It relies on negative force to pull out specific kinds of particles.
    (D) It is currently being used for separating blood cells in medical research.

42. What does **that** in the last paragraph refer to?
    (A) Transferring a massive amount of energy.
    (B) Making science fiction programs and movies.
    (C) Burning a large object into ashes.
    (D) Capturing spaceships in a beam of light.

43. What is the tone of this passage?
    (A) Objective.   (B) Suspicious.   (C) Admiring.   (D) Pessimistic.

第 44 至 47 題爲題組

Grace Wambui, a 14-year-old pupil in Nairobi, had never touched a tablet computer. But it took her only about one minute to work out how to use one when such devices arrived at Amaf School in Kawangware, a slum in the Kenyan capital. Teaching used to be conducted with a blackboard and a handful of tattered textbooks. Now children in groups of five take turns to swipe the touch screen of the devices, which are loaded with a multimedia version of Kenya's syllabus.

The tablets at Amaf School are part of a pilot project run by eLimu, a technology start-up. If it and other firms are right, tablets and other digital devices may soon be the rule in African schools. Many are betting on a boom in digital education in Kenya and elsewhere. Some executives even expect it to take off like M-Pesa, Kenya's hugely successful mobile-money service.

Such growth in digital education would be timely. The flood of new pupils has overwhelmed state schools, which were already understaffed, underfunded and poorly managed. The prospect of Africa's 300 million pupils learning digitally has caught the attention of global technology giants. Amazon has seen sales of its Kindle e-readers in Africa increase tenfold in the past year. Intel has been helping African governments buy entry-level computers. In Nigeria, Intel brought together a publisher and a telecom carrier to provide exam-preparation tools over mobile phones, a service that has become hugely popular.

A bigger question is whether digital tools actually improve education. Early results are encouraging. In Ghana, reading skills improved measurably among 350 children that had been given Kindle e-readers. In Ethiopia, in the absence of teachers, children figured out how to use tablets and learned the English ABCs. At Amaf School, average marks in science went from 58 to 73 in a single term.

44. Which of the following is the best title for this passage?
    (A) The Bestseller in Africa
    (B) Problems Plaguing Education in Africa
    (C) Schools in Africa Are Going Digital
    (D) Tablet Computers Are in Great Demand in Kenya

45. What is the author trying to convey in citing Grace Wambui's case?
    (A) Grace is a genius in computer skills.
    (B) The tablet computer is very user-friendly.

(C) The delivery system in Kenya is very poor.

(D) Tablet computers are common in Kawangware.

46. According to the passage, what is eLimu?
    (A) A company.   (B) A computer program.
    (C) An e-book.   (D) An educational project.

47. According to the passage, which of the following is true about education in Africa?
    (A) The number of students keeps dropping in recent years.
    (B) There are more than enough teachers for traditional classroom teaching.
    (C) Students have received Kindle e-readers donated by Amazon to improve reading.
    (D) Early results from use of digital tools in teaching are quite positive in some countries.

第 48 至 51 題為題組

In the Spartathlon, one of the world's toughest ultra-marathons, runners run 245 km, about six marathons, within 36 hours. The runners start in Athens, and run all the way to historical Sparta.

The Spartathlon's heritage goes back to 490 B.C., when Pheidippides, an Athenian, made the journey to Sparta to ask the Spartans for help in fighting the invading Persians. It is recorded that he reached Sparta on the day after he left Athens. In 1982, this story sparked the interest of a British air-force officer and long-distance runner called John Foden, who wondered if it really was possible to run from Athens to Sparta and arrive the next day. With four other officers, Foden decided to see for himself; after a 36-hour slog they arrived in Sparti, as the town is now called. That achievement inspired the organization of the first Spartathlon a year later.

The Spartathlon's attraction has two sources. The first is the difficulty of finishing it. The Spartathlon is not the most difficult race, but it combines lots of different tests. There is the heat of the Greek day, and then the plunge in temperatures when darkness falls. There are climbs: the route includes a series of ascents, among them a 1,200-meter mountain pass in the dead of night. Above all, there is the relentless pressure of the clock. The second reason is that the idea of retracing Pheidippides's footsteps still grips many participants. It feels like racing in history, passing through places where history began.

As finishers receive a laurel wreath and water from schoolgirls, many are overjoyed with emotion. However, **the euphoria is fleeting**. Within a few minutes, their joints and muscles start to seize up: after the race, Sparti resembles the set of a zombie film as participants lumber slowly around on legs that will not bend. But the itch to do it all over again soon appears.

48. What is the second paragraph mainly about?
    (A) The background of John Foden.
    (B) The route of an ultra-marathon.
    (C) The origin of the Spartathlon.
    (D) The story of Pheidippides in ancient Athens.

49. Why do ultra-runners choose the Spartathlon?
    (A) It is the most classical ultra-marathon in the world.
    (B) Runners feel like racing through history.
    (C) Their personal problems will be solved in the race.
    (D) They have to finish all the tests in one day.

50. What does **the euphoria is fleeting** in the last paragraph mean?
    (A) The feeling of triumph will last forever.
    (B) The race is incomprehensibly difficult to finish.
    (C) The fatigue after the race is overwhelming.
    (D) The excitement of finishing the race is soon gone.

51. According to the passage, which of the following statements is true about the Spartathlon?
    (A) The Spartathlon was first organized in 1983.
    (B) The event of the Spartathlon was made into a movie.
    (C) After completing the race, many decide not to try it again.
    (D) The runners have to endure high temperature day and night.

第貳部份：非選擇題（占 28 分）

說明： 本部分共有二題，請依各題指示作答，答案必須寫在「答案卷」上，並標明大題號（一、二）。作答務必使用筆尖較粗之黑色墨水的筆書寫，且不得使用鉛筆。

一、中譯英（占 8 分）

說明： 1. 請將以下中文句子譯成正確、通順、達意的英文，並將答案寫在「答案卷」上。
    2. 請依序作答，並標明子題號（1、2）。每題4分，共8分。

1. 對現今的許多學生而言，在課業與課外活動間取得平衡是一大挑戰。
2. 有效的時間管理是每位有責任感的學生必須學習的首要課題。

二、英文作文（占 20 分）

說明： 1. 依提示在「答案卷」上寫一篇英文作文。
    2. 文長至少 120 個單詞（words）。

提示： 以下有兩項即將上市之新科技產品：

產品一：隱形披風
（invisibility cloak）
穿上後頓時隱形，旁人看不到你的存在；同時，隱形披風會保護你，讓你水火不侵。

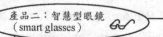

產品二：智慧型眼鏡
（smart glasses）
具有掃瞄透視功能，戴上後即能看到障礙物後方的生物；同時能完整紀錄你所經歷過的場景。

如果你有機會獲贈其中一項產品，你會選擇哪一項？請以此為主題，寫一篇至少 120 個單詞的英文作文。文分兩段，第一段說明你的選擇及理由，並舉例說明你將如何使用這項產品。第二段說明你不選擇另一項產品的理由及該項產品可能衍生的問題。

102年度指定科目考試英文科試題詳解

第壹部分：選擇題

一、詞彙：

1. (**A**) Industrial waste must be carefully handled, or it will <u>contaminate</u> the public water supply.
   工業的廢棄物必須小心處理，否則會<u>污染</u>大眾的供水系統。
   (A) ***contaminate*** 〔kənˋtæmə͵net〕 v. 污染
   (B) facilitate 〔fəˋsɪlə͵tet〕 v. 使便利
   (C) legitimate〔lɪˋdʒɪtəmɪt〕 adj. 合法的
   (D) manipulate 〔məˋnɪpjə͵let〕 v. 操縱
   * industrial 〔ɪnˋdʌstrɪəl〕 adj. 工業的　　waste〔west〕 n. 廢棄物
     handle〔ˋhændḷ〕 v. 處理　　supply〔səˋplaɪ〕 n. 供給

2. (**D**) John's vision was direct, concrete and simple and he recorded <u>faithfully</u> the incidents of everyday life.
   約翰的看法很直接、具體，又簡單，他會<u>忠實地</u>記錄日常生活的事件。
   (A) universally 〔͵junəˋvɝsḷɪ〕 adv. 普遍地
   (B) scarcely 〔ˋskɛrslɪ〕 adv. 幾乎不 (= *hardly*)
   (C) passively 〔ˋpæsɪvlɪ〕 adv. 被動地
   (D) ***faithfully*** 〔ˋfeθfəlɪ〕 adv. 忠實地
   * vision〔ˋvɪʒən〕 n. 洞察力；眼力；看法
     concrete〔kanˋkrit〕 adj. 具體的　　incident〔ˋɪnsədənt〕 n. 事件

3. (**C**) The government cannot find a good reason to <u>justify</u> its high expenses on weapons, especially when the number of people living in poverty is so high.
   政府無法找到很好的理由來<u>爲</u>高額的軍購費用<u>辯護</u>，尤其是生活貧困的人民數量如此龐大。
   (A) abolish〔əˋbalɪʃ〕 v. 廢除　　(B) escort〔ɪˋskɔrt〕 v. 護送
   (C) ***justify*** 〔ˋdʒʌstə͵faɪ〕 v. 爲…辯護；使成爲正當
   (D) mingle〔ˋmɪŋgḷ〕 v. 混合
   * expense〔ɪkˋspɛns〕 n. 費用　　weapon〔ˋwɛpən〕 n. 武器
     poverty〔ˋpavɚtɪ〕 n. 貧窮　　***live in poverty*** 過貧窮的生活

4. (**A**) The writing teacher has found that reading fantasies such as J. K. Rowling's *Harry Potter* may inspire her students to think and write with creativity.

這位教寫作的老師已經發現，閱讀像是 J.K.羅琳的「哈利波特」這樣的奇幻小說，能激發她的學生在思考和寫作方面更有創造力。

  (A) ***creativity*** (ˌkrɪeˈtɪvətɪ) *n.* 創造力；獨創力
  (B) generosity (ˌdʒɛnəˈrɑsətɪ) *n.* 慷慨；大方
  (C) superstition (ˌsupɚˈstɪʃən) *n.* 迷信
  (D) foundation (faʊnˈdeʃən) *n.* 創立；基礎

  ＊fantasy (ˈfæntəsɪ) *n.* 幻想作品；幻想小說
   inspire (ɪnˈspaɪr) *v.* 激勵；激發

5. (**B**) Since several child abuse cases were reported on the TV news, the public has become more aware of the issue of domestic violence.

因為電視新聞報導了好幾件虐童案，所以一般大眾變得更加注意家暴的問題。

  (A) blunder (ˈblʌndɚ) *n.* (愚蠢的) 錯誤
  (B) ***abuse*** (əˈbjus) *n.* 虐待　　***child abuse*** 虐待兒童
  (C) essence (ˈɛsns) *n.* 本質　　(D) defect (ˈdifɛkt) *n.* 瑕疵；缺點

  ＊case (kes) *n.* 案件　　***be aware of*** 知道；察覺到
   issue (ˈɪʃju) *n.* 議題；問題　　domestic (dəˈmɛstɪk) *adj.* 家庭的
   violence (ˈvaɪələns) *n.* 暴力

6. (**C**) Helen's doctor suggested that she undergo a heart surgery. But she decided to ask for a second opinion from another doctor.

海倫的醫生建議她動心臟手術。但是她決定問另一位醫生的意見。

  (A) purpose (ˈpɝpəs) *n.* 目的
  (B) statement (ˈstetmənt) *n.* 敘述；說法
  (C) ***opinion*** (əˈpɪnɪən) *n.* 意見　　(D) excuse (ɪkˈskjus) *n.* 藉口

  ＊undergo (ˌʌndɚˈgo) *v.* 進行　　surgery (ˈsɝdʒərɪ) *n.* 手術
   ask for 要求　　***a second*** 另一個的

7. (**A**) All candidates selected after preliminary screening will be further invited to an interview, after which the final admission decision will be made. 初選所選出來的所有候選人，將會被邀請來做更進一步的面試，然後就會做出是否准許入學的最後決定。

(A) *preliminary* 〔 prɪˋlɪməˏnɛrɪ 〕 *adj.* 初步的

(B) affectionate 〔 əˋfɛkʃənɪt 〕 *adj.* 摯愛的；充滿著愛情的

(C) controversial 〔ˏkɑntrəˋvɝʃəl 〕 *adj.* 有爭議的

(D) excessive 〔 ɪkˋsɛsɪv 〕 *adj.* 過度的

* candidatet 〔ˋkændəˏdet 〕 *n.* 候選人
  screening 〔ˋskrinɪŋ 〕 *n.* 審查；選拔
  further 〔ˋfɝðɚ 〕 *adv.* 更進一步地　　interview 〔ˋɪntɚˏvju 〕 *n.* 面試
  admission 〔 ədˋmɪʃən 〕 *n.* 入學（許可）

8. (**D**) To prevent terrorist attacks, the security guards at the airport check all luggage carefully to see if there are any <u>explosive</u> items or other dangerous objects.

為了預防恐怖攻擊，機場的安全警衛仔細檢查所有的行李，看看是否有任何<u>爆裂</u>物或危其他的危險物品。

(A) dynamic 〔 daɪˋnæmɪk 〕 *adj.* 動力的；動態的

(B) identical 〔 aɪˋdɛntɪkl̩ 〕 *adj.* 完全相同的

(C) permanent 〔ˋpɝmənənt 〕 *adj.* 永久的

(D) *explosive* 〔 ɪkˋsplosɪv 〕 *adj.* 爆炸的

* terrorist 〔ˋtɛrərɪst 〕 *adj.* 恐怖分子的
  security 〔 sɪˋkjurətɪ 〕 *adj.* 安全的；保安的
  guard 〔 gɑrd 〕 *n.* 警衛　　luggage 〔ˋlʌgɪdʒ 〕 *n.* 行李
  item 〔ˋaɪtəm 〕 *n.* 項目；物品　　object 〔ˋɑbdʒɛkt 〕 *n.* 物體

9. (**C**) In the desert, a huge mall with art galleries, theaters, and museums will be constructed to <u>shelter</u> visitors from the heat outside.

在沙漠中，將會建造一間有美術館、戲院、博物館的大型購物中心，好<u>讓</u>遊客<u>躲避</u>外面的酷熱。

(A) convert 〔 kənˋvɝt 〕 *v.* 使轉變

(B) defend 〔 dɪˋfɛnd 〕 *v.* 保衛；防禦

(C) *shelter* 〔ˋʃɛltɚ 〕 *v.* 保護；庇護；為…提供避難所
    shelter sb. from 保護某人使不受…

(D) vacuum 〔ˋvækjuəm 〕 *v.* 用吸塵器打掃

* desert 〔ˋdɛzɚt 〕 *n.* 沙漠　　huge 〔 hjudʒ 〕 *adj.* 巨大的
  mall 〔 mɔl 〕 *n.* 購物中心　　gallery 〔ˋgælərɪ 〕 *n.* 畫廊；美術館
  art gallery 美術館　　construct 〔 kənˋstrʌkt 〕 *v.* 建造
  heat 〔 hit 〕 *n.* 熱；高溫

10. (**D**) Judge Harris always has good points to make. Her arguments are very <u>persuasive</u> as they are based on logic and sound reasoning.

哈里斯法官總是能提出很好的論點。她的論點非常有說服力，因為都是根據邏輯和正確的推論。

(A) emphatic〔ɪmˈfætɪk〕 *adj.* 強調的
(B) indifferent〔ɪnˈdɪfərənt〕 *adj.* 漠不關心的
(C) dominant〔ˈdɑmənənt〕 *adj.* 支配的；統治的
(D) ***persuasive***〔pɚˈswesɪv〕 *adj.* 有說服力的

＊judge〔dʒʌdʒ〕 *n.* 法官　　point〔pɔɪnt〕 *n.* 論點
argument〔ˈɑrgjəmənt〕 *n.* 論點　　***be based on*** 以⋯爲基礎；根據
logic〔ˈlɑdʒɪk〕 *n.* 邏輯
sound〔saʊnd〕 *adj.* 正確的；有事實根據的
reasoning〔ˈriznɪŋ〕 *n.* 推論

二、綜合測驗：

<u>第 11 至 15 題爲題組</u>

The undersea world isn't as quiet as we thought, according to a New Zealand researcher. Fish can "talk" to each other and make a range of <u>noises</u>
11
by vibrating their swim bladder, an internal gas-filled organ used as a resonating chamber to produce or receive sound.

海底世界並非如同和我們想的一樣安靜，根據紐西蘭研究員調查，魚能彼此「說話」，並藉著震動魚鰾發出各種聲音。魚鰾是一種充滿氣體的內臟，當作產生或接收聲音的共鳴腔。

undersea〔ˈʌndɚˈsi〕 *adj.* 海底的　　***New Zealand*** 紐西蘭
researcher〔rɪˈsɝtʃɚ〕 *n.* 研究員　　***each other*** 彼此
range〔rendʒ〕 *n.* 範圍　　***a range of*** 各種的
vibrate〔ˈvaɪbret〕 *v.* 震動　　bladder〔ˈblædɚ〕 *n.* 鰾；膀胱
internal〔ɪnˈtɝnl̩〕 *adj.* 內部的　　gas-filled〔ˈgæsˌfɪld〕 *adj.* 充滿氣體的
organ〔ˈɔrgən〕 *n.* 器官　　resonate〔ˈrɛznˌet〕 *v.* 共鳴；回響
chamber〔ˈtʃembɚ〕 *n.* 房間；腔；室
produce〔prəˈdjus〕 *v.* 產生

11. (**D**) 依據文意，應選 (D) ***noises***，make noises 表示「製造聲音」的意思。
(A) 選擇；(B) 物體；(C) 腔調，均不符句意。

　　Fish are believed to speak to each other for a number of reasons, such as to attract mates, scare off predators, or give directions to other fish. Damselfish, for example, have been found to make sounds to scare off <u>threatening</u> fish and even divers.　Another discovery about fish sounds is
　　12
that not all fish are <u>equally</u> "talkative."　Some species talk a lot, while
　　　　　　　　　　　　13
others don't.

　　一般相信，魚會彼此交談有一些原因，像是要求偶、嚇走掠食者，或是告訴其他魚方向。例如，人們發現雀鯛會製造聲音來嚇走具威脅性的魚，甚至潛水者。另一項關於魚會發出聲音的發現是，並非所有的魚同樣「愛說話」，有些種類話很多，而有些則不然。

> ***a number of*** 一些　　　***such as*** 例如　　mate〔met〕*n.* 配偶
> ***scare off*** 嚇退　　predator〔'prɛdətə〕*n.* 掠食者
> direction〔də'rɛkʃən〕*n.* 方向
> damselfish〔'dæmzl͵fɪʃ〕*n.* 雀鯛（一種熱帶珊瑚礁魚類）
> diver〔'daɪvə〕*n.* 潛水者　　talkative〔'tɔkətɪv〕*adj.* 愛說話的

12. (**C**)　此處是用分詞當形容詞的用法，用來修飾空格後的名詞 fish。依據文意，應選現在分詞 (C) 具威脅性的；而過去分詞 (A) 受到威脅的，不符句意。

13. (**B**)　依據文意，應選 (B)。
　　(A) merely〔'mɪrlɪ〕*adv.* 僅僅；只有
　　(B) ***equally***〔'ikwəlɪ〕*adv.* 同樣地
　　(C) officially〔ə'fɪʃəlɪ〕*adv.* 正式地
　　(D) favorably〔'fevərəblɪ〕*adv.* 有利地；贊同地

The gurnard species has a wide vocal repertoire and keeps up a constant chatter.　Codfish, <u>on the other hand</u>, usually keep silent, except when they
　　　　　　　　　　　　　　　　14
are laying eggs.　Any goldfish lover who hopes to strike up a conversation with their pet goldfish is <u>out of luck</u>.　Goldfish have excellent hearing, but
　　　　　　　　　　　　　　　15
they don't make any sound whatsoever.　Their excellent hearing isn't associated with vocalization.

魴魚擁有各種聲音的技能，會一直喋喋不休。另一方面，鱈魚通常很安靜，除非是產卵的時候。想要和寵物金魚聊天的飼主，恐怕運氣沒那麼好。金魚的聽力很好，但牠們不會發出任何聲音，它們優異的聽力與發聲無關。

gurnard〔'gɜnəd〕 *n.* 魴魚　　species〔'spiʃiz〕 *n.* 品種

vocal〔'vokḷ〕 *adj.* 聲音的

repertoire〔'rɛpə,twɑr〕 *n.* 表演曲目；個人技能　　***keep up*** 保持

constant〔'kɑnstənt〕 *adj.* 持續的　　chatter〔'tʃætə〕 *n.* 喋喋不休

codfish〔'kɑd,fɪʃ〕 *n.* 鱈魚（ = *cod* ）

lay〔le〕 *v.* 產（卵）；生（蛋）　　goldfish〔'gold,fɪʃ〕 *n.* 金魚

strike up 開始　　hearing〔'hɪrɪŋ〕 *n.* 聽力

whatsoever〔,hwɑtso'ɛvə〕 *adv.* 一點也（不）（ = *at all* ）

be associated with 與…有關　　vocalization〔,vokələ'zeʃən〕 *n.* 發聲

14.（ **D** ）依據文意，應選 (D)。

　　(A) by all means　務必；一定　　(B) for example　例如

　　(C) as a result　因此　　(D) ***on the other hand***　另一方面

15.（ **A** ）依據文意，應選 (A)。

　　(A) ***out of luck***　運氣不佳　　(B) in the dark　黑暗中；不知道

　　(C) off the record　私底下；非正式的

　　(D) on the rise　上升中；增加中

第 16 至 20 題為題組

　　The U.S. Postal Service has been struggling financially for some time. It plans to stop delivering mail on Saturdays, starting Aug. 1 this year.
　　　　　　　　　　　　　　　　　　　　　　　　　　16

This decision was announced on Wednesday without congressional approval. Unless forbidden to do so by the Congress, the agency for the
　　　　　　　　17

first time will deliver mail only Monday through Friday. It is expected

that this move will save about $2 billion a year.
　　　18

　　美國郵政署面臨財政困難已經有一段時間了。他們計畫從今年八月一日起，將在周六停止遞送郵件。這項決定在沒有國會同意下，於周三宣布。除非被國會禁止，否則該機構將首度只有在周一到周五遞送郵件。預計這樣措施將能每年省下約二十億元。

service〔'sɜvɪs〕 *n.* （政府機關）部；署；局

the U.S. Postal Service 美國郵政署

struggle〔'strʌgḷ〕 *v.* 掙扎；對抗

financially〔faɪ'nænʃəlɪ〕 *adv.* 財務上

deliver〔dɪ'lɪvə〕 *v.* 遞送　　announce〔ə'naʊns〕 *v.* 宣布

congressional〔kən'grɛʃənḷ〕*adj.* 國會的

approval〔ə'pruvḷ〕*n.* 同意　　forbid〔fɚ'bɪd〕*v.* 禁止

Congress〔'kɑŋɡrəs〕*n.*（美國）國會

agency〔'edʒənsɪ〕*n.* 行政機構；代辦處　　***for the first time*** 首次

billion〔'bɪlɪən〕*n.* 十億

16. (**C**) 空格原應填入 "which will start"，省略關代 which，動詞 will start
改成 starting，即成爲分詞片語，故選 (C)。

17. (**B**) 此爲保留連接詞的分詞構句句型，依據文意，原句應爲 "Unless the
agency is forbidden to do so by the Congress, …"，應選 (B) 除非。
(A) 當；(C) 一旦；(D) 以免；均與句意不符。

18. (**A**) 依據文意，應選 (A)。

(A) ***move***〔muv〕*n.* 措施；舉動　　(B) round〔raʊnd〕*n.* 回合

(C) chance〔tʃæns〕*n.* 機會　　(D) fact〔fækt〕*n.* 事實

In recent years, the postal service has suffered tens of billions of dollars in
losses <u>with</u> the increasing popularity of the Internet and e-commerce. The
     19
postal service plans to continue Saturday delivery of packages, which
remain a profitable and growing part of the delivery business. Post offices
would remain open on Saturdays <u>so that</u> customers can drop off mail or
          20
packages, buy postage stamps, or access their post office boxes. But hours
would likely be reduced at thousands of smaller locations.

近年來，隨著網際網路及電子商務越來越普及，郵政業務遭受好幾百億的損失。
郵政署打算繼續周六遞送包裹的業務，它一直是遞送業務中有利潤且持續成長
的部分。郵局在周六仍會營業，以便顧客能寄送郵件或包裹、買郵票、或使用
郵政信箱。但營業時間在數千家較小規模的地區可能會縮短。

postal〔'postḷ〕*adj.* 郵政的

service〔'sɝvɪs〕*n.* 服務；公共事業　　suffer〔'sʌfɚ〕*v.* 遭受

tens of billiens of 數百億的　　loss〔lɔs〕*n.* 損失

popularity〔,pɑpjə'lærətɪ〕*n.* 普及；流行

Internet〔'ɪntɚˏnɛt〕*n.* 網際網路

e-commerce〔'i 'kɑmɝs〕*n.* 電子商務　　delivery〔dɪ'lɪvərɪ〕*n.* 遞送

package〔'pækɪdʒ〕*n.* 包裹　　remain〔rɪ'men〕*v.* 仍是

profitable〔'prɑfɪtəbḷ〕*adj.* 有利潤的
customer〔'kʌstəmɚ〕*n.* 顧客　　***drop off*** 放下；丟下
postage〔'postɪdʒ〕*n.* 郵資　　***postage stamp*** 郵票（＝*stamp*）
access〔'æksɛs〕*v.* 使用；取得　　reduce〔rɪ'djus〕*v.* 減少；縮小
thousands of 數以千計的　　location〔lo'keʃən〕*n.* 地點

19.(**B**) 依據文意，表示「隨著」網際網路及電子商務越來越普及，應選 (B)。

20.(**A**) 依據文意，應選 (A)。
　　(A) ***so that*** 以便　　　　　　(B) as soon as 一…（就…）
　　(C) in case 如果；（以防）萬一　　(D) ever since 自從

三、文意選填：

第 21 至 30 題為題組

　　People who want to experience an overnight stay in arctic-like cold may try the ice hotel—a building of frozen water. Despite the seemingly unattractive prospect of sleeping in a room at minus 15 degrees Celsius, every year about 4,000 people [21](C) check in to an ice hotel in a town in Canada.

　　想體驗在北極般的寒冷中過夜，可以試試冰飯店——一棟用冰所蓋成的建築，儘管要睡在攝氏零下十五度的房間，似乎不是很具吸引力，但每年有近四千人到加拿大一座小鎮的冰旅館辦理入住。

experience〔ɪk'spɪrɪəns〕*v.* 體驗
overnight〔'ovɚ'naɪt〕*adj.* 過夜的
arctic〔'ɑrktɪk〕*n.* 北極　*adj.* 北極的
despite〔dɪ'spaɪt〕*prep.* 儘管　　seemingly〔'simɪŋlɪ〕*adv.* 似乎
unattractive〔ʌnə'træktɪv〕*adj.* 不吸引人的
prospect〔'prɑspɛkt〕*n.* 預期；指望　　minus〔'maɪnəs〕*adj.* 負的
Celsius〔'sɛlsɪəs〕*adj.* 攝氏的

21.(**C**) ***check in*** 入住登記；報到

　　The only warm things at the ice hotel are the candles on the bedside tables. The air is so cold that you can see your [22](A) breath, which turns to liquid and appears as tiny droplets at the opening of your sleeping bag. The tip of your nose feels numb—almost as though it were [23](E) frozen.

Getting up for a little while—to drink a glass of water or go to the
bathroom—seems ²⁴ (F) impossible without risking death.
冰飯店中唯一溫暖的東西就是床邊桌上的蠟燭。空氣寒冷到能看到自己的氣
息，它會變成水，而且在一打開睡袋時，顯現出小水滴的形狀。鼻尖會感到麻
痺，彷彿被冰凍了。起床一下，去喝杯水或上洗手間，似乎如果不冒點生命危
險是無法辦到的。

candle〔ˋkændḷ〕n. 蠟燭　　bedside〔ˋbɛdˏsaɪd〕adj. 床邊的
turn to 轉變成　　liquid〔ˋlɪkwɪd〕n. 液體
appear〔əˋpɪr〕v. 出現；呈現　　tiny〔ˋtaɪnɪ〕adj. 微小的
droplet〔ˋdrɑplɪt〕n. 小水滴
opening〔ˋopənɪŋ〕n. 打開　　**sleeping bag** 睡袋
tip〔tɪp〕n. 頂端　　numb〔nʌm〕adj. 麻痺的；失去知覺的
as though 彷彿（= as if）　　risk〔rɪsk〕v. 冒險

22. (**A**) breath〔brɛθ〕n. 呼吸；氣息
23. (**E**) frozen〔ˋfrozṇ〕adj. 冷凍的；結冰的
24. (**F**) impossible〔ɪmˋpɑsəbḷ〕adj. 不可能的

Since an adventurous spirit alone is not enough to ²⁵ (L) withstand more
than two hours at the icy hotel, the staff briefs guests on what to wear and
how to behave. Normal winter boots and outfits ²⁶ (H) offer little protection
from the cold. The guests also learn how to ²⁷ (K) warm up quickly in their
arctic sleeping bags and how to prevent eyeglasses from freezing.
因為單單靠冒險精神，不足以在冰旅館待超過兩個小時，所以員工會向客
人簡單說明要穿什麼，以及該怎麼做。一般冬天穿的靴子和服裝不太能抵擋這
樣的嚴寒。這些客人也要學習，如何在他們於北極地區使用的睡袋中快速變溫
暖，以及如何預防眼鏡結冰。

adventurous〔ədˋvɛntʃərəs〕adj. 愛冒險的
spirit〔ˋspɪrɪt〕n. 精神
alone〔əˋlon〕adv. 單單；僅僅　　staff〔stæf〕n. 職員
brief〔brif〕v. 對…簡單說明　adj. 簡短的
behave〔bɪˋhev〕v. 行為；表現
normal〔ˋnɔrmḷ〕adj. 標準的；普通的
boots〔buts〕n. pl. 靴子　　outfit〔ˋautˏfɪt〕n. 服裝
protection from 防…【例如：protection from the sun（防曬）】
eyeglasses〔ˋaɪˏglæsɪz〕n. pl. 眼鏡　　freeze〔friz〕v. 結冰

25. (**L**) withstand〔wɪθˈstænd〕*v.* 反抗；耐得住；經得起

26. (**H**) offer〔ˈɔfɚ〕*v.* 提供

27. (**K**) *warm up* 變溫暖

For individuals who need to escape the cold for a brief period, there are outdoor hot tubs in the hotel courtyard. You should make sure you have stopped sweating before you go to bed, though, because any [28] **(G)** moisture freezes immediately. Guests who are not [29] **(B)** careful can quickly get cold feet and a blocked nose.

對於需要短暫逃避寒冷的人來說，在旅館的庭院有個戶外的熱浴缸。不過在你去睡覺之前，一定要確定自己已經停止流汗，因為任何的水分都會立刻結冰。粗心大意的客人，可能腳很快就會變冷，而且還會鼻塞。

　　individual〔ˌɪndəˈvɪdʒʊəl〕*n.* 個人
　　outdoor〔ˈaʊtˌdor〕*adj.* 戶外的　　tub〔tʌb〕*n.* 浴缸
　　courtyard〔ˈkortˌjard〕*n.* 庭院　　sweat〔swɛt〕*v.* 流汗
　　blocked〔blɑkt〕*adj.* 阻塞的

28. (**G**) moisture〔ˈmɔɪstʃɚ〕*n.* 水分

29. (**B**) careful〔ˈkɛrfəl〕*adj.* 小心的

Comfort, however, is not the [30] **(I)** purpose to stay in the ice hotel. Guests want to feel like polar explorers. For them, the first hot cup of post-expedition coffee is pure delight.

不過舒適並不是住這間旅館的目的。客人會想要覺得像是極地探險家一樣。對他們而言，遠征過後喝到的第一杯熱咖啡，真是一大享受。

　　comfort〔ˈkʌmfɚt〕*n.* 舒適　　　stay〔ste〕*v.* 暫住
　　guest〔gɛst〕*n.* (旅館的) 旅客　　polar〔ˈpolɚ〕*adj.* 極地的
　　explorer〔ɪkˈsplorɚ〕*n.* 探險家　　post- 表「…之後」。
　　expedition〔ˌɛkspɪˈdɪʃən〕*n.* 遠征；探險旅行
　　pure〔pjʊr〕*adj.* 純粹的；完全的
　　delight〔dɪˈlaɪt〕*n.* 喜悅；高興的事

30. (**I**) purpose〔ˈpɝpəs〕*n.* 目的

四、篇章結構：

第 31 至 35 題爲題組

In the Dutch colonial town later known as Albany, New York, there lived a baker, Van Amsterdam, who was as honest as he could be. He took great care to give his customs exactly what they paid for—not more not less.

在一個荷蘭殖民的城鎭，後來爲紐約州的首府奧伯尼。那裡住著一位麵包師傅，名叫阿姆斯特丹，他非常誠實。他非常注意客人們付多少錢就給剛剛好多少東西——不多也不少。

> Dutch〔dʌtʃ〕*adj.* 荷蘭（人）的　　colonial〔kə'loniəl〕*adj.* 殖民的
> later〔'letɚ〕*adv.* 後來　　***be known as*** 被稱爲
> Albany〔'ɔlbənɪ〕*n.* 奧伯尼【美國紐約州的首府】
> baker〔'bekɚ〕*n.* 麵包師傅　　***as…as one can be*** 儘可能…；非常…
> ***take great care to*** *V.* ～很小心；～很注意
> exactly〔ɪɡ'zæktlɪ〕*adv.* 剛好

One Saint Nicholas Day morning, when the baker was just ready for business, the door of his shop flew open. [31] (B) In walked an old woman wrapped in a long black shawl. She asked for a dozen of the baker's Saint Nicolas cookies. Van Amsterdam counted out twelve cookies. But the woman insisted that a dozen is thirteen. Van Amsterdam was not a man to bear foolishness. He refused. The woman turned to go without the cookies but she stopped at the door, saying, "Van Amsterdam! However honest you may be, your heart is small and your fist is tight." Then she was gone.

在一個聖尼古拉節的早晨，當這位麵包師傅開始要營業時，店的大門突然打開。一位裹著長黑色披肩的老婦人出現。她要求要一打麵包師傅做的聖尼古拉餅乾。阿姆斯特丹數了十二塊餅乾。但老婦人堅持一打是十三個。阿姆斯特丹不是一個可以忍受愚笨的男子，他拒絕了。老婦人沒有買任何餅乾轉身就走，但她停在門口並說：「阿姆斯特丹，無論你多誠實，你的心胸很狹窄，且你很吝嗇。」然後她就離開了。

> ***Saint Nicholas Day*** 聖尼古拉節【是每年 12 月 6 日德國人和荷蘭人慶祝的節日，這個節日有點類似一般人所說的耶誕節。而小朋友只要在每年的 12 月 5 日晚上，把自己的襪子掛在家裡中的窗戶或門口，裡面放一張自己想得到的禮物單子，尼古拉就會把小朋友的禮物單子交給耶誕老公公】

fly open 突然打開　　wrap〔ræp〕v. 裹；包
shawl〔ʃɔl〕n. 披肩；圍巾　　*count out* 逐一數出
dozen〔'dʌzn̩〕n. 一打
insist〔ɪn'sɪst〕v. 堅持　　bear〔bɛr〕v. 忍受
sb's fist is tight 某人很吝嗇【tightfisted〔'taɪt'fɪstɪd〕adj. 吝嗇的】

32 (D) From that day, everything went wrong in Van Amsterdam's bakery. His bread rose too high or not at all. His pies were sour or too sweet. His cookies were burnt or doughy. His customers soon noticed the difference and slipped away.

從那天起，阿姆斯特丹麵包店的所有事情都變得不對勁。他的麵包不是膨脹太多就是完全沒膨脹。他的派餅變酸或是太甜。他的餅乾烤焦或是未熟透。他的客人們很快就察覺異狀並悄悄地離開。

go wrong 出錯；不對勁　　rise〔raɪz〕v.（麵包）膨脹
not at all 完全沒有　　sour〔saʊr〕adj. 酸的
burnt〔bɝnt〕adj. 燒焦的
doughy〔'doɪ〕adj. 未熟的；含有生麵糰的【dough〔do〕n. 生麵糰】
slip away 溜走；悄悄離開

A year passed. The baker grew poorer and poorer. Finally, on the day before Saint Nicolas Day, no customers came to his shop. **33** (F) Staring at his unsold Saint Nicolas cookies, he prayed that Saint Nicolas could help him.

一年過了。麵包師傅越來越窮苦。終於，在聖尼古拉節的前一天，沒有任何客人願意光顧。盯著那些未賣出去的餅乾，他向聖尼古拉祈求幫助他。

grow〔gro〕v. 變得　　*stare at* 凝視著；盯著
pray〔pre〕v. 祈禱

That night, the baker had a dream. He saw Saint Nicholas pulling out gifts from his baskets for a crowd of happy children. No matter how many presents Nicholas handed out, there were always more to give. Then somehow, Saint Nicholas turned into the old woman with the long black shawl!

那天晚上，麵包師傅做了一個夢。他看見聖尼古拉從他的籃子裡拿出禮物給一群快樂的孩子。不論聖尼古拉分發多少禮物，總是有更多可以給。不知怎麼地，聖尼古拉變成那位裹著長黑色披肩的老婦人。

hand out 發送；分發
somehow〔ˈsʌmˌhaʊ〕*adv.* 不知道怎麼地　　***turn into*** 變成

34 **(A)** Van Amsterdam awoke with a start. He suddenly realized that he always gave his customers exactly what they paid for, "But why not give more?"

阿姆斯特丹驚醒。他突然了解到，他總是看客人們給多少錢就剛剛好給多少東西。但為何不多給一點呢？

awake〔əˈwek〕*v.* 醒來　　***with a start*** 吃驚地；猛然
suddenly〔ˈsʌdn̩lɪ〕*adv.* 突然地　　***why not V.*** 何不～

The next morning, on Saint Nicholas Day, the baker rose early to make cookies. And to his surprise, the cookies were as fine as they could be. When he had just finished, the old woman appeared at his door again. She asked for a dozen of Van Amsterdam's Saint Nicholas cookies. **35** **(E)** In great excitement, Van Amsterdam counted out twelve cookies—and one more.

隔天早上，在聖尼古拉節時，麵包師傅很早就起床做餅乾。讓他驚訝的事，餅乾的狀況非常好。當他做完餅乾時，那位老婦人再一次出現在店門口。她要求要一打麵包師傅做的聖尼古拉餅乾。很興奮地，阿姆斯特丹數了十二片餅乾—而又多一片。

rise〔raɪz〕*v.* 起床
to one's surprise 讓某人驚訝的是；某人沒想到
in excitement 興奮地

When people heard he counted thirteen a dozen, he had more customers than ever and became wealthy. The practice then spread to other towns as a common custom.

當人們聽說他一打算成十三個，他的客人比以前有更多，並變富裕。這個作法後來流傳到其他城鎮，成為常見的風俗。

比較級 + ***than ever*** 比以前更～
practice〔ˈpræktɪs〕*n.* 習慣；作法
spread〔sprɛd〕*v.* 流傳

五、閱讀測驗：

第36至39題為題組

All pop artists like to say that they owe their success to their fans. In the case of British band SVM, it's indeed true. The band is currently recording songs because 358 fans contributed the £100,000 needed for the project. The arrangement came via MMC, an online record label that uses web-based, social-network-style "crowd-funding" to finance its acts.

所有的流行音樂藝人都喜歡說，他們的成功要歸功於他們的樂迷。對於英國樂團 SVM 而言，這確實是真的。目前這個樂團正在錄製歌曲，因為 358 位樂迷貢獻了此企劃所需的十萬英鎊。這是透過 MMC 所做的安排，MMC 是一個以使用網路為基礎，社群網路模式「群眾募資」，來提供它運作所需的資金的線上唱片公司。

pop〔pɑp〕*n.* 流行音樂	artist〔'ɑrtɪst〕*n.* 藝人
owe〔o〕*v.* 歸功於 < *to* >	success〔sək'sɛs〕*n.* 成功
fan〔fæn〕*n.* 迷　　case〔kes〕*n.* 例子；情況
British〔'brɪtɪʃ〕*adj.* 英國的	band〔bænd〕*n.* 樂團
indeed〔ɪn'did〕*adv.* 的確	currently〔'kɝəntlɪ〕*adv.* 目前
record〔rɪ'kɔrd〕*v.* 錄音　　〔'rɛkəd〕*n.* 唱片
contribute〔kən'trɪbjut〕*v.* 貢獻	project〔'prɑdʒɛkt〕*n.* 企劃
arrangement〔ə'rendʒmənt〕*n.* 安排　　via〔'vaɪə〕*prep.* 藉由
online〔'ɑn,laɪn〕*adj.* 線上的　　label〔'lebl̩〕*n.* 商標
web-based〔'wɛb'best〕*adj.* 以網路為根基的
social network 社群網路　　style〔staɪl〕*n.* 風格；型式
crowd〔kraʊd〕*n.* 群眾　　fund〔fʌnd〕*v.* 提供資金
finance〔'faɪnæns〕*v.* 資助；提供資金

Here's how it works: MMC posts demos and videos of 10 artists on its website, and users are invited to invest from £10 to £1,000 in the ones they most enjoy or think are most likely to become popular. Once an act reaches £100,000, the financing process is completed, and the money is used to pay for recording and possibly a concert tour. Profits from resulting music sales, concerts, and merchandise are split three ways: investors get to divide 40%; another 40% goes to MMC; the artist pockets 20%. The payoff for investors can be big. One fan in France who contributed £4,250 got his money back 22 times over.

　　這就是它如何運作的：MMC 在它的網站上發佈十組藝人的樣本唱片和音樂錄影帶，並邀請用戶投資十到一百英鎊給他們最欣賞或是他們認為最可能變紅的藝人。一旦金額的運作達到十萬英鎊，募資的程序即完成，而這筆錢會被用來支付錄音的花費，也可能是用在巡迴演唱會上。來自於音樂銷售，演唱會，以及周邊商品的獲利，會分成三份：投資者得到其中的 40%；另外的 40% 屬於 MMC 公司；20% 則落入藝人的口袋。投資者得到的報酬可能是很大筆的。有一個在法國的樂迷捐助了 4250 英鎊，之後拿回了超過 22 倍的錢。

work〔wɝk〕*v.* 運作　　post〔post〕*v.* 發佈

demo〔'dɛmo〕*n.* 試聽帶　　invest〔ɪn'vɛst〕*v.* 投資

likely〔'laɪklɪ〕*adv.* 很可能　　popular〔'papjələ〕*adj.* 受歡迎的

reach〔ritʃ〕*v.* 達到　　process〔'prasɛs〕*n.* 過程

completed〔kəm'plitɪd〕*adj.* 完整的；完結的

pay〔pe〕*v.* 支付　　possibly〔'pasəblɪ〕*adv.* 可能地

concert〔'kansɝt〕*n.* 演唱會　　tour〔tʊr〕*n.* 巡迴

profit〔'prafɪt〕*n.* 收益

resulting〔rɪ'zʌltɪŋ〕*adj.* 因而發生的；隨後的

sale〔sel〕*n.* 銷售　　merchandise〔'mɝtʃən,daɪz〕*n.* 商品

split〔splɪt〕*v.* 分攤　　way〔we〕*n.* 方面

investor〔ɪn'vɛstə〕*n.* 投資者　　divide〔də'vaɪd〕*v.* 分配

payoff〔'pe,ɔf〕*n.* 報酬

Crowd-funding musical acts is not new. But MMC takes the concept to another level. First of all, investors can get cash rather than just goodies like free downloads or tickets. Also, MMC is a record label. It has the means to get its music distributed around the world and to market artists effectively. "Artists need professional support," says the CEO of MMC's international division.

　　群眾募資的音樂運作方式並不是新的。但是 MMC 將這樣的概念帶到另一個層次。首先，投資者可以得到現金，而非只是一些像是免費下載音樂或是門票等小甜頭。此外，MMC 是個唱片公司。它有方法使它的音樂流通到全世界，並有效地行銷藝人。MMC 國際部門的執行長這麼陳述：「藝人們需要專業的支持。」

musical〔'mjuzɪkl̩〕*adj.* 音樂的　　concept〔'kansɛpt〕*n.* 概念

level〔'lɛvl̩〕*n.* 層次　　cash〔kæʃ〕*n.* 現金

goody〔'gʊdɪ〕*n.* 甜頭　　means〔minz〕*n.* 方法；手段【單複數同型】

distribute〔dɪ'strɪbjut〕*v.* 流通　　effectively〔ə'fɛktɪvlɪ〕*adv.* 有效地

professional〔prəˋfɛʃənḷ〕*adj.* 專業的　　support〔səˋport〕*n.* 支持
CEO 執行長（= *Chief Executive Officer*）
international〔͵ɪntəˋnæʃənḷ〕*adj.* 國際的
division〔dəˋvɪʒən〕*n.* 部門

While digital technology and the Net have created a do-it-yourself boom among musicians, **success is still a long shot**. Out of the 20,000 records released in the U.S. in 2009, only 14 DIY acts made it to the Top 200. Also, with less revenue from recorded music, music companies have become less likely to take risks, which has led to fewer artists receiving funding. The crowd-funding model, however, allows for more records to be made by spreading risk among hundreds of backers. And the social-network aspect of the site helps expand fan bases; that is, investors become a promotional army.

縱使數位科技和網路已經為音樂家們創造了一種凡事可以自己來的榮景，成功還是很遙不可及。2009 年在美國所發行的兩萬張唱片中，只有 14 張自製唱片達到排行榜前 200 名。此外，隨著從錄製唱片得到的收益愈益減少，唱片公司已經變得較不可能涉險，這導致更少的藝人能得到資金。然而，群眾募資模式藉由分散風險到數以百計的支持者身上，讓更多唱片得以產生。再者，網站在社群網路方面也助長了擴張樂迷的基數；也就是說，投資者成了促銷的尖兵。

digital〔ˋdɪdʒɪtḷ〕*adj.* 數位的　　technology〔tɛkˋnalədʒɪ〕*n.* 科技
do it yourself 自己做　　boom〔bum〕*n.* 興盛
a long shot 遙不可及；不太可能　　release〔rɪˋlis〕*v.* 發行
revenue〔ˋrɛvə͵nu〕*n.* 收入　　risk〔rɪsk〕*n.* 風險
take risks 冒險　　***lead to*** 導致　　receive〔rɪˋsiv〕*v.* 收到
model〔ˋmadḷ〕*n.* 模式　　spread〔sprɛd〕*v.* 分散
backer〔ˋbækɚ〕*n.* 支持者　　aspect〔ˋæspɛkt〕*n.* 方面
expand〔ɪkˋspænd〕*v.* 擴張　　base〔bes〕*n.* 基礎
promotional〔prəˋmoʃənḷ〕*adj.* 促銷的　　army〔ˋɑrmɪ〕*n.* 軍隊

36. (**D**) 下列哪一項標題最能表達本篇文章的主旨？
(A) 以網站為基礎的音樂製作。　　(B) 為唱片公司募款。
(C) 音樂樂迷從投資中獲利。　　(D) <u>音樂產業的群眾募資。</u>

express〔ɪkˋsprɛs〕*v.* 表達　　production〔prəˋdʌkʃən〕*n.* 製作
fundraising〔ˋfʌnd͵rezɪŋ〕*n.* 募款　　industry〔ˋɪndəstrɪ〕*n.* 產業

37. (**D**) 透過 MMC 唱片公司，一個樂團要錄製自己的音樂，必須募集到多
　　 少錢？

    (A) 10 英鎊。　　　　　　　　　　(B) 1,000 英鎊。

    (C) 4,250 英鎊。　　　　　　　　　(D) 100,000 英鎊。

    raise〔rez〕*v.* 籌措（金錢）

38. (**C**) 下列對於 MMC 的敘述何項是對的？

    (A) 它幫助了很多自製唱片的音樂人達到排行榜前 200 名。

    (B) 同時有 14 位藝人的作品發佈在它的網站。

    (C) 它讓樂迷們能夠提供資金支持他們所喜愛的音樂人。

    (D) 從群眾募資企畫中獲利的最大一份，是給了音樂人。

    statement〔'stetmənt〕*n.* 敘述

    musician〔mju'zɪʃən〕*n.* 音樂家　　provide〔prə'vaɪd〕*v.* 提供

    financial〔fə'nænʃəl〕*adj.* 財務的　　share〔ʃɛr〕*n.* 部分

39. (**B**) 在第四段中，作者說「成功還是很遙不可及」，是什麼意思？

    (A) 成功的效果是永恆的。　　　　(B) 成功並不容易達到。

    (C) 成功通常以一位大人物為開端。

    (D) 成功應該是每位音樂人的長期目標。

    everlasting〔͵ɛvɚ'læstɪŋ〕*adj.* 永恆的

    effect〔ɪ'fɛkt〕*n.* 影響；效果　　achieve〔ə'tʃiv〕*v.* 達成

    big shot 大人物　　long-term〔'lɔŋ'tɝm〕*adj.* 長期的

第 40 至 43 題為題組

    In science fiction TV programs such as Star Trek, tractor beams are used to tow spaceships and move objects. For years, scientists have labored to replicate this feat. In 2013, they succeeded. A team of British and Czech scientists, led by Dr. Tomas Cizmar, say they have created a real-life "tractor beam," like the kind from Star Trek, which uses a beam of light to attract objects, at least at a microscopic level.

    在像是星艦迷航記的科幻小說電視節目裡，牽引光束被用來拖曳太空船和移動物體。多年來，科學家們已經努力複製了這項技術。在 2013 年，他們成功了。一個由托瑪斯·席茲瑪博士率領的英國和捷克的科學家團隊，說他們已經創造出一個真實的「牽引光束」，就像從星艦迷航記來的那種一樣，它用一道光束來吸引物體，至少是在細微的程度上。

science〔'saɪəns〕*n.* 科學　　fiction〔'fɪkʃən〕*n.* 小說
science fiction 科幻小說　　program〔'progræm〕*n.* 節目
Star Trek 星艦迷航記【美國科幻電視影集】
tractor〔'træktɚ〕*n.* 牽引機　　beam〔bim〕*n.* 光束
tow〔to〕*v.* 拖曳　　spaceship〔'spes.ʃɪp〕*n.* 太空船
move〔muv〕*v.* 移動　　object〔'ɑbdʒɪkt〕*n.* 物體
scientist〔'saɪəntɪst〕*n.* 科學家　　labor〔'lebɚ〕*v.* 努力做
replicate〔'rɛplɪ.ket〕*v.* 複製　　feat〔fit〕*n.* 技藝
succeed〔sək'sid〕*v.* 成功　　team〔tim〕*n.* 團隊
British〔'brɪtɪʃ〕*adj.* 英國的　　Czech〔tʃɛk〕*adj.* 捷克的
lead〔lid〕*v.* 率領　　Dr.〔'dɑktɚ〕*n.* 博士（= *doctor*）
create〔krɪ'et〕*v.* 創造　　real-life〔'rɪəl'laɪf〕*adj.* 真實的；現實的
attract〔ə'trækt〕*v.* 吸引
microscopic〔.maɪkrə'skɑpɪk〕*adj.* 顯微鏡的；細微的
level〔'lɛvl̩〕*n.* 程度

　　Light manipulation techniques have existed since the 1970s, but this is thought to be the first time a light beam has been used to draw objects towards a light source. Usually when microscopic objects are hit by a beam of light, they are forced along the direction of the beam. After many years' research, Dr. Cizmar's team discovered a technique that allows for the radiant force of light to be reversed and to use the negative force to draw out certain particles.

　　光的操縱技術自 70 年代已經存在，然而一道光束被用來將物體拉向光源則被認爲是第一次。通常當細微的物體被光束擊中的時候，它們會被迫沿著光束的方向前進。在許多年的研究以後，席茲瑪博士的團隊發現一項技術，容許光的輻射力被反轉，並且用負向力拉出某些粒子。

manipulation〔mə.nɪpjə'leʃən〕*n.* 操縱　　technique〔tɛk'nik〕*n.* 技術
exist〔ɪg'zɪst〕*v.* 存在　　***1970s*** 70 年代　　think〔θɪŋk〕*v.* 認爲
draw〔drɔ〕*v.* 拉；拖　　source〔sors〕*n.* 來源　　hit〔hɪt〕*v.* 擊中
force〔fors〕*v.* 迫使；*n.* 力　　direction〔də'rɛkʃən〕*n.* 方向
research〔'risɝtʃ〕*n.*（學術）研究　　discover〔dɪ'skʌvɚ〕*v.* 發現
allow〔ə'laʊ〕*v.* 容許　　radiant〔'redɪənt〕*adj.* 輻射的
reverse〔rɪ'vɝs〕*v.* 反轉；逆轉　　negative〔'nɛgətɪv〕*adj.* 負的
certain〔'sɝtn̩〕*adj.* 某些　　particle〔'pɑrtɪkl̩〕*n.* 粒子

Dr. Cizmar says that even though it is a few years away from practical use, the technology has huge potential for medical research. In particular, the tractor beam is highly selective in the particles it can attract, so it can pick up particles that have specific properties, such as size or composition, in a mixture. "Eventually, this could be used to separate white blood cells, for example," Dr. Cizmar told BBC News.

席茲瑪博士說，即使距離實際上的運用還有幾年，這項科技對醫學研究有著巨大的潛力。尤其，牽引光束對它能吸引的粒子是極有選擇性的，所以它可以在一團混合物當中，發現有特定屬性的粒子，例如大小或組成。席茲瑪告訴英國國家廣播公司新聞台說：「最後，舉例來說，這可以被用來分離白血球。」

even though 即使　　practical〔ˈpræktɪkḷ〕*adj.* 實際的
use〔juz〕*n.* 使用　　technology〔tɛkˈnɑlədʒɪ〕*n.* 科技
huge〔hjudʒ〕*adj.* 巨大的　　potential〔pəˈtɛnʃəl〕*n.* 潛力
medical〔ˈmɛdɪkḷ〕*adj.* 醫學的　　***in particular*** 尤其；特別地
highly〔ˈhaɪlɪ〕*adv.* 非常　　selective〔səˈlɛktɪv〕*adj.* 有選擇性的
pick up 發現　　specific〔spɪˈsɪfɪk〕*adj.* 特定的
property〔ˈprɑpɚtɪ〕*n.* 屬性　　composition〔ˌkɑmpəˈzɪʃən〕*n.* 組成
mixture〔ˈmɪkstʃɚ〕*n.* 混合物　　eventually〔ɪˈvɛntʃʊəlɪ〕*adv.* 最後
separate〔ˈsɛpəˌret〕*v.* 分離　　cell〔sɛl〕*n.* 細胞
white blood cell 白血球　　***for example*** 舉例來說
BBC 英國國家廣播公司（= *British Broadcasting Corporation*）
news〔njuz〕*n.* 新聞

It has been a primary plot device in science fiction TV programs and movies to allow objects like spaceships to be trapped in a beam of light. But Dr. Cizmar said this particular technique would not eventually lead to **that**. A transfer of energy happens in the process. On a microscopic scale that is OK, but on a large scale it would cause huge problems. A large object could be destroyed by the heating, which results from the massive amount of energy necessary to pull it.

讓像是太空船的物體陷入一道光束裡，已經是科幻電視節目和電影裡的基本劇情構想。但是席茲瑪博士說，這特別的技術最後將不會導致那個結果。在過程中會發生能量的轉移。在微小的規模上那是沒問題的，然而在大的規模上，它會造成莫大的問題。一個大的物體，可能會被要拉動它所需的大量能量引起的加熱作用給摧毀。

primary〔'praɪˌmɛrɪ〕*adj.* 基本的　　plot〔plɑt〕*n.* 情節
device〔dɪ'vaɪs〕*n.* 構想　　allow〔ə'laʊ〕*v.* 讓
trap〔træp〕*v.* 陷入　　particular〔pə'tɪkjələ〕*adj.* 特別的
lead〔lid〕*v.* 導致　　transfer〔'trænsfɝ〕*n.* 轉移
energy〔'ɛnədʒɪ〕*n.* 能量　　process〔'prɑsɛs〕*n.* 過程
scale〔skel〕*n.* 規模　　large〔lɑrdʒ〕*adj.* 大的
destroy〔dɪ'strɔɪ〕*v.* 摧毀　　heating〔'hitɪŋ〕*n.* 加熱作用
result〔rɪ'zʌlt〕*v.* 引起　　***result from*** 由~引起；起因於
massive〔'mæsɪv〕*adj.* 大量的　　amount〔ə'maʊnt〕*n.* 數量
necessary〔'nɛsəˌsɛrɪ〕*adj.* 必需的

40.（**B**）這段文章主要是關於什麼？
(A) 照明科技在現代社會的應用。
(B) 一個研究團隊所研發的一項科學發明的使用和限制。
(C) 光的操縱技術在醫學治療上的採用。
(D) 科學發展對科幻小說的影響和效果。

mainly〔'menlɪ〕*adv.* 主要地　　passage〔'pæsɪdʒ〕*n.* （文章的）段
application〔ˌæplə'keʃən〕*n.* 應用　　lighting〔'laɪtɪŋ〕*n.* 照明
modern〔'mɑdɚn〕*adj.* 現代的　　limitation〔ˌlɪmə'teʃən〕*n.* 限制
invention〔ɪn'vɛnʃən〕*n.* 發明　　adoption〔ə'dɑpʃən〕*n.* 採用
treatment〔'tritmənt〕*n.* 治療　　influence〔'ɪnfluəns〕*n.* 影響
effect〔ə'fɛkt〕*n.* 效果　　development〔dɪ'vɛləpmənt〕*n.* 發展

41.（**C**）以下關於席茲瑪博士的牽引光束，何者為真？
(A) 它像星艦迷航記裡的牽引光束一樣移動大的物體。
(B) 它是第一個將物體往前推的光束裝置。
(C) 它依靠負向力將特別種類的粒子拉出。
(D) 它目前在醫學研究上被用來分離血球。

device〔dɪ'vaɪs〕*n.* 裝置　　rely〔rɪ'laɪ〕*v.* 依靠
currently〔'kɝəntlɪ〕*adv.* 目前　　specific〔spɪ'sɪfɪk〕*adj.* 特定的

42.（**D**）最後一段的 **that** 指的是什麼？
(A) 轉移大量的能量。　　(B) 製作科幻小說的節目和電影。
(C) 將一個巨大的物體燃燒成灰燼。
(D) 用一道光束捕獲太空船。

burn〔bɝn〕*v.* 燃燒　　ash〔æʃ〕*n.* 灰燼
capture〔'kæptʃɚ〕*v.* 捕獲

43. (**A**) 這篇段落的語氣為何？

　　(A) 客觀的。　　　　　　　　　(B) 懷疑的。
　　(C) 佩服的。　　　　　　　　　(D) 悲觀的。

tone〔ton〕*n.* 語氣　　objective〔əbˋdʒɛktɪv〕*adj.* 客觀的
suspicious〔səˋspɪʃəs〕*adj.* 懷疑的
admiring〔ədˋmaɪrɪŋ〕*adj.* 佩服的
pessimistic〔͵pɛsəˋmɪstɪk〕*adj.* 悲觀的

第 44 至 47 題為題組

　　Grace Wambui, a 14-year-old pupil in Nairobi, had never touched a tablet computer. But it took her only about one minute to work out how to use one when such devices arrived at Amaf School in Kawangware, a slum in the Kenyan capital. Teaching used to be conducted with a blackboard and a handful of tattered textbooks. Now children in groups of five take turns to swipe the touch screen of the devices, which are loaded with a multimedia version of Kenya's syllabus.

　　格雷絲・萬姆布是在奈洛比的一位十四歲的學生，她從來沒碰過平板電腦。但是當這樣的東西出現在阿馬夫學校裡，這座學校位於肯亞首都裡的一處貧民區，卡旺威，她只花了大約一分鐘就了解了如何使用平板電腦。以往的教學，是用黑板和少許破爛的教科書來進行，現在孩子們五人一組，輪流滑動平板電腦的觸控螢幕，裡面裝載有肯亞多媒體形式的課程大綱。

Nairobi〔naɪˋrobɪ〕*n.* 奈洛比【東非肯亞（Kenya)的首都】
pupil〔ˋpjupl̩〕*n.* (中、小學）學生　　***tablet computer*** 平板電腦
work out 想出；解決　　device〔dɪˋvaɪs〕*n.* 器具；裝置
slum〔slʌm〕*n.* 貧民窟　　Kenyan〔ˋkɛnjən〕*adj.* 肯亞的
capital〔ˋkæpətl̩〕*n.* 首都　　***used to V.*** 過去～
conduct〔kənˋdʌkt〕*v.* 進行　　***a handful of*** 一把～；少量的
tattered〔ˋtætɚd〕*adj.* 破爛的　　textbook〔ˋtɛkst͵bʊk〕*n.* 課本
take turns 輪流　　swipe〔swaɪp〕*v.* 滑動
touch screen 觸控螢幕　　***be loaded with*** 裝載著
multimedia〔͵mʌltɪˋmidɪə〕*n.* 多媒體
version〔ˋvɝʒən〕*n.* 版本；形式　　syllabus〔ˋsɪləbəs〕*n.* 課程大綱

　　The tablets at Amaf School are part of a pilot project run by eLimu, a technology start-up. If it and other firms are right, tablets and other digital devices may soon be the rule in African schools. Many are betting on a boom in digital education in Kenya and elsewhere. Some executives even expect it to take off like M-Pesa, Kenya's hugely successful mobile-money service.

阿馬夫學校的平板電腦是試驗計畫的一部份，這是由一家新創立的科技公司艾利莫所運作。如果它們和其他公司是對的，平板電腦和其他的數位產品很快就會普及在非洲的學校裡。很多公司打賭，數位教育在肯亞和其他地方會快速成長。有些執行長甚至預期它會迅速竄紅，就像在肯亞非常成功的行動貨幣 M-Pesa 一樣。

pilot〔ˊpaɪlət〕*n.* 機師　　***pilot project*** 試驗計畫
run〔rʌn〕*n.* 經營；運作　　technology〔tɛkˊnɑlədʒɪ〕*n.* 科技
start-up〔ˊstɑrt‚ʌp〕*n.* 新成立的公司　　firm〔fɝm〕*n.* 公司
digital〔ˊdɪdʒɪtl̩〕*adj.* 數位的　　rule〔rul〕*n.* 慣例；普遍情況
bet on 打賭　　boom〔bum〕*n.* 榮景；遽增
executive〔ɪgˊzɛkjutɪv〕*n.* 執行長　　***take off*** 起飛；成功
M-Pesa 行動貨幣【M 代表 mobile，Pesa 是當地語言裡「錢」的意思】
hugely〔ˊhjudʒlɪ〕*adv.* 非常地　　successful〔səkˊsɛsfəl〕*adj.* 成功的
mobile〔ˊmobl̩〕*adj.* 可動的；行動的
mobile-money service 行動貨幣服務【讓消費者能夠在商店、餐館和交通終端用手機來為其貨物和服務付款】

Such growth in digital education would be timely. The flood of new pupils has overwhelmed state schools, which were already understaffed, underfunded and poorly managed. The prospect of Africa's 300 million pupils learning digitally has caught the attention of global technology giants. Amazon has seen sales of its Kindle e-readers in Africa increase tenfold in the past year. Intel has been helping African governments buy entry-level computers. In Nigeria, Intel brought together a publisher and a telecom carrier to provide exam-preparation tools over mobile phones, a service that has become hugely popular.

如此的數位教育的成長來得恰到好處。大量湧入的新生超出了公立學校的負荷，而這些學校原本就已經人員不足、資金短缺且經營不佳。非洲三億透過數位學習的學童的前景受到全球科技巨擘的注意。亞馬遜網站銷售的天火藏書在非洲去年增加了十倍。英代爾公司持續幫助非洲政府買基本配備的電腦。在奈及利亞，英代爾公司讓出版商和電信公司合作，來提供手機上準備考試的工具，這服務已經變得非常受歡迎。

timely〔'taɪmlɪ〕*adj.* 合適的；適時的　　flood〔flʌd〕*n.* 大量的流入
overwhelm〔‚ovə'hwɛlm〕*v.* 淹沒；壓倒　***state school*** 公立學校
understaffed〔‚ʌndə'stæft〕*adj.* 人員不足的
underfunded〔‚ʌndə'fʌndɪd〕*adj.* 資金短缺的
manage〔'mænɪdʒ〕*v.* 管理；經營
prospect〔'prɑspɛkt〕*n.* 前景；希望
catch sb's attention 吸引某人的注意
global〔'globl̩〕*adj.* 全球的　　giant〔'dʒaɪənt〕*n.* 巨人；傑出人物
Amazon 亞馬遜【美國購物網站】　　see〔si〕*v.* 見證；經歷
Kindle〔'kɪndl̩〕天火藏書【亞馬遜推出的電子書】
e-reader 電子書　　increase〔ɪn'kris〕*v.* 增加
ten-fold〔'tɛn‚fold〕*adv.* 十倍地
Intel 英代爾公司【電腦硬體生產公司】
government〔'gʌvəmənt〕*n.* 政府　　***entry-level*** *adj.* 入門的；基本的
Nigeria〔naɪ'dʒɪrɪə〕*n.* 奈及利亞【位於非洲中西部的國家】
bring together 使合作
publisher〔'pʌblɪʃə〕*n.* 出版者；出版商
telecom〔'tɛlɪkəm〕*n.* 電信；遠距通訊（= *telecommunications*）
carrier〔'kʊrɪə〕*n.* 信差；嚮導　　***telecom carrier*** 電信公司
tool〔tul〕*n.* 工具

A bigger question is whether digital tools actually improve education. Early results are encouraging. In Ghana, reading skills improved measurably among 350 children that had been given Kindle e-readers. In Ethiopia, in the absence of teachers, children figured out how to use tablets and learned the English ABCs. At Amaf School, average marks in science went from 58 to 73 in a single term.

　　一個更大的問題是，數位工具是否實際上改善了教育。早期的結果非常振奮人心，在迦納，使用天火藏書的 350 位孩童的閱讀能力顯著地增加。在衣索比亞，沒有老師的幫助，孩童學會如何使用平板電腦，和學習英文字母 ABC。在阿馬夫學校，科學的平均分數在一學期內從 58 分進步到 73 分。

actually〔'æktʃʊəlɪ〕*adv.* 實際上
improve〔ɪm'pruv〕*v.* 改善　　result〔rɪ'zʌlt〕*n.* 結果
encouraging〔ɪn'kɝdʒɪŋ〕*adj.* 鼓舞的；振奮人心的
Ghana〔'gɑnə〕*n.* 迦納【位於非洲西部的國家】

measurably〔ˈmɛʒərəblɪ〕*adv.* 顯著地
Ethiopia〔ˌiθɪˈopɪə〕*n.* 衣索比亞【埃及南方的國家】
in the absence of 沒有　　***figure out*** 想出
average〔ˈæv(ə)rɪdʒ〕*adj.* 平均的　　mark〔mɑrk〕*n.* 分數
single〔ˈsɪŋl〕*adj.* 單一的　　term〔tɜm〕*n.* 學期

44.(**C**) 以下何者是本文最佳的標題？
　　(A) 非洲的暢銷書　　　　　　(B) 非洲危害教育的問題
　　(C) <u>非洲的學校正走向數位化</u>　(D) 平板電腦在肯亞有大量的需求
　　bestseller〔ˌbɛstˈsɛlə〕*n.* 暢銷書　　plague〔pleg〕*v.* 使困擾；危害
　　in great demand 有很大的需求

45.(**B**) 作者引用格雷絲・萬姆布的例子是要傳達什麼？
　　(A) 格雷絲是電腦技能的天才。　(B) <u>平板電腦容易使用上手。</u>
　　(C) 肯亞的運送系統很差。　　　(D) 平板電腦在卡旺威很普遍。
　　convey〔kənˈve〕*v.* 傳達　　cite〔saɪt〕*v.* 引用
　　genius〔ˈdʒinjəs〕*n.* 天才　　***user-friendly*** *adj.* 容易使用的
　　delivery〔dɪˈlɪvərɪ〕*n.* 遞送；運送

46.(**A**) 根據本文，什麼是 eLimu？
　　(A) <u>一家公司。</u>　　　　　　(B) 一種電腦程式。
　　(C) 一本電子書。　　　　　　(D) 一個教育計畫。
　　program〔ˈprogræm〕*n.* 程式

47.(**D**) 根據本文，關於非洲的教育，何者為真？
　　(A) 學生的人數近幾年持續減少。
　　(B) 以傳統的課堂教學來說，老師非常足夠。
　　(C) 學生收到了由亞馬遜所捐贈的藏火天書，以改善閱讀能力。
　　(D) <u>在某些國家，教學上使用數位工具的早期結果是正面的。</u>
　　drop〔drɑp〕*v.* 掉落；下降　　***more than*** 非常地
　　donate〔ˈdonet〕*v.* 捐贈　　positive〔ˈpɑzətɪv〕*adj.* 正面的

第 48 至 51 題為題組

　　In the Spartathlon, one of the world's toughest ultra-marathons, runners run 245 km, about six marathons, within 36 hours. The runners start in Athens, and run all the way to historical Sparta.

在全世界最艱辛的超級馬拉松之一，斯巴達松的路程裡，跑者在 36 個小時之內，要跑 245 公里，大約是 6 個馬拉松的距離。跑者從雅典起跑，要一路跑到歷史上的斯巴達。

> Spartathlon〔͵spɑrt'æθlən〕 *n.* 斯巴達松【由 Sparta（斯巴達）和 athlon（競賽）組合而成】　　　　tough〔tʌf〕 *adj.* 費力的；艱辛的
> ultra〔'ʌltrə〕 表示「超…」的字根
> marathon〔'mærə͵θɑn〕 *n.* 馬拉松
> Athens〔'æθɪnz〕 *n.* 雅典【希臘首都】
> ***all the way*** 一路上；一直　　　historical〔hɪs'tɔrɪkl̩〕 *adj.* 歷史上的

The Spartathlon's heritage goes back to 490 B.C., when Pheidippides, an Athenian, made the journey to Sparta to ask the Spartans for help in fighting the invading Persians. It is recorded that he reached Sparta on the day after he left Athens. In 1982, this story sparked the interest of a British air-force officer and long-distance runner called John Foden, who wondered if it really was possible to run from Athens to Sparta and arrive the next day. With four other officers, Foden decided to see for himself; after a 36-hour slog they arrived in Sparti, as the town is now called. That achievement inspired the organization of the first Spartathlon a year later.

斯巴達松的傳統要追溯至西元前 490 年，當時一名雅典人，費底皮斯，為了尋求斯巴達人的幫助，以對抗入侵的波斯人，完成到斯巴達的這項歷程。根據記載，在他離開雅典一天後，他就抵達斯巴達。在 1982 年，這個故事激發了約翰福登的興趣，他是英國空軍軍官，也是一位長距離賽跑者，他想知道，從雅典跑步出發，是不是真的可能在隔天抵達斯巴達。福登決定親身去領會，連同其他四位軍官一起；在 36 小時之後，他們抵達了現在名為斯巴提的城鎮。那樣的成就促成了一年後第一屆斯巴達松的籌辦。

> heritage〔'hɛrətɪdʒ〕 *n.* 遺產；傳統　　***go back to*** 追溯到
> ***B.C.*** 西元前（= *before Christ*）　　Athenian〔ə'θiniən〕 *adj.* 雅典的
> ***make a journey to*** 前往　　Spartan〔'spɑrtn̩〕 *n.* 斯巴達人
> ***ask*** *sb.* ***for help*** 向某人求助　　invading〔ɪn'vedɪŋ〕 *adj.* 入侵的
> Persian〔'pɝʒən〕 *n.* 波斯人　　record〔rɪ'kɔrd〕 *v.* 紀錄
> spark〔spɑrk〕 *v.* 引起　　***air-force*** *adj.* 空軍的
> officer〔'ɔfəsɚ〕 *n.* 軍官　　***for*** *oneself* 親自
> slog〔slɑg〕 *n.* 艱難的行進　　achievement〔ə'tʃivmənt〕 *n.* 成就
> inspire〔ɪn'spaɪr〕 *v.* 鼓舞；激發
> organization〔͵ɔrgənə'zeʃən〕 *n.* 組成；籌辦

The Spartathlon's attraction has two sources. The first is the difficulty of finishing it. The Spartathlon is not the most difficult race, but it combines lots of different tests. There is the heat of the Greek day, and then the plunge in temperatures when darkness falls. There are climbs: the route includes a series of ascents, among them a 1,200-meter mountain pass in the dead of night. Above all, there is the relentless pressure of the clock. The second reason is that the idea of retracing Pheidippides's footsteps still grips many participants. It feels like racing in history, passing through places where history began.

斯巴達松吸引人的原因有兩點。第一點是它很難完成。斯巴達松並非最困難的賽跑，但它結合了許多困難的考驗。有希臘白天炎熱，當黑夜降臨時，氣溫卻驟降。有許多的爬坡，此路徑涵蓋了一連串的上坡，其中包括了在深夜時候，通過一段 1200 公尺的山路。尤其是時間的無情壓力。第二個理由是，追循著費底皮斯的腳步，這樣的構想仍舊吸引了許多參加者。感覺就像是在歷史中賽跑，經過了歷史起源的地方。

attraction〔ə'trækʃən〕n. 吸引人的地方
source〔sors〕n. 來源；原因　　combine〔kəm'baɪn〕v. 結合
Greek〔grik〕adj. 希臘的　　day〔de〕n. 白天
plunge〔plʌndʒ〕n. 突然掉落；驟降　　fall〔fɔl〕v. 降臨
route〔rut〕n. 路線　　*a series of* 一連串的
ascent〔ə'sɛnt〕n. 上坡　　pass〔pæs〕n. 山路；山頂上的通道
in the dead of night 在深夜　　*above all* 尤其是；最重要的是
relentless〔rɪ'lɛntlɪs〕adj. 無情的　　pressure〔'prɛʃɚ〕n. 壓力
clock〔klɑk〕n. 時鐘；時間　　retrace〔rɪ'tres〕v. 循著…的路
footstep〔'fʊt,stɛp〕n. 腳步；足跡　　grip〔grɪp〕v. 抓住；吸引
participant〔pɚ'tɪsəpənt〕n. 參與者

As finishers receive a laurel wreath and water from schoolgirls, many are overjoyed with emotion. However, **<u>the euphoria is fleeting</u>**. Within a few minutes, their joints and muscles start to seize up: after the race, Sparti resembles the set of a zombie film as participants lumber slowly around on legs that will not bend. But the itch to do it all over again soon appears.

當完成者接受了桂冠的殊榮以及來自女學生給予的水，許多人感動地欣喜若狂。然而，興奮的情緒卻是稍縱即逝的。在幾分鐘之內，他們的關節和肌肉

開始僵硬：在賽跑之後，當參賽者用僵直的腿緩慢四處走動時，斯巴提城就像是殭屍電影的一景。但是很快地，再參加一次的渴望又會湧現。

> laurel〔ˋlɔrəl〕*n.* 桂冠【象徵榮譽】
> wreath〔riθ〕*n.* 花圈　　*be overjoyed with* 因…而欣喜若狂
> emotion〔ɪˋmoʃən〕*n.* 感情；感動
> euphoria〔juˋforɪə〕*n.* 快樂；幸福　　fleeting〔ˋflitɪŋ〕*adj.* 短暫的
> joint〔dʒɔɪnt〕*n.* 關節　　muscle〔ˋmʌsḷ〕*n.* 肌肉
> *seize up* 僵硬；無法動彈　　resemble〔rɪˋzɛmbḷ〕*v.* 類似
> set〔sɛt〕*n.* 場景　　zombi〔ˋzɑmbɪ〕*n.* 僵屍
> lumber〔ˋlʌmbɚ〕*v.* 緩慢地移動；笨重地走　　bend〔bɛnd〕*v.* 彎曲
> itch〔ɪtʃ〕*n.* 渴望　　*all over again* 再一次
> appear〔əˋpɪr〕*v.* 出現

48.(**C**) 第二段主要是關於什麼？
　　(A) 約翰福登的生平背景。　　　(B) 超級馬拉松的路徑。
　　(C) 斯巴達松的起源。　　　　　(D) 古雅典人費底皮斯的故事。
　　background〔ˋbæk͵graʊnd〕*n.* 背景
　　origin〔ˋɔrədʒɪn〕*n.* 起源　　ancient〔ˋenʃənt〕*adj.* 古代的

49.(**B**) 為什麼超級賽跑者選擇參加斯巴達松？
　　(A) 它是全世界最正統的超級馬拉松。
　　(B) 賽跑者感覺就像是穿越了歷史。
　　(C) 他們的個人問題在賽跑中將會被解決。
　　(D) 他們必須在一天之內完成所有考驗。
　　classical〔ˋklæsɪkḷ〕*adj.* 傳統的；正統的

50.(**D**) 在最後一段中的「興奮的情緒卻是稍縱即逝的」指的是什麼？
　　(A) 勝利的感覺將持續到永遠。
　　(B) 完成這項賽跑，是不可思議的困難。
　　(C) 在賽跑之後，疲勞會排山倒海而來。
　　(D) 完成賽跑的興奮之情會消散的很快。
　　triumph〔ˋtraɪəmf〕*n.* 勝利　　last〔læst〕*v.* 持續
　　incomprehensibly〔͵ɪnkɑmprɪˋhɛnsəblɪ〕*adv.* 不可思議地
　　fatigue〔fəˋtig〕*n.* 疲勞
　　overwhelming〔͵ovɚˋhwɛlmɪŋ〕*adj.* 壓倒性的

51. (**A**) 根據本文，關於斯巴達松的敘述何者是正確的？

　　(A) 斯巴達松在 1983 年第一次被籌辦。

　　(B) 斯巴達松的活動被製作成了電影。

　　(C) 許多人在賽跑之後決定不要再次嘗試。

　　(D) 賽跑者在白天與夜晚都必須忍受高溫。

　　be made into 被製成　　endure〔ɪn'dʊr〕*v.* 忍受

第貳部分：非選擇題

一、中譯英：

1. 對現今的許多學生而言，在課業和課外活動間取得平衡是一大挑戰。

For many students nowadays, it is a big challenge to strike a balance

between ⎰ their studies and extracurricular activities.

　　　　 ⎱ their academic and extracurricular activities.

2. 有效的時間管理是每位有責任感的學生必須學習的首要課題。

Effective time management

To manage ⎱

Managing ⎰ time effectively ⎰ is a top priority for

⎰ every student with a sense of responsibility ⎱

⎱ every responsible student ⎰ to learn.

二、英文作文：

【範例】

　　If I were lucky enough to win either prize, I would definitely prefer the smart glasses. ***First of all***, I think I could put them to better use than the invisibility cloak. ***For instance***, with the smart glasses, I could potentially use them to help people. If someone had an injury, I could identify the problem and possibly give them assistance before they could reach a hospital. ***Another benefit*** of the glasses would be the recording feature. ***For example***, if I witnessed a traffic accident, I could provide the recording to the police so they could take appropriate action.

　　The invisibility cloak is not without its merits, but I think it would be used for more negative things like sneaking around or spying on people. Although the idea of being invisible is attractive, I personally can't think of a positive use for it. If such a thing existed, it would almost certainly fall into the wrong hands. People would go around robbing banks and committing other crimes, ***and worst of all***, get away with it. ***So in conclusion***, I would prefer the prize that did the most good for society in general.

> prize〔praɪz〕*n.* 獎；獎品
> definitely〔'dɛfənɪtlɪ〕*adv.* 明確地；一定
> prefer〔prɪ'fɝ〕*v.* 較喜歡；偏好　　***first of all*** 首先
> ***put⋯to use*** 使用　　invisibility〔ɪn,vɪzə'bɪlətɪ〕*n.* 看不見；隱形
> cloak〔klok〕*n.* 斗篷　　***for instance*** 舉例來說（= *for example*）
> potentially〔pə'tɛnʃəlɪ〕*adv.* 可能地　　injury〔'ɪndʒərɪ〕*n.* 受傷
> identify〔aɪ'dɛntə,faɪ〕*v.* 辨識；看出
> assistance〔ə'sɪstəns〕*n.* 幫助
> meanwhile〔'min,hwaɪl〕*adv.* 同時　　benefit〔'bɛnəfɪt〕*n.* 好處
> recording〔rɪ'kɔrdɪŋ〕*adj.* 記錄的；自動記錄裝置的
> feature〔'fitʃə〕*n.* 特色　　witness〔'wɪtnɪs〕*v.* 目擊
> appropriate〔ə'proprɪɪt〕*adj.* 適當的
> action〔'ækʃən〕*n.* 行動　　merit〔'mɛrɪt〕*n.* 好處；優點
> negative〔'nɛɡətɪv〕*adj.* 負面的
> sneak〔snik〕*v.* 偷偷摸摸；鬼鬼祟祟　　***spy on*** 暗中監視；偷窺
> invisible〔ɪn'vɪzəbḷ〕*adj.* 看不見的；隱形的
> personally〔'pɝsṇlɪ〕*adv.* 對個人而言　　***think of*** 想到
> positive〔'pɑzətɪv〕*adj.* 正面的　　exist〔ɪɡ'zɪst〕*v.* 存在
> ***fall into the wrong hands*** 落入不當的人手中；被不當使用
> rob〔rɑb〕*v.* 搶劫　　***commit crimes*** 犯罪
> ***worst of all*** 最糟的是　　***get away with***⋯ 做⋯而未受懲罰
> ***in conclusion*** 總而言之　　***in general*** 一般來說；大體上

102年指定科目考試英文科試題修正意見

題　　號	修　　正　　意　　見
一、詞彙 　　第 2 題	…simple and he *recorded faithfully* the incidents of everyday life. → …simple**,** and he ***faithfully recorded*** the incidents of everyday life ＊要用逗點分隔所連接的獨立子句。（詳見「文法寶典」p.39） 及物動詞 + { 受詞 + 副詞 　　　　　　 副詞 + 長受詞（子句） 副詞修飾及物動詞，如副詞語氣較弱時，可置於動詞之前。 （詳見「文法寶典」p.264）
第 6 題	Helen's doctor suggested that she undergo *a heart surgery*. → Helen's doctor suggested that she undergo ***heart surgery***. ＊surgery（手術）為不可數名詞，故須去掉冠詞 a。
三、文意選填 　　最後一段 　　倒數第 2 行	Comfort, however, is not the *purpose to stay* in the ice hotel. → Comfort, however, is not the ***purpose of staying*** in the ice hotel ＊purpose 後面須接 of + V-ing，表「目的」。
五、閱讀測驗 　　第 38 題 　　（D）	The biggest share of *its* profits…. → The biggest share of ***the*** profits…. ＊依句意，應是這個 project 賺到的錢，並不是 MMC 這家公司賺到的。
第 40 題 （B）	The uses and limitations of a scientific invention *by* a research team. → The uses and limitations of a scientific invention ***developed by*** a research team. ＊加 developed 句意才清楚。

題　　號	修　正　意　見
第 41 題 (A)	It moves big objects as the tractor beam *did in Star Trek.* → It moves big objects as the tractor beam *in Star Trek did.* * 依句意，in Star Trek 修飾 tractor beam。
第 47 題 (A)	The number of students *keeps dropping in recent years.* → The number of students *has been dropping* in recent years. 或→ The number of students *keeps dropping.* * in recent years 應和現在完成式或現在完成進行式連用。
第 48 題至 51 題 最後一段 第一行	…, many are *overjoyed with emotion.* → …, many are *overcome with emotion.* 或→ …, many are *overjoyed.* * overjoyed（非常高興的），不需要再加 with emotion，句意重覆。 overcome〔͵ovɚˋkʌm〕*v.* 克服；使無法承受 *be overcome with emotion* 很感動
第 49 題 (B)	Runners *feel like racing* through history. → Runners *feel like they are racing* through history. * 文章中是用 It feels like racing in history.（這使人覺得像是在歷史中賽跑。）在此用 Runners 當主詞，feel like 接子句，作「感覺像…」解。 feel like + V-ing 表「想要…」。
第 51 題 (D)	The runners have to endure high *temperature* day and night. → The runners have to endure high *temperatures* day and night. * high temperatures　高溫 low temperatures　低溫 這兩個成語中的 temperature 都要用複數形式。

※ 此次題目出得很好，有深度，沒有經過嚴格模考訓練，很難得到高分。

102 年指定科目考試英文科出題來源

題　　號	出　　　　　　　　處
一、詞彙 第 1～10 題	今年所有的詞彙題，選項均出自「新版高中常用 7000 字」。
二、綜合測驗 第 11～20 題	11~15 題改寫自 Fish Talk to One Another（魚兒細語）一文，敘述魚彼此如何製造聲音來彼此溝通。 16~20 題改寫自 Postal Service to cut Saturday mail（郵政系統刪除週六郵件）一文，描述美國郵政系統如何要去掉週六遞送服務來節省開支。
三、文意選填 第 21～30 題	改寫自 For North America's only ice hotel, b-r-r-r-ing warm clothes（北美唯一的冰製旅館），敘述位於加拿大冰製旅館的熱潮。
四、篇章結構 第 31～35 題	改寫自 The Baker's Dozen: A Saint Nicholas Tale（麵包師傅的一打餅乾）一文，敘述一位麵包師傅如何多做給一個餅乾而致富。
五、閱讀測驗 第 36～39 題	改寫自「時代雜誌」I'm with the Band（樂團與我同在）一文，敘述樂團如何透過樂迷的捐贈來發行專輯。
第 40～43 題	改寫自 BBC 的 Star Trek style 'tractor beam' created by scientists（星際大戰牽引光束）一文，用科學方式說明實際上不可能創造出電影裡的光束來移動物體。
第 44～47 題	改寫自「經濟學人」Tablet teachers（平板電腦老師）一文，敘述平板電腦如何改善了非洲學童的閱讀能力。
第 48～51 題	改寫自 The Spartathlon, a long distance run for true masochists（斯巴達馬拉松，受虐者的一場長途賽跑），敘述斯巴達馬拉松的歷史，以及其吸引人之處。

【102 年指考】綜合測驗：11-15 出題來源：

　　　　　—— http://news.discovery.com/animals/whales-dolphins/
　　　　　fish-talk-communication.htm

Fish Talk to One Another

THE GIST

- Fish can not only hear, but also communicate by vibrating their swim bladder.
- Some reef fish even made sounds to attempt to scare off threatening fish and even divers.
- Not all fish can talk, however, so it's probably not worth attempting to strike up a conversation with your goldfish.

　　The undersea world isn't as quiet as we thought, according to a New Zealand researcher who found fish can "talk" to each other.

　　Fish communicate with noises including grunts, chirps and pops, University of Auckland marine scientist Shahriman Ghazali has discovered according to newspaper reports Wednesday.

　　"All fish can hear, but not all can make sound -- pops and other sounds made by vibrating their swim bladder, a muscle they can contract," Ghazali told the New Zealand Herald.

　　Fish are believed to communicate with each other for different reasons, including attracting mates, scaring off predators or orienting themselves.

　　The gurnard species has a wide vocal repertoire and keeps up a constant chatter, Ghazali found after studying different species of fish placed into tanks.

　　On the other hand, cod usually kept silent, except when they were spawning.

　　Some reef fish, such as the damselfish, made sounds to attempt to scare off threatening fish and even divers, he said.

⋮

【102 年指考】綜合測驗：11-15 出題來源：

—— http://www.ctpost.com/news/article/Postal-Service-
to-cut-Saturday-mail-4255254.php

Postal Service to cut Saturday mail

The financially struggling U.S. Postal Service says it plans to stop delivering mail on Saturdays, but continue delivering packages six days a week.

In an announcement scheduled for later Wednesday, the service is expected to say the cut, beginning in August, would mean a cost saving of about $2 billion annually. The move accentuates one of the agency's strong points—package delivery has increased by 14 percent since 2010. The delivery of letters and other mail has declined with the increasing use of email and other Internet use.

Under the new plan, mail would be delivered to homes and businesses only from Monday through Friday, but would still be delivered to post office boxes on Saturdays. Post offices now open on Saturdays would remain open on Saturdays.

The move is the latest cutback by the struggling U.S. Postal Service. Bridgeport has had its own mail woes, with two of the city's five post offices repeatedly in the crosshairs of cost-cutters. The Noble Avenue and Barnum Avenue branches were on a list of planned closures in 2009 and again in 2011, but a public outcry and opposition from U.S. Rep. Jim Himes and Mayor Bill Finch won them a reprieve.

Stamford's Glenbrook post office was also targeted in 2011. Bridgeport lost its Processing and Distribution Centerin 2006, when the facility's functions were consolidated into the Stamford P&DC. An investigation by the Office of the Inspector General a year later determined that the move was justified for efficiency reasons and could save the postal service $17 million over 10 years.

⋮

【102 年指考】文意選填：21-30 出題來源：

—— http://topnews.in/north-americas-only-ice-hotel-brrring-warm-clothes-294535

For North America's only ice hotel, b-r-r-r-ing warm clothes

　　Quebec City, Canada-Many travellers to Scandinavia are familiar with ice hotels, edifices of frozen water that beckon guests with the prospect of an overnight stay in arctic-like cold. There is one such hotel in North America-in the predominantly French-speaking Canadian province of Quebec.

　　This winter, it will be open from January 4 to March 29.

　　The only warm things at the Hotel de Glace are the candles on the bedside tables. The air is so cold you can see your breath, which adheres in tiny droplets to the opening of your sleeping bag. The tip of your nose feels numb—almost as though it were frozen. Getting up for a little while, drinking a glass of milk or going to the toilet seem impossible without risking death.

　　Despite the seemingly uninviting prospect of sleeping in a room at minus 15 degrees Celsius, every year about 4,000 people do just that at the Hotel de Glace, in the town of Sainte-Catherine-de-la-Jacques-Cartier, near the provincial capital Quebec City.

　　From the outside, it looks like an oversized igloo. Inside, variously coloured lamps make the walls, columns and statues glow—sometimes in green, then in red and yellow. With its hand-carved, ice chandeliers, the hotel resembles a fairy-tale castle for snow kings.

：

【102 年指考】篇章結構：31-35 出題來源：

—— http://www.aaronshep.com/stories/020.html

The Baker's Dozen A Saint Nicholas Tale Told by Aaron Shepard

In the Dutch colonial town later known as Albany, New York, there lived a baker, Van Amsterdam, who was as honest as he could be. Each morning, he checked and balanced his scales, and he took great care to give his customers exactly what they paid for—not more and not less.

Van Amsterdam's shop was always busy, because people trusted him, and because he was a good baker as well. And never was the shop busier than in the days before December 6, when the Dutch celebrate Saint Nicholas Day.

At that time of year, people flocked to the baker's shop to buy his fine Saint Nicholas cookies. Made of gingerbread, iced in red and white, they looked just like Saint Nicholas as the Dutch know him—tall and thin, with a high, red bishop's cap, and a long, red bishop's cloak.

One Saint Nicholas Day morning, the baker was just ready for business, when the door of his shop flew open. In walked an old woman, wrapped in a long black shawl.

"I have come for a dozen of your Saint Nicholas cookies."

Taking a tray, Van Amsterdam counted out twelve cookies. He started to wrap them, but the woman reached out and stopped him.

"I asked for a dozen. You have given me only twelve."

"Madam," said the baker, "everyone knows that a dozen is twelve."

"But I say a dozen is thirteen," said the woman. "Give me one more."

Van Amsterdam was not a man to bear foolishness. "Madam, my customers get exactly what they pay for—not more and not less."

"Then you may keep the cookies."

The woman turned to go, but stopped at the door.

"Van Amsterdam! However honest you may be, your heart is small and your fist is tight. Fall again, mount again, learn how to count again!"

Then she was gone.

⋮

【102 年指考】閱讀測驗：36-39 出題來源：

—— http://topnew.time.com/time/magazine/article 2050052,00.h tml

I'm with the Band

All pop artists like to say they're indebted to their fans. But in the case of British band Some Velvet Morning, it's literally true. The trio is currently recording songs because 358 fans ponied up the £100,000 ($160,000) needed to pay for the project. The arrangement came via My Major Company (MMC), an online record label that uses Web-based, social-network-style "crowdfunding" to finance its acts. While the firm has just started in the U.K., it's already huge and quite profitable in France, where it has 116,000 registered users and 34 funded acts.

Here's how it works: MMC posts demos and videos of 10 artists on its website, and users are invited to invest anywhere from £10 to £1,000 ($16 to $1,600) in the ones they most enjoy or think are most likely to score a hit. Once an act reaches £100,000, the financing is locked in, and the money is used to pay for recording and possibly a tour. Net revenue from resulting music sales, concerts and merchandise is split three ways: investors get to divide 40%; another 40% goes to MMC; the artist pockets 20%. Some Velvet Morning hit the jackpot in a mere seven weeks; label mate Ivyrise, an indie-rock band, reached the magic number in just four days. MMC's other eight acts—whose styles range from soul to pop to folk—each have a six-month window in which to secure funding. The payoff for investors can be big. One fan in France who contributed $6,850 got his money back 22 times over.

⋮

【102 年指考】閱讀測驗：40-43 出題來源：

— http://www.bbc.co.uk/news/uk-scotland-tayside-central-21187598

Star Trek style 'tractor beam' created by scientists

A real-life "tractor beam," which uses light to attract objects, has been developed by scientists.

It is hoped it could have medical applications by targeting and attracting individual cells.

The research, published in Nature Photonics and led by the University of St Andrews, is limited to moving microscopic particles.

In science fiction programmes such as Star Trek, tractor beams are used to move much more massive objects.

It is not the first time science has aimed to replicate the feat-albeit at smaller scales.

In 2011, researchers from China and Hong Kong showed how it might be done with laser beams of a specific shape—and the US space agency Nasa has even funded a studyto examine how the technique might help with manipulating samples in space.

The new study's lead researcher Dr Tomas Cizmar, research fellow in the School of Medicine at the University of St Andrews, said while the technique is very new, it had huge potential.

He said: "The practical applications could be very great, very exciting. The tractor beam is very selective in the properties of the particles it acts on, so you could pick up specific particles in a mixture."

"Eventually this could be used to separate white blood cells, for example."

⋮

【102 年指考】閱讀測驗：44-47 出題來源：

　── http://www.economist.com/news/business/21567972-schools-africa-are-going-dig italwith-encouraging-results-tablet-teachers

Tablet teachers

UNTIL recently Grace Wambui, a 14-year-old pupil in Nairobi, had never touched a tablet computer. But it took her about "one minute," she says, to work out how to use one when such devices arrived at her school, a tin shack in Kawangware, a slum in the Kenyan capital.

Other students at Amaf School were no slower to embrace the new tool. Teaching used to be conducted with a blackboard and a handful of tattered textbooks. Now children in groups of five take turns to swipe the touch screen of the devices, which are loaded with a multimedia version of Kenya's syllabus.

The tablets at Amaf School are an exception; they are part of a pilot project run by eLimu, a technology start-up. But if it and other firms are right, tablets and other digital devices may soon be the rule in African schools: many are betting on a boom in digital education in Kenya and elsewhere. Some executives even expect it to take off like M-Pesa, Kenya's hugely successful mobile-money service.

Such growth in digital education would be timely. The number of children in Africa without school places may have dropped in recent years, but the flood of new pupils has overwhelmed state schools, which were already underfunded and poorly managed. "Business as usual is not working," says Mike Trucano, an education and technology expert at the World Bank.

A for-profit venture, eLimu ("education" in Swahili) is one of several local publishers which are looking to disrupt the business of traditional textbook vendors, which are often slow and expensive. It aims to show that digital content can be cheaper and better.

：

【102 年指考】閱讀測驗：48-51 出題來源：

—— http://quotulatiousness.ca/blog/2012/12/31/the-spartathlon-a-long-distan ce-run-for-true-masochists/

The Spartathlon, a long distance run for true masochists

This year's Spartathlon, which took place in late September, was the 30th. Its heritage goes back much further. The most famous ultra-marathon in history was that run by Pheidippides, an Athenian who made the journey to Sparta in 490BC. His mission was to ask the Spartans for their help in fighting the invading Persians; Herodotus, a historian, records that he reached Sparta on the day after he left Athens. (The Spartans were celebrating a religious festival, so could not offer help until after the Athenians had dispatched the Persians at the battle of Marathon.)

Herodotus did not appear particularly taken by Pheidippides's feat of endurance. Since his "Histories" also includes tales of ants bigger than foxes, it probably seemed rather unimpressive. But in 1982 his terse description sparked the interest of a British air-force officer and long-distance runner called John Foden, who wondered if it really was possible to run from Athens to Sparta and arrive the next day. With four other officers, Mr Foden decided to see for himself; after 36 hours' slog they arrived in Sparti, as the town is now called.

Racing through history

That achievement inspired the organisation of the first Spartathlon a year later; the race now ranks as one of the world's classic ultra-marathons. The Spartathlon's allure has two sources. The first is the difficulty of finishing it. Any race that is longer than a marathon can call itself an ultra-marathon, but no self-respecting ultrarunner gets excited about finishing, say, a 48km course. The most talked-about events in the calendar are the ones that look most incomprehensible to the average person.

⋮

102 年指考英文科非選擇題閱卷評分原則說明

閱卷召集人：張武昌〈中國文化大學外國語文學院院長〉

　　102 學年度指定科目考試英文考科的非選擇題共有兩大題，第一大題是中譯英，考生需將兩個中文句子譯成正確而通順達意的英文，題型與過去幾年相同，兩題合計八分。第二大題是引導式的作文，考生需從「隱形披風」及「智慧型眼鏡」兩項新科技產品中擇一，寫一篇至少 120 個單詞（words）的作文，文分兩段；作文滿分為二十分。

　　關於閱卷籌備工作，在正式閱卷前，於 7 月 7 日先召開評分標準訂定會議，由正、副召集人及協同主持人共 14 位，參閱了 3000 份試卷，經過一天的討論，訂定評分標準，並選出合適的樣卷，編製成閱卷參考手冊，供閱卷委員共同參閱。

　　7 月 9 日上午 9：00 到 11：00，118 位大學教授分組進行試閱會議，根據閱卷參考手冊的樣卷，分別評分，並討論評分準則，務求評分標準一致，確保閱卷品質。為求慎重，試閱會議之後，正、副召集人及協同主持人進行第一次評分標準再確定會議，確認評分原則後才開始正式閱卷。

　　關於評分標準，在中譯英部分，每小題總分 4 分，原則上是每個錯誤扣 0.5 分。作文的評分標準是依據內容、組織、文法句構、字彙拼字、體例五個項目給分，字數明顯不足則扣總分 1 分。依閱卷流程，每份試卷皆會經過兩位委員分別評分，最後以二人平均分數計算。如果第一閱與第二閱分數差距超過標準，再請第三位委員（正、副召集人或協同主持人）評分。

今年的中譯英與「有效的時間管理」有關，句型及詞彙皆爲高中生所熟悉的；評量的重點在於考生能否能運用所學的詞彙與基本句型將中文翻譯成正確達意的英文句子；測驗之詞彙皆控制在大考中心詞彙表四級內之詞彙，中等程度以上的考生如果能使用正確句型並注意用字、拼字，應能得到理想的分數。但在選取樣卷時，仍發現有以下的缺失：例如拼字的錯誤（「挑戰」誤寫爲 chellege，「平衡」誤寫爲 bellence 等）；也有少部分考生的翻譯有中式英文的錯誤，例如將「對現今的許多學生而言」翻譯成 "For many today student to say"；此外也有考生粗心漏譯了「許多學生」的「許多」及「一大挑戰」中的形容詞「大」等，相當可惜。

作文題目的主題爲科技產品，與考生的生活經驗息息相關，考生多能發揮。考生作文應分兩段，第一段說明選擇的科技產品及理由，並舉例說明將如何使用這項產品，第二段說明不選擇另一項產品的理由及該項產品可能衍生的問題。從樣卷發現：英文寫作能力中等以上之考生皆能針對兩項產品發揮創意，在第一段舉例說明選擇「隱形披風」或「智慧型眼鏡」的原因，並在第二段說明未選擇另一項產品的理由。有考生選擇了「隱形披風」且所提出的理由是穿上披風後可以免費看電影、欣賞音樂會或球賽，雖然這些理由並不全然妥適，但只要考生用字及結構正確，並有清楚的敘述，不會因此而扣分。

102 年指考英文科試題或答案之反映意見回覆

※ 題號：6

【題目】

1. Helen's doctor suggested that she undergo a heart surgery. But
   she decided to ask for a second _____ from another doctor.
   (A) purpose　　　　　　(B) statement
   (C) opinion　　　　　　(D) excuse

【意見內容】

(B) 選項的 statement（觀點、陳述、指令）代進去應該也通才對。

【大考中心意見回覆】

本題評量考生能否掌握 opinion 的用法，作答線索為前一句中 …
suggested … ；選項 (B) statement 雖可譯為「觀點」，但屬於透過
書寫文字或動作（而非口頭形式）呈現的觀點，而這些觀點多屬於
較公開正式或強烈的看法與醫生對病患的診療建議不同，因此選項
(C) opinion 為最適當的選項。

※ 題號：36

【題目】

第 36 至 39 題為題組

　　All pop artists like to say that they owe their success to their
fans. In the case of British band SVM, it's indeed true. The band
is currently recording songs because 358 fans contributed the
£100,000 needed for the project. The arrangement came via
MMC, an online record label that uses Web-based, social-network-
style "crowd-funding" to finance its acts.

Here's how it works: MMC posts demos and videos of 10 artists on its website, and users are invited to invest from £10 to £1,000 in the ones they most enjoy or think are most likely to become popular. Once an act reaches £100,000, the financing process is completed, and the money is used to pay for recording and possibly a concert tour. Profits from resulting music sales, concerts, and merchandise are split three ways: investors get to divide 40%; another 40% goes to MMC; the artist pockets 20%. The payoff for investors can be big. One fan in France who contributed £4,250 got his money back 22 times over.

Crowd-funding musical acts is not new. But MMC takes the concept to another level. First of all, investors can get cash rather than just goodies like free downloads or tickets. Also, MMC is a record label. It has the means to get its music distributed around the world and to market artists effectively. "Artists need professional support," says the CEO of MMC's international division.

While digital technology and the Net have created a do-it-yourself boom among musicians, **success is still a long shot**. Out of the 20,000 records released in the U.S. in 2009, only 14 DIY acts made it to the Top 200. Also, with less revenue from recorded music, music companies have become less likely to take risks, which has led to fewer artists receiving funding. The crowd-funding model, however, allows for more records to be made by spreading risk among hundreds of backers. And the social-network aspect of the site helps expand fan bases; that is, investors become a promotional army.

36. Which of the following titles best expresses the main idea of the passage?
   (A) Web-based Music Production
   (B) Fundraising for Music Companies
   (C) Music Fans Profiting from Investments
   (D) Crowd-funding in the Music Industry

【意見內容】

1. (C) 選項亦合全文之主旨，且較 (D) 恰當。粉絲們（music fans）確實由此投資（investments）行為獲得利益（profit），且與本文主旨相扣，並無偏離或僅具片面之詞之現象。雖然文中有提到 crowd-funding，但只是簡介其來源及新發展，且 crowd-funding 為有一歷史之制度，非新奇事物，當然也不是本文的主旨；反之，本文在強調介紹這讓粉絲投資藝人的機制與幫助藝人成名的方法，並且可以得到一定比例的利潤，由文中強調投資的方法與歌手的發展可看出，故答案應為 (C)。參考資料：Beitz, C. R. (2009). *The idea of human rights*. Oxford: Oxford University Press.

2. (D) "Crowd-funding in the Music Industry" did not clearly show the precise main idea of this passage since crowd funding has been working for a long time

【大考中心意見回覆】

選文內容關於英國的「網路集資發行音樂」。本題評量考生能否掌握文章的主旨（main idea）。作答線索從第一段文意中即以 MMC 為例說明 crowd-funding（大眾集資）在音樂產業的運用，第二、三段說明其進行的方式，第四段說明其發展。全文著重於音樂家因此得以獲益，不致埋沒才華，才會有第一段第一句及第三段最後一句"Artists need professional support," ⋯及"⋯ investors become a promotional army.",選項 (C) 僅論及部分細節而非主旨，因此選項 (D) 為最適當的答案。

※ 題號：**43**

【題目】

第 40 至 43 題為題組

In science fiction TV programs such as Star Trek, tractor beams are used to tow spaceships and move objects. For years, scientists have labored to replicate this feat. In 2013, they succeeded. A team of British and Czech scientists, led by Dr. Tomas Cizmar, say they have created a real-life "tractor beam," like the kind from Star Trek, which uses a beam of light to attract objects, at least at a microscopic level.

Light manipulation techniques have existed since the 1970s, but this is thought to be the first time a light beam has been used to draw objects towards a light source. Usually when microscopic objects are hit by a beam of light, they are forced along the direction of the beam. After many years' research, Dr. Cizmar's team discovered a technique that allows for the radiant force of light to be reversed and to use the negative force to draw out certain particles.

Dr. Cizmar says that even though it is a few years away from practical use, the technology has huge potential for medical research. In particular, the tractor beam is highly selective in the particles it can attract, so it can pick up particles that have specific properties, such as size or composition, in a mixture. "Eventually, this could be used to separate white blood cells, for example," Dr. Cizmar told BBC News.

It has been a primary plot device in science fiction TV programs and movies to allow objects like spaceships to be trapped in a beam of light. But Dr. Cizmar said this particular technique would not eventually lead to **that**. A transfer of energy happens in the process. On a microscopic scale that is OK, but on a large scale it would cause huge problems. A large object could be destroyed by the heating, which results from the massive amount of energy necessary to pull it.

43. What is the tone of this passage?
   (A) Objective.   (B) Suspicious.
   (C) Admiring.   (D) Pessimistic.

【意見內容】

文中第四段 "On a microscopic scale that is OK, but on a large scale it would cause huge problems. A large object could … ",該文若以研究結果來看,則 (A) 可以正確,而若以作者的角度 "but" 這個字可能是對此項發明提出疑惑則 (B) Suspicious 也正確,因此竊自認為 (A)、(B) 皆可給分。

【意見回覆】

本題評量考生能否掌握作者的態度、文章敘述的立場。作答線索為作者對於全文中 light beam 正、反兩面看法並陳,其中第一段中 In 2013, they succeeded. A team of British and Czech scientists, led by Dr. Tomas Cizmar, say they have created a real-life "tractor beam," like the kind from Star Trek … 、第二段中 After many years' research, Dr. Cizmar's team discovered a technique that allows for the radiant force of light to be reversed and to use the negative force to draw out certain particles. 屬正面看法,第三段中 Dr. Cizmar 提及距離實際運用仍待多年以後,正、反兩面看法並陳,事實上正面看法甚至略較反面看法多。因此選項 (A) 為最適當的答案。

※ 題號：**50**

【題目】

<u>第 48 至 51 題爲題組</u>

In the Spartathlon, one of the world's toughest ultra-marathons, runners run 245 km, about six marathons, within 36 hours. The runners start in Athens, and run all the way to historical Sparta.

The Spartathlon's heritage goes back to 490 B.C., when Pheidippides, an Athenian, made the journey to Sparta to ask the Spartans for help in fighting the invading Persians. It is recorded that he reached Sparta on the day after he left Athens. In 1982, this story sparked the interest of a British air-force officer and long-distance runner called John Foden, who wondered if it really was possible to run from Athens to Sparta and arrive the next day. With four other officers, Foden decided to see for himself; after a 36-hour slog they arrived in Sparti, as the town is now called. That achievement inspired the organization of the first Spartathlon a year later.

The Spartathlon's attraction has two sources. The first is the difficulty of finishing it. The Spartathlon is not the most difficult race, but it combines lots of different tests. There is the heat of the Greek day, and then the plunge in temperatures when darkness falls. There are climbs: the route includes a series of ascents, among them a 1,200-meter mountain pass in the dead of night. Above all, there is the relentless pressure of the clock. The second reason is that the idea of retracing Pheidippides's footsteps still grips many participants. It feels like racing in history, passing through places where history began.

　　As finishers receive a laurel wreath and water from schoolgirls, many are overjoyed with emotion.　However, **the euphoria is fleeting**.　Within a few minutes, their joints and muscles start to seize up: after the race, Sparti resembles the set of a zombie film as participants lumber slowly around on legs that will not bend. But the itch to do it all over again soon appears.

50. What does **the euphoria is fleeting** in the last paragraph mean?
　(A) The feeling of triumph will last forever.
　(B) The race is incomprehensibly difficult to finish.
　(C) The fatigue after the race is overwhelming.
　(D) The excitement of finishing the race is soon gone.

【意見內容】

此題題幹敘述 "the euphoria is fleeting"，雖中譯和 (D) 吻合沒錯，但這題主要應是要考學生用上下文去推敲文句意思，而這句話在文章後接的是一連串的「肌肉痠痛」、「不能彎曲」等，似乎在暗示考生要選 (C) 這個描述「疲勞」的選項。因這題不是純粹考考生認字而是要從上下文推理，出現 (C) 這個選項說「賽後的疲勞是壓倒性的，不可擋的」，若引以為誘答似乎有點過當，建議 (C) 選項送分。

【意見回覆】

本題評量考生能否根據上下文猜測字詞或句意。作答線索為the euphoria is fleeting 後之進一步闡述句 Within a few minutes, their joints and muscles start to seize up: after the race, Sparti resembles the set of a zombie film as participants lumber slowly around on legs that will not bend.，說明「完成賽程的喜悅」因為「身體的疲憊」隨即消逝，因此選項 (D) 為最適當的選項。

102 年大學入學指定科目考試試題
數學甲

第壹部分：選擇題（單選題、多選題及選填題共占 76 分）

一、單選題（占 24 分）

說明：第 1 題至第 4 題，每題有 5 個選項，其中只有一個正確或最最適
當的選項，請畫記在答案卡之「選擇（填）題答案區」。各題答
對者，得 6 分；答錯、未作答或畫記多於一個選項者，該題以零
分計算。

1. 設 z 爲一複數，且 $\dfrac{z-2}{z+2}=i$（其中 $i=\sqrt{-1}$ 爲虛數單位）。試問 z 的
   絕對值 $|z|$ 爲下列哪一個選項？

   (1) $\dfrac{1}{2}$　　　(2) $\dfrac{\sqrt{2}}{2}$　　　(3) 1　　　(4) $\sqrt{2}$　　　(5) 2

2. 坐標平面上，直線 $x=2$ 分別交函數 $y=\log_{10}x$、$y=\log_{2}x$ 的圖形於
   P、Q 兩點；直線 $x=10$ 分別交函數 $y=\log_{10}x$、$y=\log_{2}x$ 的圖形於
   R、S 兩點。試問<u>四邊形</u> $PQSR$ 的面積最接近下列哪一個選項？
   （$\log_{10}2 \approx 0.3010$）

   (1) 10　　　(2) 11　　　(3) 12　　　(4) 13　　　(5) 14

3. 袋中有大小相同編號 1 到 8 號的球各一顆。小明自袋中隨機一次取
   出兩球，設隨機變數 X 的值爲取出兩球中的較小號碼。若 P_k 表 X
   取值爲 k 的機率（$k=1,2,\cdots,8$），試問有幾個 P_k 的值大於 $\dfrac{1}{5}$ ？

   (1) 1 個　　　(2) 2 個　　　(3) 3 個　　　(4) 4 個　　　(5) 5 個

4. 考慮所有由 1、2、3、4、5、6 各一個與三個 0 所排成形如 $\begin{bmatrix} 0 & a & b \\ c & 0 & d \\ e & f & 0 \end{bmatrix}$

對角線均為 0 的三階方陣。今隨機選取這樣一個方陣，試問其行列

式值 $\begin{vmatrix} 0 & a & b \\ c & 0 & d \\ e & f & 0 \end{vmatrix}$ 為奇數的機率為下列哪一個選項？

(1) $\dfrac{1}{20}$　　　(2) $\dfrac{1}{10}$　　　(3) $\dfrac{1}{2}$　　　(4) $\dfrac{9}{10}$　　　(5) $\dfrac{19}{20}$

二、多選題（占 40 分）

說明：第 5 題至第 9 題，每題有 5 個選項，其中至少有一個是正確的選
項。請將正確選項畫記在答案卡之「選擇（填）題答案區」。各
題之選項獨立判定，所有選項均答對者，得 8 分；答錯 1 個選項
者，得 4.8 分；答錯 2 個選項者，得 1.6 分；答錯多於 2 個選項或
所有選項均未作答者，該題以零分計算。

5. 令 $A(-2, 0)$、$B(0, 1)$、$C(2, 1)$、$D(4, 3)$ 為坐標平面上四點。請選出正
確的選項。

(1) 恰有一直線通過 A、B、C 三點

(2) 恰有一圓通過 A、B、D 三點

(3) 恰有一個二次多項式函數的圖形通過 B、C、D 三點

(4) 恰有一個三次多項式函數的圖形通過 A、B、C、D 四點

(5) 可找到兩平行直線，其聯集包含 A、B、C、D 四點

6.　設 c 爲實數，E_1、E_2、E_3 皆爲坐標空間中的平面，其方程式如下：

$$E_1 : \qquad cx + y = c$$

$$E_2 : \qquad cy + z = 0$$

$$E_3 : \qquad x + cz = 1$$

已知 E_1、E_2、E_3 有一個交點的 z 坐標爲 1，請選出正確的選項。

(1)　(1,0,0) 是 E_1、E_2、E_3 的一個交點

(2)　E_1、E_2、E_3 有無窮多個交點

(3)　E_1、E_2、E_3 中一定有兩個平面重合

(4)　$c = 1$

(5)　E_1、E_2、E_3 有一個交點的 z 坐標爲 2

7.　令 $f(x) = x^3 - x^2 - 2x + 1$。設 a、b、c 爲方程式 $f(x) = 0$ 的三個實根，且 $a < b < c$，請選出正確的選項。

(1)　極限 $\lim\limits_{x \to 1} \dfrac{f(x)}{x-1}$ 存在

(2)　a、b、c 至少有一個在 0 與 1 之間

(3)　$a, a^2, a^3, \ldots, a^n, \ldots$ 爲收斂數列

(4)　$b, b^2, b^3, \ldots, b^n, \ldots$ 爲收斂數列

(5)　$c, c^2, c^3, \ldots, c^n, \ldots$ 爲收斂數列

8.　已知函數 $f(x) = |\sin x| + |\cos x|$，其中 x 爲任意實數。請選出正確的選項。

(1)　$f(-x) = f(x)$ 對所有實數 x 均成立

(2)　f 的最大值爲 $\sqrt{2}$

(3) f 的最小值為 0

(4) $f(\frac{\pi}{10}) > f(\frac{\pi}{9})$

(5) 函數 f 的（最小正）週期為 π

9. 考慮向量 $\vec{u} = (a,b,0)$、$\vec{v} = (c,d,1)$，其中 $a^2 + b^2 = c^2 + d^2 = 1$。請選出正確的選項。

(1) 向量 $\vec{v}$ 與 z 軸正向的夾角恆為定值（與 c、d 之值無關）

(2) $\vec{u} \cdot \vec{v}$ 的最大值為 $\sqrt{2}$

(3) $\vec{u}$ 與 $\vec{v}$ 夾角的最大值為 $135°$

(4) $ad - bc$ 的值可能為 $\frac{5}{4}$

(5) $|\vec{u} \times \vec{v}|$ 的最大值為 $\sqrt{2}$

三、選填題（占 12 分）

說明： 1. 第 A 與 B 題，將答案畫記在答案卡之「選擇（填）題答案區」所標示的列號（10 − 15）。

　　　 2. 每題完全答對給 6 分，答錯不倒扣，未完全答對不給分。

A. 設 A、B、C、D 為空間中四個相異點，且直線 CD 垂直平面 ABC。

$\overline{AB} = \overline{BC} = \overline{CD} = 10$，$\sin \angle ABC = \frac{4}{5}$，且 $\angle ABC$ 為銳角，

則 $\overline{AD} = $ ⑩ $\sqrt{}$ ⑪ 。（化成最簡根式）

B. 設 m 爲實數。若圓 $x^2 + y^2 + 4x - 7y + 10 = 0$ 與直線 $y = m(x + 3)$ 在坐標平面上的兩個交點位於不同的象限,而滿足此條件的 m 之最大範圍爲 $a < m < b$,則 $a = \dfrac{⑫}{⑬}$, $b = \dfrac{⑭}{⑮}$。(化成最簡分數)

-------- 以下第貳部分的非選擇題,必須作答於答案卷 --------

第貳部分:非選擇題(占 24 分)

說明: 本部分共有二大題,答案必須寫在「答案卷」上,並於題號欄標明大題號(一、二)與子題號((1)、(2)、……),同時必須寫出演算過程或理由,否則將予扣分甚至給零分。作答務必使用筆尖較粗之黑色墨水的筆書寫,且不得使用鉛筆。每一子題配分標於題末。

一、 設 $p(x)$ 爲一實係數多項式,其各項係數均大於或等於 0。在坐標平面上,已知對所有的 $t \geq 1$,函數 $y = p(x)$、$y = -1-x^2$ 的圖形與直線 $x = 1$、$x = t$ 所圍成有界區域的面積爲 $t^4 + t^3 + t^2 + t + C$(其中 C 爲常數)。

(1) 試說明 $p(x) > -1-x^2$ 對所有的 $x \geq 1$ 均成立。(2 分)

(2) 設 $t \geq 1$,試求 $\int_1^t (-1 - x^2)dx$。(3 分)

(3) 試求 C。(2 分)

(4) 試求 $p(x)$。(5 分)

二、設 $A(1,0)$、$B(0,1)$ 為坐標平面上兩點，C 為直線 AB 外一點。經平面線性變換 M 作用後，A 被映射至 $A'(1,\sqrt{2})$、B 被映射至 $B'(-1,\sqrt{2})$，而 C 被映射至 C'。

(1) 試問變換 M 的矩陣為何？（4 分）

(2) 試證明變換 M 將 ΔABC 的重心映射至 $\Delta A'B'C'$ 的重心。
（4 分）

(3) 若 ΔABC 的面積為 3，試求點 C' 與直線 $A'B'$ 的距離。
（4 分）

102年度指定科目考試數學(甲)試題詳解

第壹部分：選擇題

一、單選題

1. 【答案】 (5)

    【解析】 已知 $\dfrac{z-2}{z+2}=i \Rightarrow z-2=iz+2i \Rightarrow (1-i)z=2+2i$

    $$\Rightarrow z=\dfrac{2+2i}{1-i}$$

    所求 $|z|=\left|\dfrac{2+2i}{1-i}\right|=\dfrac{|2+2i|}{|1-i|}=\dfrac{\sqrt{8}}{\sqrt{2}}=2$ ，故選 (5)

2. 【答案】 (3)

    【解析】 由條件可得 P, Q, S, R 座標及相關位置如右圖

    四邊形 $PQSR$ 為一梯形，

    $\Rightarrow$ 且 $\overline{PQ}=1-\log 2$ ，

    $\overline{SR}=\dfrac{1}{\log 2}-1$ ， $\overline{QR}=8$

    ∴四邊形 $PQSR$ 面積

    $$=\dfrac{\left[(1-\log 2)+(\dfrac{1}{\log 2}-1)\right]\times 8}{2}=4\left(\dfrac{1}{\log 2}-\log 2\right)$$

    $\fallingdotseq 12.0836$ ，故選 (3)

3. 【答案】(2)

　　【解析】8 球任取 2 球的樣本空間 $n(S) = C_2^8 = 28$

　　　　　依題意隨機變數 X 的值表示兩球中較小的號碼

　　　　　$p_k = P(X = k)$ 可得：

　　　　　$p_1 = \dfrac{C_1^7}{C_2^8} = \dfrac{1}{4} > \dfrac{1}{5}$，$p_2 = \dfrac{C_1^6}{C_2^8} = \dfrac{3}{14} > \dfrac{1}{5}$，$p_3 = \dfrac{C_1^5}{C_2^8} = \dfrac{5}{28} < \dfrac{1}{5}$，

　　　　　其餘 $p_4 \cdots p_7 < \dfrac{1}{5}$，故選 (2)

4. 【答案】(2)

　　【解析】依題意：$\begin{vmatrix} 0 & a & b \\ c & 0 & d \\ e & f & 0 \end{vmatrix} = ade + bcf$

　　　　　（其中 a, b, c, d, e, f 為相異正整數且 $1 \le a, b, c, d, e, f \le 6$）

　　　　　則 $\begin{vmatrix} 0 & a & b \\ c & 0 & d \\ e & f & 0 \end{vmatrix} = ade + bcf$ 為奇數的機率 $= \dfrac{3 \times 3! + 3 \times 3!}{6!} = \dfrac{1}{10}$，

　　　　　故選 (2)

二、多選題

5. 【答案】(3) (4) (5)

　　【解析】已知 $A(-2,0)$、$B(0,1)$、$C(2,1)$、$D(4,3)$ 可得

　　　　　斜率 $m_{AB} = \dfrac{1}{2}$、$m_{AC} = \dfrac{1}{4}$、$m_{AD} = \dfrac{1}{2}$

(1) $\because m_{AB} = \dfrac{1}{2} \neq m_{AC} = \dfrac{1}{4}$

　　$\therefore A$、B、C 三點不共線

(2) $\because m_{AB} = \dfrac{1}{2} = m_{AD}$

　　$\therefore A$、B、D 三點共線，故不可能找到一圓同時通過

　　　A、B、D 三點

(3) $\because B$、C、D 三點不共線且 x 坐標皆不同

　　$\therefore$ 通過 B、C、D 三點可唯一決定一個二次函數，

　　　正確

(4) $\because A$、B、C、D 四點不共線且 x 坐標皆不同

　　$\therefore$ 通過 A、B、C、D 三點可唯一決定一個三次函數，

　　　正確

(5) 由 (2) 知 A、B、D 三點共線，設該線為 L，過 C 做

　　一直線 L' 使得 $L' /\!/ L$，則 L, L' 兩直線即為所求，正確

故選 (3) (4) (5)

6. 【答案】 (1) (2) (5)

　　【解析】 已知 E_1, E_2, E_3 有一個交點的 z 坐標為 1

　　　　　且由平面方程式可取各平面法向量如下：

　　　　　$E_1 : cx + y = c \Rightarrow \overrightarrow{n_1} = (c,1,0)$

　　　　　$E_2 : cy + z = 0 \Rightarrow \overrightarrow{n_2} = (0,c,1)$，可得三平面任兩平面不平行

　　　　　$E_3 : x + cz = 1 \Rightarrow \overrightarrow{n_3} = (1,0,c)$

　　　　　(1) $(1,0,0)$ 代入 E_1, E_2, E_3 三平面方程式皆符合

　　　　　　　$\Rightarrow (1,0,0)$ 為 E_1, E_2, E_3 的一個交點，正確

(2) $\because E_1, E_2, E_3$ 有一個交點的 z 坐標爲 1

　　且由 (1) 得 $(1,0,0)$ 亦爲其交點

　　$\therefore E_1, E_2, E_3$ 三平面有無窮多個交點，正確

(3) 由三平面的法向量可知 E_1, E_2, E_3 三平面任兩平面皆

　　不重合

(4) 由 (2) 以及克拉瑪定理可得 $\Delta = \begin{vmatrix} c & 1 & 0 \\ 0 & c & 1 \\ 1 & 0 & c \end{vmatrix} = 0$，

　　得 $c = -1$

(5) 由 (4) 得 $c = -1$ 代回聯立方程式得 $\begin{cases} E_1 : -x + y = -1 \\ E_2 : -y + z = 0 \\ E_3 = x - z = 1 \end{cases}$，

　　可得解 $\begin{cases} x = 1 + t \\ y = t \\ z = t \end{cases}$，$t \in R$

　　令 $t = 2$ 得一交點 $(3,2,2)$，正確

故選 (1) (2) (5)

7. 【答案】 (2) (4)

　　【解析】 已知 $f(x) = x^3 - x^2 - 2x + 1$ 且 $a < b < c$ 爲 $f(x) = 0$ 的實根

　　　　利用勘根定理可得三實根所落的區間如下：

x	-2	-1	0	1	2
$f(x)$	-7	3	1	-1	1

　　得 $-2 < a < -1$，$0 < b < 1$，$1 < c < 2$

(1) $f(1) = 1 - 1 - 2 + 1 = -1 \neq 0$ $\therefore \lim_{x \to 1} \dfrac{f(x)}{x-1} = \dfrac{-1}{0}$ 不存在

(2) 實根 b 在 0 與 1 之間，正確

(3) $\because -2 < a < -1 \Rightarrow |a| > 1$

$\therefore a, a^2, a^3, \cdots, a^n, \cdots$ 爲發散數列

(4) $\because 0 < b < 1 \Rightarrow |b| < 1$

$\therefore b, b^2, b^3, \cdots, b^n, \cdots$ 爲收斂數列，正確

(5) $\because 1 < c < 2 \Rightarrow |c| > 1$ $\therefore c, c^2, c^3, \cdots, c^n, \cdots$ 爲發散數列

故選 (2) (4)

8. 【答案】 (1) (2)

　　【解析】 已知 $f(x) = |\sin x| + |\cos x|$，$x \in R$，可得 $f(x)$ 函數圖形
　　　　　　如下：

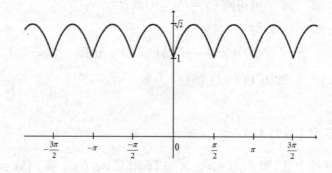

(1) $f(-x) = |\sin(-x)| + |\cos(-x)| = |-\sin x| + |\cos x|$

$= |\sin x| + |\cos x| = f(x)$，正確

(2) 由函數圖形可得 f 的最大值爲 $\sqrt{2}$，正確

(3) 由函數圖形可得 f 的最小值爲 1

(4) 由函數圖形可得 $x \in (0, \dfrac{\pi}{4})$ 時 $f(x)$ 遞增，

又 $0 < \dfrac{\pi}{10} < \dfrac{\pi}{9} < \dfrac{\pi}{4}$，得 $f(\dfrac{\pi}{10}) < f(\dfrac{\pi}{9})$

(5) 由函數圖形可得 f 的最小正週期為 $\dfrac{\pi}{2}$　故選 (1) (2)

9. 【答案】(1) (3) (5)

【解析】已知 $\vec{u} = (a,b,0)$，$\vec{v} = (c,d,1)$，且 $a^2 + b^2 = c^2 + d^2 = 1$

(1) 取 z 軸正向的方向向量 $\vec{w} = (0,0,1)$，設 $\vec{v}$ 與 $\vec{w}$ 夾角

為 θ，則 $\cos\theta = \dfrac{\vec{v} \cdot \vec{w}}{|\vec{v}||\vec{w}|} = \dfrac{(c,d,1)\cdot(0,0,1)}{\sqrt{c^2+d^2+1}\sqrt{1}} = \dfrac{1}{\sqrt{2}}$ 為一定

值，正確

(2) $\vec{u} \cdot \vec{v} = (a,b,0) \cdot (c,d,1) = ac + bd$，由柯西不等式可得：

$(ac+bd)^2 \le (a^2+b^2)(c^2+d^2) = 1\times1 \Rightarrow -1 \le \vec{u} \cdot \vec{v} \le 1$，

得 $\vec{u} \cdot \vec{v}$ 最大值為 1

(3) 設 $\vec{u}$ 與 $\vec{v}$ 夾角為 φ，由 (2) 得 $\vec{u}$ 與 $\vec{v}$ 夾角最大時，

$\vec{u} \cdot \vec{v} = -1$，此時 $\cos\varphi = \dfrac{-1}{\sqrt{1}\times\sqrt{1+1}} = \dfrac{-1}{\sqrt{2}} \Rightarrow \varphi = 135°$，

正確

(4) 由柯西不等式可得：

$(ad-bc)^2 \le (a^2+b^2)(d^2+(-c)^2) = 1\times1$

$\Rightarrow -1 \le ad-bc \le 1$，故 $ad-bc$ 最大值為 1

(5) $\vec{u} \times \vec{v} = (b,-a,ad-bc)$

$\Rightarrow |\vec{u} \times \vec{v}| = \sqrt{b^2+(-a)^2+(ad-bc)^2}$

由 (4) 得當 $(ad-bc)^2 = 1$ 時

$|\vec{u} \times \vec{v}| = \sqrt{b^2+(-a)^2+(ad-bc)^2}$

$= \sqrt{1+1} = \sqrt{2}$ 為最大值，正確

故選 (1) (3) (5)

三、選填題

A. 【答案】　$6\sqrt{5}$

　　【解析】　過 C 點作 $\overline{CE} \perp \overline{AB}$ 於 E 點

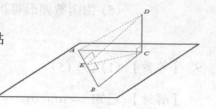

　　　　　　連 $\overline{CE}$ $\overline{DE}$ 與 $\overline{AD}$，

　　　　　　根據三垂線定理：

　　　　　　∵ $\overline{DC} \perp \overline{CE}$ 且 $\overline{CE} \perp \overline{AB}$

　　　　　　∴ $\overline{DE} \perp \overline{AB}$

　　　　　　又 $\overline{DC} = \overline{AB} = \overline{BC} = 10$ 且 $\sin \angle ABC = \dfrac{4}{5}$，

　　　　　　得 $\overline{CE} = 8$，$\overline{EB} = 6$，$\overline{AE} = 4$

　　　　　　∵ $\triangle DCE$ 為直角三角形，得 $\overline{DE} = \sqrt{10^2 + 8^2} = \sqrt{164}$

　　　　　　又∵ $\triangle AED$ 為直角三角形，得 $\overline{AD} = \sqrt{164 + 4^2}$

　　　　　　　　$= \sqrt{180} = 6\sqrt{5}$

B. 【答案】　2，3，5，3

　　【解析】　已知圓 $x^2 + y^2 + 4x - 7y + 10 = 0$

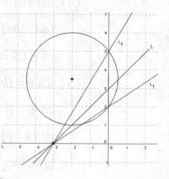

　　　　　　可得圓標準式：

　　　　　　$(x+2)^2 + (y - \dfrac{7}{2})^2 = \dfrac{25}{4}$，

　　　　　　圓心 $(-2, \dfrac{7}{2})$，半徑為 $\dfrac{5}{2}$

　　　　　　令 $x = 0$ 代入圓方程式

　　　　　　得圓與 y 軸交點為 $(0,2)$ 與 $(0,5)$，

　　　　　　直線 $L : y = m(x+3)$ 恆過定點 $(-3,0)$

若直線 $L: y = m(x+3)$ 與圓的交點在不同象限，

如右圖所示可知直線 $L: y = m(x+3)$ 的斜率介於直線 L_1

與 L_2 的斜率之間　$\Rightarrow \dfrac{2}{3} < m < \dfrac{5}{3}$

第貳部分：非選擇題

一、【解析】(1) $\because p(x)$ 為一實係數多項式且各項係數皆大於或

　　　　　等於 0　$\Rightarrow x \geq 1$ 時 $p(x) \geq 0$

　　　　又 $y = -1 - x^2$ 為一開口向下之二次函數，其函數

　　　　最大值為 -1（此時 $x = 0$）

　　　　$\therefore$ 當 $x \geq 1$ 時，$p(x) \geq 0 > -1 > -1 - x^2$，

　　　　即 $p(x) > -1 - x^2$ 恆成立

(2) $\displaystyle\int_1^t (-1 - x^2)\,dx = \left.\left(-x - \dfrac{1}{3}x^3\right)\right|_1^t = \left(-t - \dfrac{1}{3}t^3\right) - \left(-1 - \dfrac{1}{3} \times 1^3\right)$

$= -\dfrac{1}{3}t^3 - t + \dfrac{4}{3}$

(3) 設 $p(x)$ 的反導函數為 $P(x)$，

　　由已知條件 $y = p(x)$、$y = -1 - x^2$ 與直線 $x = 1$、

　　$x = t$ 所圍的區域面積為 $t^4 + t^3 + t^2 + t + C$

　　可得 $\displaystyle\int \left[p(x) - (-1 - x^2)\right]dx = \int p(x)\,dx - \int (-1 - x^2)\,dx$

　　$= P(t) - P(1) - \left(-\dfrac{1}{3}t^3 - t + \dfrac{4}{3}\right) = t^4 + t^3 + t^2 + t + C \cdots (*)$

　　令 $t = 1$ 代入，可得 $P(1) - P(1) - \left(-\dfrac{1}{3} - 1 + \dfrac{4}{3}\right)$

　　$= 1^4 + 1^3 + 1^2 + 1 + C \Rightarrow C = -4$

(4) 將 (3) 中的方程式 (*) 左右對 t 作微分可得：

$P'(t) - (-t^2 - 1) = 4t^3 + 3t^2 + 2t + 1$，

整理得 $P'(t) = p(t) = 4t^3 + 2t^2 + 2t$

$\therefore p(x) = 4x^3 + 2x^2 + 2x$

二、【解析】(1) 由題意條件得：

$$M\begin{bmatrix} 1 \\ 0 \end{bmatrix} = \begin{bmatrix} 1 \\ \sqrt{2} \end{bmatrix}，M\begin{bmatrix} 0 \\ 1 \end{bmatrix} = \begin{bmatrix} -1 \\ \sqrt{2} \end{bmatrix} \Rightarrow M\begin{bmatrix} 1 & 0 \\ 0 & 1 \end{bmatrix}$$

$$= \begin{bmatrix} 1 & -1 \\ \sqrt{2} & \sqrt{2} \end{bmatrix}，得 M = \begin{bmatrix} 1 & -1 \\ \sqrt{2} & \sqrt{2} \end{bmatrix}$$

(2) 已知 $A' = MA$，$B' = MB$，$C' = MC$，

ΔABC 重心 $G = \dfrac{A + B + C}{3}$

考慮 $\Delta A'B'C'$ 重心坐標

$$G' = \frac{A' + B' + C'}{3} = \frac{MA + MB + MC}{3} = \frac{M(A + B + C)}{3}$$

$= MG$，得證

(3) 設點 C' 到直線 $A'B'$ 距離為 x，

$$M = \begin{bmatrix} 1 & -1 \\ \sqrt{2} & \sqrt{2} \end{bmatrix} \Rightarrow \det(M) = 2\sqrt{2}$$

$\Rightarrow \Delta A'B'C'$ 面積 $= \det(M) \times \Delta ABC$ 面積

$= 2\sqrt{2} \times 3 = 6\sqrt{2}$

又已知 $A'(-1, \sqrt{2})$，$B'(1, \sqrt{2}) \Rightarrow \overline{A'B'} = 2$

得 $\Delta A'B'C'$ 面積 $= 6\sqrt{2} = \dfrac{1}{2} \cdot x \cdot 2 \Rightarrow x = 6\sqrt{2}$

102 年大學入學指定科目考試試題
數學乙

第壹部分：選擇題（單選題、多選題及選填題共占 76 分）

一、單選題（占 12 分）

說明：第 1 題至第 2 題，每題有 5 個選項，其中只有一個是正確或最
　　　適當的選項，請畫記在答案卡之「選擇（填）題答案區」。各
　　　題答對者，得 6 分；答錯、未作答或畫記多於一個選項者，該
　　　題以零分計算。

1. 設 a,b,c 為實數，且二次多項式 $f(x) = ax(x–1) + bx(x–3) + c(x–1)$
$(x–3)$ 滿足 $f(0) = 6$、$f(1) = 2$、$f(3) = –2$。請問 $a + b + c$ 等於下列
哪一個選項？

(1) 0　　　　(2) $\dfrac{2}{3}$　　　　(3) 1　　　　(4) $-\dfrac{1}{2}$　　　　(5) $-\dfrac{4}{3}$

2. 綜合數種糧食的【糧食自給率】定義為 $\dfrac{A}{B}$，其中 A 為「每一種糧
食之<u>國內生產量</u>乘以該糧食每單位產生熱量之後的總和」，B 為
「每一種糧食之<u>國內消費量</u>乘以該糧食每單位產生熱量之後的總
和」。已知甲、乙、丙三種糧食相關數據如下表：

糧食	國內生產量 （單位：千公噸）	國內消費量 （單位：千公噸）	單位糧食產生的熱量 （單位：大卡/每百公克）
甲	1000	1200	300
乙	280	320	100
丙	100	1000	600

請問綜合甲、乙、丙這三種糧食的【糧食自給率】最接近下列哪
一個選項？

(1) 37%　　　(2) 39%　　　(3) 41%　　　(4) 43%　　　(5) 45%

二、多選題（占 40 分）

說明： 第 3 題至第 7 題，每題有 5 個選項，其中至少有一個是正確的選項。請將正確選項畫記在答案卡之「選擇（填）題答案區」。各題之選項獨立判定，所有選項均答對者，得 8 分；答錯 1 個選項者，得 4.8 分；答錯 2 個選項者，得 1.6 分；答錯多於 2 個選項或所有選項均未作答者，該題以零分計算。

3. 坐標平面上兩點 $(4,1)$ 和 $(5,9)$ 在直線 $3x - y - k = 0$ 的兩側，其中 k 為整數。請選出正確的選項：

   (1) 滿足上式的 k 最少有 5 個

   (2) 所有滿足上式的 k 的總和是 35

   (3) 所有滿足上式的 k 中，最小的是 7

   (4) 所有滿足上式的 k 的平均是 9

   (5) 所有滿足上式的 k 中，奇數與偶數的個數相同

4. 下列有關循環小數的敘述中，請選出正確的選項。

   (1) $0.\overline{7} + 0.\overline{3} = 0.\overline{6} + 0.\overline{4}$

   (2) $0.\overline{72} + 0.\overline{28} = 1.\overline{1}$

   (3) $0.\overline{7} + 0.\overline{3} = 1$

   (4) $0.\overline{5} + 0.\overline{5} = 1.\overline{1}$

   (5) $0.4\overline{9} = 0.5$

5. 某研究所處理個人申請入學，其甄選總成績係探計測驗 A 分數及測驗 B 分數各占 50%。50 位申請同學依甄選總成績高低排序，錄取前 20 名。現依准考證號碼順序，將這些同學的成績列表如下：（例如，第一位同學的測驗 A 分數及測驗 B 分數分別為 93 分及 28 分）

測驗 A	93	98	100	100	100	98	96	96	98	96	96	98	98
測驗 B	28	50	59	22	52	67	30	15	46	11	72	21	59
測驗 A	93	100	100	100	100	98	98	96	98	100	96	100	96
測驗 B	24	13	53	33	61	57	55	26	35	40	9	60	23
測驗 A	96	96	96	100	100	96	98	98	91	100	96	100	98
測驗 B	66	29	34	58	55	35	16	28	28	72	51	39	40
測驗 A	98	96	96	93	98	96	98	98	98	98	93		
測驗 B	18	43	8	38	32	53	38	53	30	54	72		

所有學生測驗 A 分數的平均數為 97.38，而測驗 B 分數的平均數
為 40.22。現從甄選總成績、測驗 A 分數及測驗 B 分數之中任選
兩種成績作散佈圖，圖甲及圖乙為其中之二；兩圖中各有 50 個
資料點，每一點代表一位同學；兩個橫軸與縱軸之單位長可能
皆不同。請選出正確的選項。

(1) 圖乙的橫軸為測驗 A 分數

(2) 圖乙的縱軸為甄選總成績

(3) 圖甲的橫軸為甄選總成績

(4) 若只以測驗 B 分數高低錄取 20 位同學 (不採計測驗 A 分數)，
錄取的同學與以甄選總成績高低錄取的同學完全相同

(5) 甄選總成績的平均數為 97.38 及 40.22 的平均數

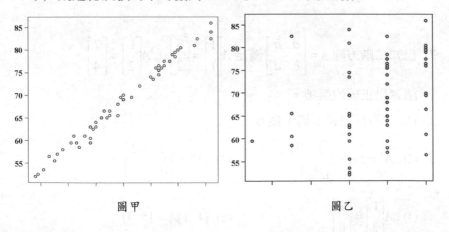

圖甲　　　　　　　　　　　圖乙

6. 想要了解選民對某候選人真正的支持度（支持率）p，四家媒體所做的民意調查結果如下表所示：

	媒體 A	媒體 B	媒體 C	媒體 D
$\hat{p}$	0.30	0.40	0.30	0.28
$\hat{\sigma}$	0.02	$\hat{\sigma}_B$	0.01	0.01

其中 $\hat{p}$ 表示抽樣支持度，$\hat{\sigma} = \sqrt{\dfrac{\hat{p}(1-\hat{p})}{n}}$，$n$ 為抽樣人數。請選出

正確的選項。

(1) 在 95% 的信心水準之下，媒體 A 抽樣所得 p 的信賴區間為 [0.28 , 0.32]

(2) 如果媒體 B 抽樣的人數與媒體 A 相同，則 $\hat{\sigma}_B$ 大於 0.02

(3) 媒體 C 抽樣人數約為媒體 A 抽樣人數的兩倍

(4) 媒體 A 的抽樣支持度比媒體 B 的抽樣支持度更接近候選人真正的支持度 p

(5) 在 95% 的信心水準之下，至少有一家媒體抽樣所得 p 的信賴區間會包含真正的支持度 p

7. 已知二階方陣 $A = \begin{bmatrix} a & b \\ c & d \end{bmatrix}$ 滿足 $A\begin{bmatrix} 1 \\ 1 \end{bmatrix} = \begin{bmatrix} 5 \\ 2 \end{bmatrix}$，$A\begin{bmatrix} 1 \\ 2 \end{bmatrix} = \begin{bmatrix} 7 \\ 4 \end{bmatrix}$。

請選出正確的選項。

(1) A 的行列式（值）為 6

(2) $A^2 = 5A - 6\begin{bmatrix} 1 & 0 \\ 0 & 1 \end{bmatrix}$ (3) $A^{-1} = \begin{bmatrix} 2 & -2 \\ 0 & 3 \end{bmatrix}$

(4) $A\begin{bmatrix} 1 \\ 3 \end{bmatrix} = \begin{bmatrix} 9 \\ 6 \end{bmatrix}$ (5) $[1 \ \ 1]A = [5 \ \ 7]$

三、選填題（占 24 分）

說明：1. 第 A 至 C 題，將答案畫記在答案卡之「選擇（填）題答案
　　　　區」所標示的列號（8–14）。

　　　2. 每題完全答對給 8 分，答錯不倒扣，未完全答對不給分。

A. 從玫瑰、菊花、杜鵑、蘭花、山茶、水仙、繡球等七盆花中選出
四盆靠在牆邊排成一列，其中杜鵑及山茶都被選到，且此兩盆花
位置相鄰的排法有 ⑧⑨⑩ 種。

B. 袋中有 3 顆白球與 1 顆黑球，每次隨機從袋中抽出 1 球，袋中每
一球被抽到的機率皆相同，抽出後不放回，直到抽中黑球時遊戲
結束。若在第 k 次抽到黑球，則得到 k 元獎金。此遊戲可獲得獎
金的數學期望值為 $\dfrac{⑪}{⑫}$ 元（化為最簡分數）。

C. 在坐標平面上，設 O 為原點，向量 $\vec{a} = (1,2)$，$\vec{b} = (2,1)$，$\vec{c} = (1,1)$，
$\vec{d} = (-1,1)$。P 為平面上的動點，令點集合 $A = \{P \mid \overrightarrow{OP} = x\vec{a} + y\vec{b}$ 且
$0 \le x \le 1$ 且 $0 \le y \le 1\}$，點集合 $B = \{P \mid \overrightarrow{OP} = x\vec{c} + y\vec{d}$ 且 $0 \le x \le 1$ 且
$0 \le y \le 1\}$，則區域 $A \cap B$ 的面積為 $\dfrac{⑬}{⑭}$ （化為最簡分數）。

- - - - - - - - 以下第貳部分的非選擇題，必須作答於答案卷 - - - - - - - -

第貳部分：非選擇題（占 24 分）

說明： 本部分共有二大題，答案必須寫在「答案卷」上，並於題號
欄標明大題號（一、二）與子題號（(1)、(2)、……），同
時必須寫出演算過程或理由，否則將予扣分甚至零分。作答
務必使用筆尖較粗之黑色墨水的筆書寫，且不得使用鉛筆。
每一子題配分標於題末。

一、 已知 $\log 2 \approx 0.3010$，$\log 3 \approx 0.4771$。

(1) 請以對數律計算 $\log 1.5$（不必四捨五入）。（3 分）

(2) 請以對數律計算 $\log (1.5)^{60}$（不必四捨五入）。（3 分）

(3) 請問 $(1.5)^{60}$ 的整數部分是幾位數？請說明理由。（3 分）

(4) 請問 $(1.5)^{60}$ 的整數部分中，最左邊的數字是幾？請說明理
由。（3 分）

二、 某工廠使用三種貴金屬元素合成兩種合金，其中每單位的甲合
金是由 5 公克的 A 金屬、3 公克的 B 金屬以及 3 公克的 C 金屬
組成，而每單位的乙合金是由 3 公克的 A 金屬、6 公克的 B 金
屬與 3 公克的 C 金屬所組成。已知甲、乙合金每單位的獲利分
別為 600、700 元。若工廠此次進了 1000 公克的 A 金屬、1020
公克的 B 金屬與 660 公克的 C 金屬投入生產這兩種合金，試問
甲、乙兩種合金各應生產多少單位，才能獲得最大利潤？又此
時利潤為多少？（12 分）

102年度指定科目考試數學(乙)試題詳解

第壹部分：選擇題

一、單選題

1. 【答案】 (2)

　　【解析】 由已知條件 $f(0) = 6$、$f(1) = 2$、$f(3) = -2$

　　　　　　代入 $f(x) = ax(x-1) + bx(x-3) + c(x-1)(x-3)$ 得：

　　　　　　$f(0) = 6 \Rightarrow c(-1) \cdot (-3) = 6$，得 $c = 2$

　　　　　　$f(1) = 2 \Rightarrow b(1) \cdot (1-3) = 2$，得 $b = -1$

　　　　　　$f(3) = -2 \Rightarrow a(3) \cdot (3-1) = -2$，得 $a = \dfrac{-1}{3}$

　　　　　　$\therefore a + b + c = 2 - 1 + \dfrac{-1}{3} = \dfrac{2}{3}$，

　　　　　　故選 (2)

2. 【答案】 (2)

　　【解析】 由題意及數據可知綜合甲、乙、丙三種糧食之【糧食自給率】即為：

$$\frac{(1000 \cdot 3000 + 280 \cdot 1000 + 100 \cdot 6000) \times 1000 [\text{大卡／公斤}]}{(1200 \cdot 3000 + 320 \cdot 1000 + 1000 \cdot 6000) \times 1000 [\text{大卡／公斤}]}$$

$$= \frac{388}{992} \doteqdot 39.1\%，故選 (2)$$

二、多選題

3. 【答案】 (3) (5)

 【解析】 已知 $(4,1)$ 與 $(5,9)$ 在直線 $3x - y - k = 0$ 的兩側且 $k \in Z$

 $\Rightarrow (12 - 1 - k)(15 - 9 - k) < 0$，得 $6 < k < 11$

 $\therefore k = 7, 8, 9, 10$

 (1) 滿足條件的 k 值僅有 4 個

 (2) 滿足條件的 k 值總和為 $7 + 8 + 9 + 10 = 34$

 (3) 滿足條件的 k 值最小為 7，正確

 (4) 滿足條件的 k 值的平均為 $\dfrac{7 + 8 + 9 + 10}{4} = 8.5$

 (5) 滿足條件的 k 值中奇數有 2 個，偶數有 2 個，正確

 故選 (3) (5)

4. 【答案】 (1) (4) (5)

 【解析】 (1) $0.\overline{7} + 0.\overline{3} = \dfrac{7}{9} + \dfrac{3}{9} = \dfrac{10}{9}$，$0.\overline{6} + 0.\overline{4} = \dfrac{6}{9} + \dfrac{4}{9} = \dfrac{10}{9}$ 正確

 (2) $0.\overline{72} + 0.\overline{28} = \dfrac{72}{99} + \dfrac{28}{99} = \dfrac{100}{99}$，$1.\overline{1} = 1 + 0.\overline{1} = 1 + \dfrac{1}{9} = \dfrac{10}{9}$，

 得 $0.\overline{72} + 0.\overline{28} \neq 1.\overline{1}$

 (3) $0.\overline{7} + 0.\overline{3} = \dfrac{7}{9} + \dfrac{3}{9} = \dfrac{10}{9} \neq 1$

 (4) $0.\overline{5} + 0.\overline{5} = \dfrac{5}{9} + \dfrac{5}{9} = \dfrac{10}{9} = 1.\overline{1}$，正確

 (5) $0.4\overline{9} = \dfrac{49 - 4}{90} = \dfrac{45}{90} = 0.5$，正確

 故選 (1) (4) (5)

5. 【答案】(1) (2) (4) (5)

　　【解析】由題意與數據可得圖甲圖乙之橫軸與縱軸的成績類別
　　　　　　如下圖所示：

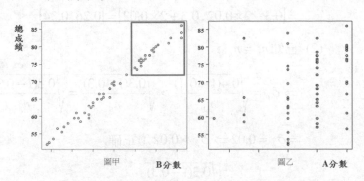

　　　(1) 圖乙的橫坐標為 A 分數，正確

　　　(2) 圖乙的縱軸為總成績，正確

　　　(3) 圖甲的橫軸為 B 分數

　　　(4) 由上圖圖甲右上方框中可知：由上而下數 20 人與由
　　　　　右而左數 20 人皆為同一群人，正確

　　　(5) ∵ 甄選總成績 $= A×50\% + B×50\%$

　　　　　∴ 甄選總成績的平均 $= \bar{A}×50\% + \bar{B}×50\% = \dfrac{\bar{A}+\bar{B}}{2}$

　　　　　　$= \dfrac{97.38+40.22}{2}$，正確

　　　故選 (1) (2) (4) (5)

6. 【答案】(2)

　　【解析】由題意與數據可得：

　　　(1) 在 95% 的信心水準之下，媒體 A 抽樣所得 p 的信賴

區間為

$$\left[\hat{p}_A - 2\sqrt{\frac{\hat{p}_A(1-\hat{p}_A)}{n}} \ , \ \hat{p}_A + 2\sqrt{\frac{\hat{p}_A(1-\hat{p}_A)}{n}}\right]$$

$$= [0.3 - 2 \times 0.02, 0.3 + 2 \times 0.02] = [0.26, 0.34]$$

(2) 已知 $n_B = n_A$，

$$\Rightarrow \hat{\sigma}_B = \sqrt{\frac{0.4(1-0.4)}{n_B}} > \sqrt{\frac{0.3(1-0.3)}{n_B}} = \sqrt{\frac{0.3(1-0.3)}{n_A}}$$

$$= \hat{\sigma}_A = 0.02 \Rightarrow \hat{\sigma}_B > 0.02 \ ， 正確$$

(3) $\dfrac{\hat{\sigma}_A}{\hat{\sigma}_C} = \dfrac{0.02}{0.01} = \dfrac{\sqrt{\dfrac{0.3(1-0.3)}{n_A}}}{\sqrt{\dfrac{0.3(1-0.3)}{n_C}}} = \sqrt{\dfrac{n_C}{n_A}}$ ，得 $n_C = 4n_A$

(4) ∵ 候選人真正的支持度 p 未知，

∴ 無法判定 $\hat{p}_A$ 與 $\hat{p}_B$ 何者與 p 較接近

(5) ∵ 候選人真正的支持度 p 未知，而且各家媒體抽樣

所得的 95% 信賴區間包含 p 的機率不是 0 就是 1。

∴ 無法保證至少有一家媒體抽樣所得 p 的信賴區間

會包含真正的支持度 p

故選 (2)

7. 【答案】(1)(2)(4)

【解析】 $A\begin{bmatrix} 1 & 1 \\ 1 & 2 \end{bmatrix} = \begin{bmatrix} 5 & 7 \\ 2 & 4 \end{bmatrix} \Rightarrow A = \begin{bmatrix} 5 & 7 \\ 2 & 4 \end{bmatrix}\begin{bmatrix} 1 & 1 \\ 1 & 2 \end{bmatrix}^{-1}$

$$= \begin{bmatrix} 5 & 7 \\ 2 & 4 \end{bmatrix}\begin{bmatrix} 2 & -1 \\ -1 & 1 \end{bmatrix} = \begin{bmatrix} 3 & 2 \\ 0 & 2 \end{bmatrix}$$

(1)　$\det(A) = \begin{vmatrix} 3 & 2 \\ 0 & 2 \end{vmatrix} = 6$，正確

(2)　$A^2 = \begin{bmatrix} 3 & 2 \\ 0 & 2 \end{bmatrix}\begin{bmatrix} 3 & 2 \\ 0 & 2 \end{bmatrix} = \begin{bmatrix} 9 & 10 \\ 0 & 4 \end{bmatrix}$，

$5A - 6\begin{bmatrix} 1 & 0 \\ 0 & 1 \end{bmatrix} = \begin{bmatrix} 15 & 10 \\ 0 & 10 \end{bmatrix} - \begin{bmatrix} 6 & 0 \\ 0 & 6 \end{bmatrix} = \begin{bmatrix} 9 & 10 \\ 0 & 4 \end{bmatrix}$，正確

(3)　$A^{-1} = \dfrac{1}{\det(A)}\begin{bmatrix} 2 & -2 \\ 0 & 3 \end{bmatrix} = \begin{bmatrix} \dfrac{1}{3} & \dfrac{-1}{3} \\ 0 & \dfrac{1}{2} \end{bmatrix}$

(4)　$A\begin{bmatrix} 1 \\ 3 \end{bmatrix} = \begin{bmatrix} 3 & 2 \\ 0 & 2 \end{bmatrix}\begin{bmatrix} 1 \\ 3 \end{bmatrix} = \begin{bmatrix} 9 \\ 6 \end{bmatrix}$，正確

(5)　$[1\ \ 1]A = [1\ \ 1]\begin{bmatrix} 3 & 2 \\ 0 & 2 \end{bmatrix} = [3\ \ 4]$

故選 (1) (2) (4)

三、選填題

A.　【答案】　120 種

　　【解析】　依題意可得，所求 $= C_2^2 \cdot C_2^5 \cdot (3!) \cdot (2!) = 120$ 種

B. 【答案】 $\dfrac{5}{2}$

【解析】 設隨機變數 K 表示第 K 次抽到黑球，依題意可得下表：

K	1	2	3	4
P(K)	$\dfrac{1}{4}$	$\dfrac{3}{4}\cdot\dfrac{1}{3}=\dfrac{1}{4}$	$\dfrac{3}{4}\cdot\dfrac{2}{3}\cdot\dfrac{1}{2}=\dfrac{1}{4}$	$\dfrac{3}{4}\cdot\dfrac{2}{3}\cdot\dfrac{1}{2}\cdot\dfrac{1}{1}=\dfrac{1}{4}$
得獎金K	1	2	3	4

$$\Rightarrow E(K)=\dfrac{1}{4}\cdot 1+\dfrac{1}{4}\cdot 2+\dfrac{1}{4}\cdot 3+\dfrac{1}{4}\cdot 4=\dfrac{5}{2}$$

C. 【答案】 $\dfrac{1}{3}$

【解析】 依題意畫圖可得右圖，其中 ΔOPC 面積即為所求

由 $\begin{cases} L_1 : y = 2x \\ L_2 : x+y = 2 \end{cases}$

可解得 $P(\dfrac{2}{3}, \dfrac{4}{3})$

故 ΔOPC 面積

$$=\dfrac{1}{2}\begin{vmatrix} \dfrac{2}{3} & \dfrac{4}{3} \\ 1 & 1 \end{vmatrix}=\dfrac{1}{3}$$

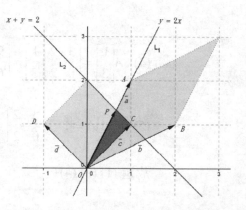

第貳部分：非選擇題

一、 【解析】 (1) $\log 1.5 = \log\dfrac{3}{2}=\log 3-\log 2=0.4771-0.301=0.1761$

(2) $\log(1.5)^{60}=60\times\log 1.5=60\times 0.1761=10.566$

(3) 由 (2) 得 $\log(1.5)^{60}=10.566=10+0.566$，首數 $=10$，

尾數 $=0.566$

故 $(1.5)^{60}$ 的整數部分為 $10+1=11$ 位數

(4) 由 (3)得 $\log(1.5)^{60}$ 的尾數 $=0.566$，

又 $\log 3=0.4771<0.566<0.602=\log 4$

故 $(1.5)^{60}$ 的整數部分最左邊的數字為 3

二、【解析】 設甲合金生產 x 單位，乙合金生產 y 單位

依題意條件可得聯立不等式：

$$\begin{cases} 5x+3y\le 1000 \\ 3x+6y\le 1020 \\ 3x+3y\le 660 \\ x\ge 0,y\ge 0 \end{cases} \Rightarrow \begin{cases} 5x+3y\le 1000 \\ x+2y\le 340 \\ x+y\le 220 \\ x\ge 0,y\ge 0 \end{cases}$$

其目標利潤函數

$f(x,y)=600x+700y$

由聯立不等式可得可行

解區域如右圖所示，得

各頂點所對應之利潤函

數值如下：

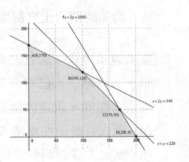

頂點	A(0,170)	B(100,120)	C(170,50)	D(200,0)
目標函數值	119000	144000	137000	120000

故甲合金生產 100 單位，乙合金生產 120 單位時，

可得最大利潤 144000 元

102年大學入學指定科目考試試題
歷史考科

第壹部分：選擇題（占 80 分）

一、單選題（占 72 分）

說明：第 1 題至第 36 題，每題有 4 個選項，其中只有一個是正確或
最適當的選項，請畫記在答案卡之「選擇題答案區」。各題
答對者，得 2 分；答錯、未作答或畫記多於一個選項者，該
題以零分計算。

1. 某一時期中，商人可以透過競標，取得徵稅的權利，並用各種日
   常所需用品到各社換取鹿肉，製成鹿脯上繳，做為部分稅收。此
   徵稅方式為：
   (A) 荷治時期的贌社制度　　　(B) 鄭氏時期的五商制度
   (C) 清領時期的土官制度　　　(D) 日治時期的保甲制度

2. 某人說：本島人諸君，要自己省察，你們對帝國盡忠只有二十餘
   年，「內地」人已有二千餘年，所以不應奢望權利與待遇與「內
   地」人相同。說這段話的人應是：
   (A) 鄭氏官員對在臺漢人所說的話
   (B) 施琅入臺對明鄭遺民所說的話
   (C) 日本殖民官員對臺民所說的話
   (D) 戰後陳儀政府對臺人所說的話

3. 一個工業國家在第二次世界大戰中，受到戰火破壞，戰後經濟困
   苦。藉著韓戰爆發的時機，迅速復興其工業，到 1970 年代成為
   經濟大國。1990 年後，該國經濟發展則陷入停滯，但其科技研發

仍居領先。這個國家是：

(A) 德國　　　　　　　　　　(B) 蘇聯

(C) 日本　　　　　　　　　　(D) 中華民國

4. 孔子作《春秋》，不欲載之空言，主張見諸行事，通過具體史事呈現微言大義，有褒有貶，使亂臣賊子知所戒懼。司馬遷繼承春秋學傳統，作《史記》，是爲中國史學的起源。從《春秋》、《史記》以來，中國史學的主要功能爲何？

(A) 考據、求眞　　　　　　　(B) 求眞、鑑戒

(C) 鑑戒、陶冶　　　　　　　(D) 陶冶、考據

5. 一個宗教團體出版信仰手册，要求信徒崇拜聖人遺骨、向遺骨祈禱、到羅馬朝聖、肯定羅馬教宗的赦罪權、主張教義須遵循羅馬教廷的解釋。這個團體最可能是：

(A) 喀爾文教派　　　　　　　(B) 英國國教派

(C) 長老會　　　　　　　　　(D) 耶穌會

6. 某一時期中，學者強調分析與研究，在探討不同因素對制度發展的影響時，還努力找出這些影響背後的規律和因果關係。這最可能是哪個時期學者思考問題的傾向？

(A) 中古時期　　　　　　　　(B) 文藝復興時期

(C) 教改革時期　　　　　　　(D) 啓蒙運動時期

7. 中國歷史上某一時期，士人和小吏要在仕途上求發展，多以孝廉爲階梯。學者指出，此時孝廉以家貲豐厚，累世仕宦，研讀經書，曉習律令，且經過地方吏職歷練的，占大多數；來自貧寒之家，但才德兼備的，則很少。這一時期最可能是：

(A) 東漢　　　　(B) 東晉　　　　(C) 北周　　　　(D) 北宋

8. 某位史家說：「十字軍對歐洲文明影響是否很大，是有爭論的。
   毫無疑問，十字軍有助於義大利港口城市的經濟成長，尤其是熱
   那亞、比薩和威尼斯。然而重要的是，十二世紀財富和人口的增
   加先使得十字軍運動成為可能。十字軍也許促進商業復興，但確
   實並未引發商業的復甦。」這位史家要說明的最可能是：
   (A) 有關十字軍運動對於東方世界的影響
   (B) 十字軍運動對於歐洲文明並沒有影響
   (C) 義大利商業復興是十字軍運動的結果
   (D) 商業和人口復興是十字軍運動的背景

9. 某國政府重視貴重金屬，除立法禁止輸出金、銀外，還規定外國
   商人前來貿易時，須以金、銀支付貨款。為振興經濟，又取消國
   內貿易障礙，以建立單一市場，並補貼本國商品獎勵出口，同時
   還限制殖民地僅能與母國貿易。某國是指：
   (A) 十五世紀的荷蘭　　　　(B) 十七世紀的法國
   (C) 十九世紀的日本　　　　(D) 二十世紀的英國

10. 一位臺灣歷史人物歷經兩個不同時期，他雖未曾擔任過官職，掌
    握過實權，卻是舉足輕重的政治人物，動見觀瞻的社會領袖，他
    用溫和的方式來抵抗日本殖民政府與國民黨的統治。他是：
    (A) 辜顯榮　　(B) 林獻堂　　(C) 蔣渭水　　(D) 謝雪紅

11. 某一皇帝下詔，隴西李氏、太原王氏、滎陽鄭氏等七姓十家，不
    得「自為婚」（相互聯姻），又禁止「賣婚」（與非世族的富人
    聯姻，以獲取豐厚的聘金或嫁妝）。但七姓十家自封為「禁婚家」，
    私下仍相互聘娶，只是不敢公開舉行婚禮而已。此一記載反映的
    時代與現象最可能是：
    (A) 秦漢時期，世族勢力仍然強固

(B) 魏晉時期，世族勢力已經衰弱

(C) 唐代世族在社會上仍有其地位

(D) 宋代世族受到打壓，漸趨崩解

12. 《元史・泰不華傳》記載：「泰不華字兼善，伯牙台氏，父塔不台，歷仕台州錄事判官，遂居於台。家貧好讀書，年十七，江浙鄉試第一，明年至治元年，進士及第。至正元年，泰不華除（担任）紹興路總管，行鄉飲酒禮，教民興讓，越俗大化。」下列論述或論著，何者最有可能引以上文字作為證據？

(A) 〈元初州縣多世襲〉　　(B) 《元西域人華化考》

(C) 〈色目人隨便居住〉　　(D) 《元典章校補》

13. 在一場內戰中，全國分為兩個陣營，戰後，戰勝陣營主張：各邦人民不僅是邦的公民，也是聯邦公民；邦政府未經法律程序，不得剝奪該邦人民的生命、自由或財產，但「法律程序」須由聯邦政府制訂。這場內戰是：

(A) 英國光榮革命　　　　(B) 法國大革命

(C) 美國南北戰爭　　　　(D) 俄國大革命

14. 一位十九世紀初期的政治人物表示：人民以為談一談社會契約，革命就完成了！事實上，對於所有國家而言，最重要的絕對不是改變，而是保持體制的穩定，以及不中斷地執行既有法律，因此應該讓現存的政府繼續執政。此人的政治觀點最可能屬於：

(A) 保守主義　　　　　　(B) 民族主義

(C) 自由主義　　　　　　(D) 社會主義

15. 中國古代的某一宗教，其經典不少是學習、摹仿，甚至借用其他宗教經典的內容而成。《玉清經本地品》就是一例，如：品中述

及元始天尊的十戒，第一戒，不得違戾父母師長，反逆不孝；第二戒，戒殺生。這個例子的情形，應作怎樣的解讀？

(A) 道教取佛教經典爲本，增添儒家觀念

(B) 佛教取道教經典爲本，增添儒家觀念

(C) 道教取儒家經典爲本，增添佛教觀念

(D) 佛教取儒家經典爲本，增添道教觀念

16. 某一時期，臺灣當局公布：糾衆集夥而以暴行或脅迫手段達成目的者，皆屬「匪徒」，依下列情節分別論處。一、爲首及敎唆者處以死刑；二、參與策畫者或擔任指揮者處以死刑；三、附從者處有期徒刑或重勞役。這個法令的目的是：

(A) 清領初期，爲了防止漳泉械鬥

(B) 清領中期，爲了避免原漢衝突

(C) 日治初期，爲了鎮壓武裝抗日

(D) 日治後期，爲阻止原住民起事

17. 司馬光在《資治通鑑》中說：「三代之前，海內諸侯，何啻萬國，有民人、社稷者，通謂之（甲）。合萬國而君之，立法度，班號令，而天下莫敢違者乃謂之（乙）。王德旣衰，強大之國能帥諸侯以尊天子者，則謂之（丙）。」甲、乙、丙各應塡入何字？

(A) 霸、王、君　　　　　　(B) 王、霸、君

(C) 君、王、霸　　　　　　(D) 君、霸、王

18. 清朝末年，中國人開始與西方工業文明接觸，如李鴻章已深感「洋機器於耕、織、印刷、陶埴諸器，皆能製造，有裨民生日用。妙在借水火之力，以省人之勞費。」於是主張「設機器局自爲製造，輪船、鐵路自爲轉運」以便「爲內地開拓生計。」但當時朝野人

士，鑒於時局的嚴峻，亦贊成利用機器，但多主張以製造何者為
先？

(A) 輪船、鐵路　　　　　(B) 鐵路、織機

(C) 織機、槍礮　　　　　(D) 槍礮、輪船

19. 圖一是歷史上某一戰爭路線圖的一部分。圖中，黑色線條表示戰
爭進行的路線，箭頭指示戰爭進行的方向。根據圖中資訊判斷，這應
是哪次戰爭的一部分？

(A) 亞歷山大東征

(B) 阿拉伯帝國的擴張

(C) 十字軍東征

(D) 蒙古人西征

圖一

20. 東晉的孫盛討論《三國志》與《世語》有關袁紹出兵人數的差異。
　　《三國志》寫到：「袁紹簡精卒十萬，騎萬匹，將攻（曹操根據地）
　　許」。《世語》則記載：「袁紹僅有步卒五萬，騎八千。」孫盛
　　指出：「根據曹操曾對崔琰說，冀州戶籍中有人口三十萬，再加上
　　幽、并、青等州，更是不少。袁紹用兵，必然大舉出動，所以他
　　出兵十萬攻打曹操應屬可信。」上述孫盛所說的內容，在歷史學中
　　稱為：

(A) 敘事　　　　(B) 考證　　　　(C) 褒貶　　　　(D) 史論

21. 越戰期間，美國派軍支援南越政府，美國記取韓戰的教訓，不允
　　許其地面部隊越過北緯十七度線，以避免刺激某國，讓戰爭擴大。
　　此處某國是指：

(A) 中共　　　　(B) 印度　　　　(C) 菲律賓　　　　(D) 北韓

22. 總督府視鴉片吸食是一種疾病,吸食者是身心不健全的中毒者。
　　因此,在制訂鴉片政策時,規定只提供鴉片給經醫師認可的中毒
　　者,避免其苦痛或猝死。如此不但可以減少民眾對新政策的抗拒,
　　也將鴉片吸食者控制在一定範圍之內以期自然消滅,同時也可以
　　經由鴉片販賣增加總督府的收入。從以上文字來看,總督府鴉片
　　政策所採取的手段為:
　　(A) 放任與自由買賣
　　(B) 治療與自由買賣
　　(C) 漸禁與專賣制度
　　(D) 嚴禁與專賣制度

23. 某位學者比較人類四大古文明時,提及其中兩個文明:這兩個文
　　明基本上都是土生土長地自行發展出來的,也都有自然天險屏障
　　或地理上的偏安,讓它們自成一個世界,為統一政權的出現提供
　　有利養分。學者所指稱的兩大文明最可能是:
　　(A) 印度、埃及古文明
　　(B) 兩河、中國古文明
　　(C) 埃及、中國古文明
　　(D) 印度、兩河古文明

24. 一位新文化運動的主導人物,主張改良,反對革命,對當時許多
　　人受到俄國十月革命鼓舞宣傳馬克思主義,介紹階級鬥爭與唯物
　　史觀的作法,並不贊成,認為變革需要一點一滴的累積,因此反
　　對急進。他最可能是:
　　(A) 李大釗　　　　　　　　(B) 陳獨秀
　　(C) 胡適　　　　　　　　　(D) 魯迅

25. 圖二是十六世紀初東南亞
某一國家都城的格局圖。
從圖中內容判斷，這最可
能是下列哪座都城？

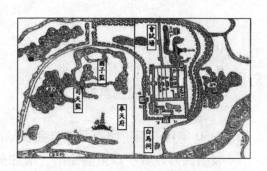

圖二

(A) 呂宋的馬尼拉

(B) 暹邏的阿瑜陀耶

(C) 緬甸的蒲甘

(D) 越南的升龍

26. 太平軍起事期間，西方各國希望維持中立，英國駐華公使文翰於
1853 年 4 月抵達「天京」，東王楊秀清與其有書函往來。江蘇巡
撫得訊後，為此深感緊張，也特別行文照會英、美兩國領事。以
下是當時三方往來的書信資料：

甲：希念兩國通商和好已久，今商民被擾，貿易不通，希速發火
輪來江剿擊。

乙：爾遠人願為藩屬，天下歡樂。既忠心歸順，是以降旨爾頭人
及眾兄弟，可隨意來天京。

丙：來書言語無狀，不能理會，中國既准吾通商，則無論何人，
有損我商務，我國惟以兵戈從事。

三段資料的先後次序排列應是：

(A) 乙甲丙　　　　　　　(B) 乙丙甲

(C) 丙甲乙　　　　　　　(D) 丙乙甲

27. 「吠陀經」和「奧義書」都是古代印度婆羅門信仰的重要經典。
「吠陀經」是婆羅門信仰的基礎，「奧義書」則是針對婆羅門信
仰流弊而起的反省與改進。從「吠陀經」到「奧義書」，印度婆
羅門信仰有何變化？

(A) 從一神信仰到多神崇拜

(B) 從犧牲獻祭到哲學思辯

(C) 從消極出世到積極入世

(D) 從有神主義到無神主義

28. 1950 年代末期,國內面臨資金短缺問題,政府為改善投資環境,吸引僑外投資,以拓展輸出,增加外匯收入,特別制定一項「有利政策」,克服了制度困難,終於在 1966 年創設高雄加工出口區。這項「有利政策」是指:

(A) 獎勵投資條例　　　　　　(B) 幣制改革方案

(C) 促進產業升級條例　　　　(D) 十大建設

29. 某位史家比較近代史上兩種政治經濟制度,指出:「『乙主義』可算是因著『甲主義』而產生的一種變態。『甲主義』提倡各種經濟因素公平而自由的交換,是以個人的私利觀作主宰。『乙主義』則從專制體制出發,以政治力量強迫將民間經濟組成集團,干預所有權與雇傭的關係。」在上文中,「甲主義」、「乙主義」分別是指:

(A) 封建主義、資本主義

(B) 資本主義、法西斯主義

(C) 法西斯主義、共產主義

(D) 共產主義、新保守主義

30. 某位史家稱伊斯蘭世界為「居於中間的文明」,因其地理疆界處各文明中間,並兼納許多文明的元素,如接受印度的阿拉伯數字、中國的造紙術。然而,伊斯蘭社會卻是遲至十八世紀才逐漸接受印刷術,且早期印製的都屬辭典、數學類作品。推測其因最可能是:

(A) 懼怕褻瀆經文　　　　(B) 輕視學術發展

(C) 施行愚民政策　　　　(D) 鄙視異國發明

31. 明朝末年，內有盜寇流竄，外有強敵壓境，賦役繁急，百姓負担
沉重。大臣上奏指出：「官員不宜隨便保舉邊地的將才，監察官
員也不宜一下子就派任爲巡撫。」又如：「邊地官員的升遷，應
該在任滿之後，看他的表現再做決定，不要隨便升任地方要員。」
三如：「地方的總督、巡撫，大多由監察官員出任，朝廷商議時，
很少討論，吏部提出名單，大家也只得答應。」利用這三則奏疏，
可以推論出當時邊地的情況最可能是：

(A) 軍情緊急，倉促用人

(B) 戰術運用，攻守兼施

(C) 軍費籌措，民窮財盡

(D) 工事修築，無地不防

32. 第二次世界大戰結束後，亞非各殖民地的獨立運動風起雲湧。有
些殖民地母國在本國實行民主法治，重視人權，卻對殖民地追求
獨立施以軍事鎮壓。殖民地經歷漫長而激烈的鬥爭始獲得獨立。
以下哪組殖民母國與殖民地屬於這種情況？

(A) 法國：阿爾及利亞　　(B) 英國：印度

(C) 美國：菲律賓　　　　(D) 日本：韓國

33. 一位演說家稱許：我們的政治體制最完美，政府由國王、貴族、
平民三者組成，互相制衡，法律保障人人平等，以確保社會秩序，
人民享有自由。這位演說家所說的體制最可能發生在：

(A) 五世紀的東羅馬帝國　(B) 八世紀的查理曼帝國

(C) 十六世紀的法蘭西王國　(D) 十八世紀的大英帝國

34. 某年，中國發生重大事件，引起蘇聯關切：《消息報》指出該事件將打擊中國反日力量的團結；《眞理報》更認爲該事件將造成中國分裂，使日本進一步侵略中國。此一重大事件爲何？
    (A) 甲午戰爭，日本要求中國割讓遼東半島及臺灣
    (B) 袁世凱稱帝，日本提出二十一條要求作爲交換
    (C) 五四運動，學生認爲政府對日軟弱，主張抗日
    (D) 西安事變，張學良要求停止剿共，以共同抗日

35. 1940 年代，南非通過了「某項政策」，導致內部反抗不斷。自 1960 年代起，對該政策的大規模抗爭運動逐漸展開。至 1980 年代，許多西方國家認爲，只有藉由外界施加壓力，如金融與其他經濟制裁，始能解除南非的動盪不安；1986 年時，大約有五十家美國公司撤離南非。在這些壓力下，南非政府自 1980 年代末，開始放鬆甚至廢除該項政策。「某項政策」是指：
    (A) 發展核武　　　　　　　　(B) 政敎合一
    (C) 黑金政治　　　　　　　　(D) 種族隔離

36. 民國時期，西醫界提出所謂「廢止中醫」的主張，引起中醫界的強力反對，形成論戰。以下是當時論戰的相關資料：
    資料一：古人《內經》之五臟非血肉之五臟，乃四時之五臟。
    資料二：所謂陰陽者，猶物之有表裡、動靜，動植物之有男女、雄雌。凡物之相反者皆得而名之，其意不過如此，其用不過止此，非有神妙不測之玄機包於其中。
    資料三：中西文化背景不同，中西醫學的基礎也不同，西方科學不是學術唯一之途徑，東方醫學自有其立足點。
    資料四：所謂「歷著明效」，所謂「成效已著」者，無他，多言幸中也，貪天之功以爲己也，以言乎實驗，渺乎遠矣。

以下何者最可能是中醫界對「廢止中醫」所提出的反駁言論？

(A) 資料一、二　　　　(B) 資料一、三

(C) 資料二、四　　　　(D) 資料三、四

二、多選題（占 8 分）

說明：　第 37 題至第 40 題，每題有 5 個選項，其中至少有一個是正確的選項，請將正確選項畫記在答案卡之「選擇題答案區」。各題之選項獨立判定，所有選項均答對者，得 2 分；答錯 1 個選項者，得 1.2 分；答錯 2 個選項者，得 0.4 分；答錯多於 2 個選項或所有選項均未作答者，該題以零分計算。

37. 後藤新平治臺時提出：「治理臺灣的方式絕對不是把成功的日本經驗套在臺灣人民身上。我們以生物學上的比目魚為例，比目魚的兩眼長在身體的同一邊。若你一定要把比目魚的眼睛改裝在身體的兩邊，那就是違反了生物學的原則。所以，我們必須先了解臺灣人的習性，依據其習性定出一套管理辦法才有效。」此一想法與他的哪些施政內容有關？

(A) 舊慣調查　　　　(B) 戶口調查　　　　(C) 神道信仰

(D) 同化政策　　　　(E) 南進政策

38. 以下為北宋末年「聯金滅遼」政策的討論，有正、反兩種意見。

資料一：「今日之舉，譬如盜入鄰家，不能救，又乘之而分其室焉，怎麼可以呢！」

資料二：「中國與遼雖為兄弟之邦，然百餘年間，彼之擾我者多矣。今遼已衰弱而不取燕、雲，女真即強，中原故地將不復為我所有。」

資料三：「兩國之誓，敗盟者禍及九族。陛下以孝理天下，其忍
　　　　忘列聖之靈乎！」
下列有關這三則資料的解讀，哪些是正確的？
(A) 贊成者是資料一與資料二，反對者是資料三
(B) 贊成者是資料二，反對者是資料一與資料三
(C) 贊成者是資料二與資料三，反對者是資料一
(D) 贊成政策者的理由是：取得燕雲十六州，建立前代所無的
　　大功
(E) 反對政策者的理由有：「澶淵之盟」與遼結爲兄弟，不可
　　背叛

39. 十九世紀中葉基督宗教進入臺灣傳教時，面臨許多阻力，臺灣民
　　衆往往抗拒基督宗教的傳播，他們拒絕傳教士進入村莊布教，更
　　拒絕將屋舍租與傳教者。面對民衆的反對，爲降低衝突，教會有
　　哪些因應方式？
(A) 建立醫館利用醫療傳教
(B) 停止向平埔族地區傳教
(C) 廣召洋人擔任傳教工作
(D) 培養本地信徒爲傳教士
(E) 設立學校藉以傳播福音

40. 以下是兩則有關羅馬帝國時代的資料：
資料甲：「羅馬前期皇帝甚少主動採取影響全帝國的措施，通常
　　　　於地方社群或個人要求後才做出回應。皇帝與人民接觸
　　　　最主要的模式爲『要求與回應』。」
資料乙：西元 112 年小亞細亞總督蒲林尼寫信向羅馬皇帝圖拉眞

請示如何對待基督徒。圖拉眞回覆：「你處理基督徒的方式很正確；要規定一個普遍原則，以爲處理這類事的標準是不可能的。」

比較兩則資料，下列哪些說法較合理？

(A) 兩者全無關連，甲談羅馬帝國皇權特性，乙則呈現帝國處理基督教的問題

(B) 兩者角度不同，甲是整體地概論皇帝作爲，乙是一則皇帝作爲的具體例證

(C) 兩者觀點不同，甲說明羅馬皇帝角色較爲消極，乙凸顯皇帝角色較爲積極

(D) 兩者可以印證，甲有關羅馬皇帝的分析論點能從乙的具體實例中得到支持

(E) 兩者可以對應，甲對皇帝角色的分析有助於理解乙中地方官和皇帝的關係

第貳部分：非選擇題（佔 20 分）

說明： 本部分共有四大題，每大題包含若干子題。各題應在「答案卷」所標示大題號（一、二、……）之區域內作答，並標明子題號（1、2、……），違者將酌予扣分。作答務必使用筆尖較粗之黑色墨水的筆書寫，且不得使用鉛筆。每一子題配分標於題末。

一、 以下是一則與臺灣有關的資料，根據資料回答問題。

「小的三十二歲，乾隆三十八年，隨父母來臺，趕車度日。時常聽見漳、泉兩府，設有天地會，邀集多人，立誓結盟，患難相救。我與同伙，平日意氣相投，遂拜盟起會。後因斗六有人立會入夥被人告發，並牽連我們一齊呈告。彰化官衙，差人到

處查辦，衙役等從中勒索，無論好人、歹人，紛紛亂拿，以致各村莊俱被滋擾，我等只好抗拒官兵。」

1. 這則資料應與哪個歷史事件有關？（2分）

2. 就資料內容來看，資料中的主角「只好抗拒官兵」的原因為何？（不可抄題幹，請用自己的話語歸納說明。）（2分）

3. 就史料性質來看，這則資料是一手史料？還是二手史料？（1分）你／妳如何判斷？（1分）

二、閱讀下列三段資料，回答問題。

資料一：乾隆十三年，湖南巡撫楊錫紱指出：「國初地餘于人，則地價賤。承平以後，地足以養人，則地價平。承平既久，人餘于地，則地價貴。向日每畝一二兩者，今至七八兩；向日七八兩者，今至二十餘兩。」

資料二：乾隆十三年，雲貴總督張允隨指出：「天下沃野，首稱巴蜀，在昔田多人少，米價極賤，雍正八、九年間，每石尚止四五錢，今則動至一兩。」

資料三：「臺灣地廣民稀，所出之米，一年豐收，足供四、五年之用。民人用力耕田，固然是為自用，也希望賣米換錢。雍正三（1725）年以後，臺米年年運送福建漳州、泉州、福州等地，亦達浙江、天津、廣東。乾隆年間，臺灣米價逐漸上揚，道光初期（1820年代）起，米價騰貴。」

1. 根據資料一、二，從清初到乾隆十三年間米價日漸上揚的原因為何？（2分）

2. 根據上述資料，臺灣地區米價逐漸上升的最主要原因為何？（2分）

三、閱讀下列資料，回答問題。

十六世紀初，一位歐洲學者寫了《騎士手冊》，談到研究《聖經》的方法：「《聖經》裡包含著耶穌的教義，沒有人為摻染。但我們需先有古代文學的訓練，因古代文學滋養人的思想，使其能理解神聖教義。」他指出：「一個基督教徒應通過詩人和演說家，來研究哲學家的著作，最好是柏拉圖學派，因他們更接近《福音書》……他須懷著虔敬心情研究《聖經》，堅信能從中找到可靠的真理。」又說「《騎士手冊》是要糾正一些人的錯誤，他們把宗教說成是由清規、戒律和外在的宗教儀式組成，他們完全不懂虔敬的真正本質。」

1. 文中提及「古代文學」，其所稱的「古代」，應是指歐洲史上的哪一時期？（2分）

2. 這位學者的觀點反映了當時的哪種思潮？（2分）

3. 這種思潮影響了後來哪個運動的發生？（2分）

四、一本書談到俄羅斯教士對土耳其帝國的宗教怨懟，說道：「四百年來，俄羅斯帝國官方信仰的精神首都，一直落在可恨的土耳其人的控制之下。將這個聖城從伊斯蘭異教徒的掌握中解放，長久以來一直是俄羅斯教會人士的一個頗孚眾望的原則。」請問：

1. 文中所說「精神首都」、「聖城」，其「現在」的名稱為何？（2分）

2. 文中所說俄羅斯帝國「官方信仰」所指為何？（2分）

102年度指定科目考試歷史科試題詳解

第壹部分：選擇題

一、單選題

1. **A**

　　【解析】(A) 題幹中提到「某一時期中，商人可以透過競標，取
　　　　　　得徵稅的權利，並用各種日常所需用品到各社換取
　　　　　　鹿肉，製成鹿脯上繳，做為部分稅收」，此即荷治
　　　　　　時期的　社制度；
　　　　　　(B) 鄭氏時期的「五商制度」，在清廷未能有效控制
　　　　　　前，鄭氏利用總部設於杭州之「山路五商」及廈門
　　　　　　之「海路五商」，從事國內外貿易；
　　　　　　(C) 「土官制度」施琅在台灣設土官（即頭目），施行
　　　　　　「授田產安定生活」政策，清朝沿襲之；
　　　　　　(D) 「保甲制度」類似今日守望相助制度，定十戶為甲，
　　　　　　十甲為保，設甲長、保正，實行連保連坐責任。

2. **C**

　　【解析】(A) 日本統治台灣時期，「內地」指母國－日本，台灣
　　　　　　島是殖民地，故日本官員會對臺灣人講『你們對帝
　　　　　　國盡忠只有二十餘年，「內地」人已有二千餘年，
　　　　　　所以不應奢望權利與待遇與「內地」人相同』；
　　　　　　1919 年一次戰後日本還在台灣推動同化政策（內
　　　　　　地延長主義），台灣從甲午戰後馬關條約 1895 年割
　　　　　　讓給日本到 1919 年約 20 多年，故說『對帝國盡忠
　　　　　　只有二十餘年』。

3. **C**

【解析】 (C) 第二次世界大戰中日本是侵略國，後因美國在日本
　　　　　　廣島和長期投擲原子彈，日本戰敗，戰後經濟困苦；
　　　　　　後因 1950 年韓戰爆發，美國需借助日本，使日本
　　　　　　迅速復興其工業，到 1970 年代成為經濟大國；後
　　　　　　因泡沫經濟影響，1990 年後，該國經濟發展則陷
　　　　　　入停滯，但其科技研發仍居領先。

4. **B**

【解析】 (B) 由題幹中「孔子作《春秋》，不欲載之空言，主張
　　　　　　見諸行事，通過具體史事呈現微言大義，有褒有貶，
　　　　　　使亂臣賊子知所戒懼。司馬遷繼承春秋學傳統，作
　　　　　　《史記》」，可知中國史學的主要功能為「求真、
　　　　　　鑑戒」；「通過具體史事呈現微言大義」即為「求
　　　　　　真」，「有褒有貶，使亂臣賊子知所戒懼」即為
　　　　　　「鑑戒」。

5. **D**

【解析】 (D) 由題幹「到羅馬朝聖、肯定羅馬教宗的赦罪權、主
　　　　　　張教義須遵循羅馬教廷的解釋」可知這是宗教改革
　　　　　　後舊教（天主教）的主張；新教派通稱「基督新
　　　　　　教」，有共通理念：他們重信仰輕事功，提出「因
　　　　　　信得救」的觀念，認為個人只要靠對上帝的信心
　　　　　　即可得救；他們奉聖經為唯一權威，否定教宗的權
　　　　　　威；他們崇尚樸素的方式，希望回復儉樸教會；答
　　　　　　案中只有 (D) 耶穌會屬於舊教（天主教），其他都屬
　　　　　　於新教派。

6. **D**

【解析】(D) 啓蒙運動是十七、八世紀在歐洲知識界的一種思想運動，它研究的是理性、自然、人類等；啓蒙運動強調理性精神，通常又被稱為「理性時代」（Age of Reason）；學者強調分析與研究，在探討不同因素對制度發展的影響時，還努力找出這些影響背後的規律和因果關係；

(A) (C)都著重於神學的研究；

(B) 文藝復興中心思想為人文主義，著重古典（古希臘羅馬）文化的研究探討，加以復興或創新。

7. **A**

【解析】(A) 由題幹「士人和小吏要在仕途上求發展，多以孝廉為階梯」，可知為東漢時期的選舉（察舉徵辟、鄉舉里選）制度，「孝廉」屬於「常舉」(歲舉)：是各地向中央推舉人才，州舉「秀才」，郡國每年推薦「孝廉」；

(B) (C)魏晉南北朝時期以九品官人法（九品中正制度）選舉人才；

(D) 北宋以科舉制度為主要的選才法。

8. **D**

【解析】(D) 此題關鍵處在「重要的是，十二世紀財富和人口的增加先使得十字軍運動成為可能」，故選 (D)「商業和人口復興是十字軍運動的背景」；

(A) 題目中未提及對東方世界的影響，而是對義大利港口城市的影響；

(B) 題目未否認十字軍運動對歐洲的影響；

(C) 題幹認為「商業和人口復興是十字軍運動的背景」而非結果。

9. B

【解析】 (B) 從題目中有「政府重視貴重金屬，除立法禁止輸出金、銀外，還規定外國商人前來貿易時，須以金、銀支付貨款」、「限制殖民地僅能與母國貿易」可知此為十六世紀商業革命時代，歐洲各國為採取「重商主義」(mercantilism)；各國政府想盡辦法來提升本國貨品的競爭力，如高築關稅壁壘，以累積國力；

(B) 法國於十六世紀投入海外探險與貿易，並於十七世紀在加拿大魁北克建立殖民地，與題幹吻合；

(A) 十五世紀「重商主義」尚未興起；

(C) 十九世紀的日本早期鎖國，故無保護本國貿易的政策，故不符題義；

(D) 二十世紀英國經歷二次大戰後，英國的殖民地多已獨立，不可能「限制殖民地僅能與母國貿易」。

10. B

【解析】 (B) 此題關鍵處在「他用溫和的方式來抵抗日本殖民政府與國民黨的統治」；

(B) 林獻堂在日治時期發起「議會設置請願運動」(1921－34年)，向殖民政府要求在臺灣設置議會，主張非武裝的方式爭取台灣殖民地的民族自決；國民黨來台發生二二八事件後他避難到日本作詩文對國民黨政府做相當沉痛的抗議，被稱為「夾縫中的民族主義者」；

(A) 辜顯榮因甲午戰爭後開臺北城引日軍入城與日本關
　　係密切，甚至協助日本打壓「議會設置請願運動」，
　　1937 年死亡，未經國民黨政府統治；

(C) 蔣渭水、林獻堂同樣是日治時期台灣政治、社會領
　　袖，但蔣渭水死於 1931 年，未經國民黨政府統治；

(D) 謝雪紅曾在日治時期組織激進的「臺灣共產黨」，
　　也在二二八事件中以武力抵抗國民黨政府，與題幹
　　中「用溫和的方式來抵抗日本殖民政府與國民黨的
　　統治溫和的方式」的敘述不符。

11. **C**

【解析】 (C) 唐太宗定《氏族志》，以李唐宗室爲主對抗山東士
　　　　族，效果不大；唐高宗在位時，下詔隴西李氏、太
　　　　原王氏、滎陽鄭氏等七姓十家，不得「自爲婚」
　　　　（相互聯姻），又禁止「賣婚」（與非世族的富人
　　　　聯姻，以獲取豐厚的聘金或嫁妝）；但七姓十家自
　　　　封爲「禁婚家」，私下仍相互聘娶，只是不敢公開
　　　　舉行婚禮而已；事實證明此項政策並未達到效果，
　　　　反而使世族在社會上仍有其地位；

　　　(A) 東漢來因察舉敗壞，名實不符，出現世代爲官家族
　　　　－「士族」或「世族」，但尚未形成強固的勢力；

　　　(B) 魏晉後期，世族的勢力雖開始衰落，但世族成爲魏
　　　　晉政權人才的主要來源，尤其永嘉之亂後，東晉政
　　　　權有賴南渡士族與江南士族的擁護，皇帝不可能下
　　　　詔禁止世族聯姻；

　　　(D) 唐末五代時世族已沒落，宋代社會公平，皇帝亦不
　　　　可能下詔禁止世族聯姻。

12. **B**

【解析】 (B) 《元西域人華化考》為史家陳垣的代表作，由題幹
中『泰不華』『父塔不台』的姓氏可知他們是非漢
民族的人，從泰不華「家貧好讀書，年十七，江浙
鄉試第一，明年至治元年，進士及第」、「泰不華除
（擔任）紹興路總管，行鄉飲酒禮，教民興讓，越
俗大化」，這些都可說明泰不華深受華化影響；

(A) 〈元初州縣多世襲〉與題幹敘述無關；

(C) 〈色目人隨便居住〉與題義不符，因「父塔不台，
歷仕台州錄事判官，遂居於台」；

(D) 《元典章校補》與題幹敘述無關。

13. **C**

【解析】 (C) 題幹中「全國分為兩個陣營」、「各邦人民不僅是邦
的公民，也是聯邦公民」，這場內戰是「聯邦政府」
與「邦政府」的衝突，可知為「美國南北戰爭」
（1861-65年）；

(A) 英國光榮革命（1688年）為英國國王與國會間的衝
突；

(B) 法國大革命（1789年）為平民不滿教士與貴族不繳
稅等社會不公平而起；

(D) 俄國大革命（1917年），因第一次世界大戰戰敗，
加上經濟不佳，群眾推翻俄羅斯帝國沙皇統治，後
來列寧領導共產黨政變，建立世界上第一個共產政
權－蘇聯（蘇俄）。

14. **A**

【解析】 (A) 由題幹中「對於所有國家而言，最重要的絕對不是

改變，而是保持體制的穩定，以及不中斷地執行既有法律，因此應該讓現存的政府繼續執政」，可知為「保守主義」，因「保守主義」強調保持現狀，維護傳統；

(B) 「民族主義」強調自己民族的優越或特色，追求民族的獨立或統一，往往會推翻傳統王朝，與題意不符；

(C) 「自由主義」以改革創新為特徵，會不斷的批判傳統，與題意不符；

(D) 「社會主義」主張廢除私有財產的共產主義，與題意不符。

15. **A**

【解析】 (A) 題目中有「元始天尊」，可知是道教的經典，因「三清」是道教地位最為高的神祇，包括玉清元始天尊、上清太上大道君、太清太上老君（道德天尊，即老子），「第一戒，不得違戾父母師長，反逆不孝」即是增添儒家觀念；「第二戒，戒殺生」取佛教經典為本。

16. **C**

【解析】 (C) 日治初期，為了鎮壓武裝抗日，初採報復性鎮壓，結果抗日日熾；乃木希典總督後採「三段警備制」，分全島為三區，但效果不好；總督兒玉源太郎改採鎮撫兼施策略，頒布「匪徒刑罰令」，警察加保甲助鎮壓，抗日勢力瓦解，題幹中有處罰「匪徒」者即是「匪徒刑罰令」；

(A) 清領初期消極治台，頒布「移民三禁」等造成後
　　來的漳泉械鬥等；

(B) 清領時期，只有以「土牛紅線」（「土牛地界」）
　　分隔漢番，並禁墾番地，但漢人移墾，仍不斷跨越，
　　形成漢番雜處的社會；

(D) 經過日治初期的武裝鎮壓，日治後期已有效控制
　　原住民，不需要頒布「匪徒刑罰令」阻止原住民
　　起事。

17. **C**

【解析】 (C) 此題關鍵處在於題幹第三句：「王德既衰，強大之
　　　　　 國能帥諸侯以尊天子者，則謂之 (丙)」，指明春秋
　　　　　 時期周天子衰弱，齊桓公、晉文公「尊王攘夷」而
　　　　　 成為「霸」主，則謂之「霸」，答案中只有 (C) (丙)
　　　　　 是「霸」，故選 (C)；題幹第二句：「合萬國而君之，
　　　　　 立法度，班號令，而天下莫敢違者乃謂之 (乙)」指
　　　　　 商與西周時商王、周王為諸侯共主；題幹第一句：
　　　　　 「三代之前，海內諸侯，何啻萬國，有民人、社稷
　　　　　 者，通謂之 (甲)」，指三代之前王權尚未集中，「海
　　　　　 內諸侯，何啻萬國」，以「君」來稱呼有民人、社
　　　　　 稷者較適合。

18. **D**

【解析】 (D) 清末中國國勢衰敗，在英法聯軍、太平天國後李
　　　　　 鴻章等人推動自強運動，目標要「師夷長技以制
　　　　　 夷」，當時學習西洋事務者普遍認為西方人確實
　　　　　 「船堅炮利」，故多主張以製造槍礮、輪船為先，

先有上海江南機器製造局、福州船政局等成立，
任務爲製造軍械和造輪船，後來才有交通、工礦、
織機等的建設。

19. **A**

【解析】 (A) 亞歷山大東征從征波斯、佔領小亞細亞開始，征服
範圍包括敘利亞、腓尼基、埃及、巴比倫，又揮兵
向東佔領印度河流域，路線與圖一符合；

(B) 阿拉伯帝國的擴張起自阿拉伯半島，路線與圖一不
符合；

(C) 十字軍東征的目標爲收復聖地－耶路撒冷（巴勒斯
坦地區），未攻入埃及，路線與圖一不符合；

(D) 蒙古西征起兵於蒙古，經過中亞後攻入東歐，還攻
入莫斯科等地；另一路往西南征服波斯、兩河流
域，還佔領今日伊拉克等地，但未進入巴勒斯坦與
埃及，路線與圖一不符合。

20. **B**

【解析】 (B) 題幹先列舉兩條史料，說明袁紹進攻曹操根據地－
許（昌）的軍隊有「卒十萬、騎萬匹」以及「步卒
五萬，騎八千」兩種說法，後又根據根據曹操曾對
崔琰說法，考證「袁紹用兵，必然大舉出動，所以
他出兵十萬攻打曹操應屬可信」，此爲史學考證過
程，並非(A) 敘事或 (D) 史論，且題幹未見 (C) 褒貶
之意，故選 (B)。

21. **A**

【解析】 (A) 1950 年韓戰發生，中共毛澤東以「抗美援朝」名

義出兵攻打南韓，使戰爭擴大，後麥克阿瑟率領聯合國部隊越過兩韓邊界的北緯三十八度線，更抵中韓邊境－鴨綠江、圖們江；所以越戰期間，美國派軍支援南越政府，美國記取韓戰的教訓，不允許其地面部隊越過北緯十七度線，以避免刺激中共，讓戰爭擴大；

(B) 印度未參與韓越戰；

(C) 菲律賓一直與美軍合作；

(D) 北韓金日成先攻擊南韓，非受到美國越過北緯三十八度線的影響。

22. **C**

【解析】 (C) 1897 年臺灣日本總督府將鴉片收歸專賣，並採漸禁政策，規定吸食者須憑證才能買鴉片；總督府藉鴉片專賣賺取豐厚利潤，並沒有根絕鴉片的誠意，引起知識分子的批評；1928 年台灣民眾黨向國際聯盟控訴台灣總督府以鴉片膏買賣所得為日本本國的財政收入；為免爭議，台灣總督府公佈「台灣新鴉片令」，『凡是向官府登記在案，並繳納稅金者，即可合法吸食鴉片。」但是日本人不准吸食，如供應這種人吸食工具者，皆處以死刑』；日方統治者除更嚴格控制鴉片證數量外，並成立更生院擴大戒癮活動。

23. **C**

【解析】 (C) 人類四大古文明是西亞、埃及、印度和中國文明，題幹提及「其中兩個文明： 這兩個文明基本上都

是土生土長地自行發展出來的,也都有自然天險屏障或地理上的偏安,讓它們自成一個世界,爲統一政權的出現提供有利養分」,埃及與中國文明具有以上特色,如埃及文明南邊有高山屏障,北面有地中海阻隔,東西兩邊都是沙漠,外族的侵襲不易,古埃及文化的發展,具有單純、穩定的特色,曾建立統一政權;中國文明偏安東亞,以黃河、長江流域爲中心,也曾建立統一政權;兩河流域東北方是高原和山區,在河流和高山間沒有天然險阻可以抵擋入侵者,居住在山區地帶的民族自古以來就是兩河流域的大患,南方是阿拉伯沙漠,在沙漠邊緣的游牧民族也時侵入農耕地帶,不符題幹提及的敘述;印度達羅毗荼人(Dasas)定居於印度河河谷地區,曾發展出哈拉帕文化的城市文明,後來遭阿利安人入侵出現阿利安文明,也未出現統一政權,亦與題義不符。

24. **C**

【解析】(C) 新文化運動的主導人物有胡適之與陳獨秀,他們檢討傳統中國文化-打倒孔家店、新思想的引進-民主與科學、新文學的提倡-主張寫白話文;惟胡適「對當時許多人受到俄國十月革命鼓舞宣傳馬克思主義,介紹階級鬥爭與唯物史觀的作法,並不贊成」,是此題答案;

(A)(B) 陳獨秀受到馬克思主義的影響,與李大釗是中國共產黨創始人;

(D) 魯迅在新文化運動時對中國儒家文化批判不遺餘

力，曾講中國文化是「吃人的禮教」，思想相當左
傾，中共建國後標榜魯迅為中國偉大文學家，但他
非新文化運動的主導人物，故不選。

25. **D**

【解析】 (D) 由圖中看到此都城設立的各種機構，可知此地受中
國影響很深，才有如中國設置的「司天監」（天文
曆法機構）、「國子監」（教育行政機構）、「奉天府」
（一般行政機構）、「會試場」（科舉考試場地）、
「白馬祠」（佛寺）等的設立，答案中只有越南從
秦漢到隋唐漢化甚深，尤其隋唐中國文化影響朝
鮮、日本及越南最明顯，形成「東亞世界」，亦稱
「漢文化圈」；朝鮮、日本及越南建立中國式的教
育，亦受唐朝開始與孔廟結合－稱為「廟學」影
響，形成「儒家文化區」，故答案應為 (D)；升龍
為今日的河內，曾為越南的首都。

26. **B**

【解析】 (B) 由題義可知三段資料的先後次序是東王楊秀清先寫
信給英國駐華公使文翰，次為文翰回函，最後是江
蘇巡撫行文照會英、美兩國領事；乙資料中有「可
隨意來天京」一定是東王楊秀清書函；丙資料中有
「中國既准吾通商」可知為文翰回函；甲資料中有
「希念兩國通商和好已久」為江蘇巡撫行文照會
英、美兩國領事書函，三段資料的先後次序排列應
是正確答案 (B) 乙丙甲。

27. **B**

【解析】 (B) 印度婆羅門教重視祭典儀式，流於形式主義，與一般民眾漸行漸遠；爲祭神而濫用犧牲，也對農民造成經濟負擔；婆羅門教的變質引起學者的反感，他們認爲＜奧義書＞所探索的「梵」，代表宇宙終極眞理，位在神明之上；要掌握「梵」的本質須靠心智的探求而非祭典的形式從「吠陀經」到「奧義書」，印度婆羅門信仰從犧牲獻祭到哲學思辯；

(A) 從「吠陀經」到「奧義書」始終爲多神信仰；

(C) 「吠陀經」或「奧義書」都兼有出世和入世之法；

(D) 從「吠陀經」到「奧義書」皆是有神主義。

28. **A**

【解析】 (A) 1950 年代末期，政府由 40 年代的進口替代期轉變成出口擴張(經濟起飛期)，爲改善投資環境，吸引僑外投資，以拓展輸出，增加外匯收入，特別制定「獎勵投資條例」，降低關稅，放寬進口限制，終於在 1966 年創設高雄加工出口區；

(B) 「改革幣制方案」是 1949 年因通貨膨脹，物價飛漲，因此政府發行新台幣，1 元換舊台幣 4 萬元，通貨膨脹現象趨緩和；

(C) 「促進產業升級條例」公布於 1990 年，目的在推動發展通訊、資訊等新興工業，促進產業升級；

(D) 1960 年代，因 62、64 年兩次石油危機，世界景氣不振，加上退出聯合國，投資意願低落，故蔣經國院長推動「十大建設」大型公共投資。

29. **B**

【解析】 (B) 資本主義（Capitalism），其特色是強調私人擁有資本財產（反對共產），且投資活動由個人決定，非由國家控制，經濟行為以尋求私人利潤為目標；法西斯主義（Fascism）可視為極端形式的集體主義，反對個人主義，出現在 1922 年至 1943 年間的墨索里尼政權統治下的義大利，類似的包含納粹主義，法西斯主義通常結合獨裁主義、極端民族主義、軍國主義、反對自由放任的資本主義、反共產主義，題幹這位史家講的「甲主義」、「乙主義」分別指資本主義，和法西斯主義；

(A) 資本主義的出現，並非延伸自封建主義，中古封建社會出現，資本主義的興盛在於工業革命以後；

(C) 共產主義的出現早於法西斯主義；

(D) 共產主義主張廢除私有財產－公有財產，與題幹「甲主義」不符，新保守主義（Neoconservatism）指六○及七○年代在美國興起的一種政治思想，強調西方價值，敵視共產主義，擁護資本主義、市場經濟、自由競爭，力主對傳統宗教、道德及家庭觀念的維護，不可能是共產主義的變態。

30. **A**

【解析】 (A) 《古蘭經》以阿拉伯文寫成，為伊斯蘭教的經典，有利於穆斯林間的溝通，阿拉伯人認為這是屬於自己的宗教，為避免產生不同的解釋，用抄寫方式流傳，伊斯蘭社會遲至十八世紀才逐漸接受印刷術，且早期印製的都屬辭典、數學類作品，即

懼怕褻瀆經文；

(B) 阿拉伯人相當重視學術發展，如化學、數學、天文、醫學等科學，都有相當高的成就，絕無輕視學術發展；

(C) 回教徒必須具備閱讀《古蘭經》的能力，因此伊斯蘭世界識字率相當高，絕無施行愚民政策；

(D) 阿拉伯人接受中國造紙術、火藥和印度數字與零的觀念，且將之傳播至西方，絕無鄙視異國發明。

31. **A**

【解析】 (A) 由題目中三封奏章，可看出 (A) 軍情緊急，倉促用人，如第一封「官員不宜隨便保舉邊地的將才，監察官員也不宜一下子就派任為巡撫。」，第二封「不要隨便升任地方要員」，第三封「朝廷商議時，很少討論，吏部提出名單，大家也只得答應」；其他答案明顯不對。

32. **A**

【解析】 (A) 第二次大戰後新興國家獨立方式有三種：

(1) 經聯合國協助：在第二次世界大 戰戰敗的德、義、日等國，它們的殖民地大都是經由聯合國託管理事會協助獲得獨立，如北非的利比亞原屬義大利殖民地，二次戰後義大利戰敗，遂交予聯合國大會討論，允其獨立；

(2) 經由和平談判：美、英兩國對殖民地的獨立運動採取較開明的態度；菲律賓是以和平談判的方式在 1946 年脫離美國獨立；印度獨立運動

　　　領袖甘地提倡「不合作運動」，讓印度人恢復民
　　　族自尊心，1947 年印度終獲獨立；

　(3) 經由武裝革命：法、荷、比等國的殖民地大都
　　　是以武裝革命獨立，如印尼原屬於荷蘭的殖民
　　　地，在蘇卡諾（Sukarno）領導下驅逐荷蘭人；
　　　後經聯合國的調解，荷蘭才停戰撤兵，並承認
　　　印尼的獨立，(A) 法國殖民地阿爾及利亞是經由
　　　武裝革命而獨立；

(B) (C) 經由和平談判而獨立；

(D) 經聯合國協助。

32. D

【解析】(D) 題幹中「政府由國王、貴族、平民三者組成，互相
　　　制衡，法律保障人人平等，以確保社會秩序，人民
　　　享有自由」，可知此國家為民主國家，(D) 英國在
　　　1689 年光榮革命後英王簽署《權利法案》，國會
　　　成為最高的權力機構，英國專制王權結束，國會分
　　　為上下兩院，上議院由世襲貴族和高階教士出任，
　　　下議院議員由平民選出，十八世紀的大英帝國延續
　　　此體制，為正確答案；

(A) 東羅馬帝國皇帝為政治和宗教最高領導人，非民主
　　　國家；

(B) 法蘭克國王查理曼受教宗加冕為「羅馬人的皇帝」，
　　　查理曼權大，非民主國家；

(C) 十六世紀的法蘭西王國為中央集權的君主專制國
　　　非民主國家。

34. **D**

【解析】 (D) 題幹中有「蘇聯關切」、「該事件將造成中國分裂，使日本進一步侵略中國」，(D) 1936 年西安事變爆發前，日本已侵略中國，國民政府此時實行攘外（抗日）必先安內（剿共）政策，張學良受共黨影響發動「西安事變」，挾持蔣中正要求停止剿共，以共同抗日，《消息報》指出該事件將打擊中國反日力量的團結，故引起蘇聯關切，怕日本勢力在中國擴張，傷害蘇聯的利益；

(A) 甲午戰爭清廷戰敗，中日簽訂《馬關條約》，日本沒有進一步侵略中國；

(B) 袁世凱想稱帝，1915年日本提出二十一條要求作爲交換，蘇聯關切無用；

(C) 「五四運動」是中國北京地區大學生等抗議日本在巴黎和會中繼德國在山東的權益的遊行，蘇聯關切無用。

35. **D**

【解析】 (D) 南非「種族隔離政策」白人掌握政治經濟的權力，有色人種成爲廉價勞動力的來源；其中的黑人多在白人擁有的農場工作，但是只拿到白人八分之一的工資，而且工資通常無法養家；也有不少黑人失業；這個制度在 1948 年被以法律方式執行；受差別待遇的黑人有 2500 萬人，白人只有 400 萬人，南非的種族隔離政策不但引發國內的反彈與抗爭，更引發國際社會的攻擊與經濟制裁；1989 年戴克拉克（Frederik Willem de Klerk）擔任南非總統後，釋放反對種族隔離政策而入獄的黑人領袖－曼德拉

　　（N. Mandela），並且於1991 年取消種族隔離政策，

　　曼德拉於 1994 年成為南非第一位民選黑人總統；

(A) 南非曾發展核武，1990 年南非總統戴克拉克宣布
　　銷毀南非擁有的核武，成為世界上第一個放棄核
　　武的國家；

(B) 南非非政教合一；

(C) 南非貪污情形嚴重，並未導致外界施加壓力。

36. **B**

【解析】(B) 民國初年西醫取代中醫的呼聲，可說是新文化運
　　　　　動中「全盤西化」的語言，留學歐美與日本的新
　　　　　式知識分子逐漸成為知識界的主流，二十世紀初
　　　　　葉留學歸國的新式西醫，撐起反對中醫的旗幟，
　　　　　余巖（雲岫）成為反中醫運動中最重要的人物，
　　　　　以惲鐵樵為代表的中醫，陸續回應廢除中醫的挑
　　　　　戰，惲鐵樵說明傳統中醫和西醫的思維、理論不
　　　　　同，不能一概而論；資料一說「古人《內經》之
　　　　　五臟非血肉之五臟，乃四時之五臟」，說明人體
　　　　　健康不僅受到人的感情、思想或飲食起居的影響，
　　　　　也和四時、日月星辰的變動有感應關係；資料三
　　　　　「西方科學不是學術唯一之途徑，東方醫學自有
　　　　　其立足點」，這兩項都是中醫界對「廢止中醫」
　　　　　所提出的反駁言論；資料二認為「陰陽…凡物之
　　　　　相反者皆得而名之，其意不過如此，其用不過止此，
　　　　　非有神妙不測之玄機包於其中」；資料四提到所謂
　　　　　「成效已著者，無他，多言幸中也，貪天之功以
　　　　　為己也，以言乎實驗，渺乎遠矣」，認為中醫治

病成效只是運氣好，並歸功於經驗，其實兩者根本無關，資料二和資料四都是批判中醫之論。

二、多選題

37. AB

【解析】 (A)(B) 日治時期統治台灣以兒玉源太郎總督、後藤新平（Got－Sinpei）民政長官　時代最有成就，尤其後藤新平提出「生物學原則」，主張如自然生態一樣，要了解順應台灣生態，他的 (A) 舊慣調查 (B) 戶口調查、林野調查、人口調查與土地改革等都與此一想法有關；

(C) 神道信仰、(E) 南進政策都是在 1937 年二次大戰開始後的「皇民化運動」推行；

(D) 同化政策則於 1919－1936 年一次大戰結束後的「內地延長主義」推動。

38. BDE

【解析】 (B) 資料二贊成「聯金滅遼」的言論，提及「中國與遼雖為兄弟之邦，然百餘年間，彼之擾我者多矣」，「今遼已衰弱而不取燕、雲，女真即強，中原故地將不復為我所有」，故「聯金滅遼」應該；

(D) 資料二亦提及「取得燕雲十六州，建立前代所無的大功」；

(A)(C) 資料一為對「聯金滅遼」表示反對，認為「今日之舉，譬如盜（金）入鄰（遼）家，不能救，又乘之而分其室焉，怎麼可以呢！」；資料三亦對「聯金滅遼」表示反對，提及「兩國之誓，敗盟者禍及九族」，

(E) 反對「聯金滅遼」政策者的理由有：「澶淵之盟」
　　與遼結爲兄弟，不可背叛，以免禍延後代子孫。

39. **ADE**

【解析】(A) 十九世紀中葉基督教進入臺灣傳教時，面臨許多阻
　　　　力，爲推動傳教，傳教士多以建立醫館利用醫療傳
　　　　教爭取臺灣人好感，如馬雅各在府城創辦臺灣史上
　　　　第一所西醫館（即今台南新樓醫院前身），馬偕雖
　　　　然本人不是醫生，馬偕在北臺灣引進拔牙技術及治
　　　　療瘧疾的特效藥－金雞納霜，馬偕成立偕醫館秉持
　　　　「寧願燒盡，不願鏽壞」的精神，爲臺灣西醫開新
　　　　局面；

　　　　(D) 培養本地信徒爲傳教士，藉由臺灣人傳教士來宣
　　　　教，對台灣民衆更具說服力；

　　　　(E) 教會積極設置西式學堂，如馬偕的理學堂大書院
　　　　（牛津學堂）、女學堂，長老教會在臺南成立學校
　　　　長老教會中學、臺南女中（今長榮中學、長榮女中），
　　　　特殊教育方面還有甘爲霖的盲人學校，巴克禮創辦
　　　　「臺南神學院」，這是臺灣第一所近代形式的大學，
　　　　都是從教育開始播下信仰的種子；

　　　　(B) 傳教士並未因此停止向平埔族地區傳教，仍積極傳
　　　　教；

　　　　(C) 未廣召洋人擔任傳教工作。

40. **BDE**

【解析】(B)(D)(E) 資料甲說明「羅馬前期皇帝甚少主動採取影
　　　　響全帝國的措施」，整體上皇帝通常是被動的角色，
　　　　「皇帝與人民接觸最主要的模式爲『要求與回
　　　　應』」；資料乙敘述地方官員（小亞細亞總督）請

示皇帝對待基督徒特定事件的處理方式，這兩項資料都是提供關於羅馬帝國的皇帝與人民接觸主要的模式，兩者角度不同，甲是整體地概論皇帝作為，乙是一則皇帝作為的具體例證；兩者可以印證，甲有關羅馬皇帝的分析論點能從乙的具體實例中得到支持；兩者可以對應，甲對皇帝角色的分析有助於理解乙中地方官和皇帝的關係；

(A) 兩者有關連；

(C) 兩者觀點並無不同，只是角度不同。

第貳部分：非選擇題

一、【解答】　1. 林爽文事件；

2. 官逼民反；

3. 一手史料，當事人自述。

二、【解答】　1. 人口增加，糧食不足；

2. 台灣米運送到中國，台米減少，造成臺灣米價逐漸上揚。

三、【解答】　1. 古希臘、羅馬時期；

2. 基督教人文主義；

3. 宗教改革。

四、【解答】　1. 伊斯坦堡；

2. 東正教（希臘正教）。

102 年大學入學指定科目考試試題
地理考科

壹、單選題（占 76 分）

說明：第 1 題至第 38 題，每題有 4 個選項，其中只有一個是正確或
　　　最適當的選項，請畫記在答案卡之「選擇題答案區」。各題
　　　答對者，得 2 分；答錯、未作答或畫記多於一個選項者，該
　　　題以零分計算。

1. 在民國 99 年的《國土空間發展策略計畫》中，主張將原來由臺
   北市、新北市與基隆市構成的區域生活圈擴大，進一步納入宜蘭
   縣。此一主張最可能和下列哪項因素造成的空間關連改變有關？
   (A) 知識經濟　　(B) 交通革新　　(C) 工業連鎖　　(D) 人口轉型

2. 土壤的發育是土質、氣候、水文、地形、植生等環境要素綜合作
   用的結果。其中黑鈣土分布的地理環境，最可能具有下列哪兩項
   特色？
   甲、夏暖冬冷，草類一歲一枯榮；
   乙、全年氣候溫和，草類終年繁茂；
   丙、年雨量略少於年可能蒸發散量；
   丁、土壤透水性差，降雨聚積於表土；
   戊、坡度較大，有利於雨季時的排水。
   (A) 甲丙　　　　(B) 甲戊　　　　(C) 乙丁　　　　(D) 乙戊

3. 進行地理實察，若欲使用全球衛星定位系統（GPS）進行位置測
   定，下列何種環境條件最可能影響訊號接收而「無法」定位？
   (A) 星空籠罩的平原　　　　　(B) 森林茂密的山谷
   (C) 雲霧繚繞的山峰　　　　　(D) 風勢強勁的台地

4. 表（一）為臺灣本島六座國家公園管理處的橫麥卡托投影二度分帶座標。其中哪三個國家公園園區內有照片（一）中野生動物的活動？

表（一）

	X 座標	Y 座標
甲	305216	2783145
乙	227404	2427884
丙	163091	2543768
丁	237676	2704896
戊	234746	2634355
己	313167	2672604

照片（一）

(A) 甲乙丙　　　(B) 乙丙丁　　　(C) 丙丁戊　　　(D) 丁戊己

5. 近年來，一些國家因人口結構快速轉變，使工作年齡人口相較於受撫養人口快速成長，且受過良好教育，將有利於經濟發展，成為「人口機會窗」。人口機會窗通常出現在人口轉型階段的哪個階段？
(A) 高穩定階段
(B) 低穩定階段
(C) 早期擴張階段
(D) 晚期擴張階段

6. 我國是世界重要的面板製造地，國內面板產業的上、下游廠商，主要分布於科學工業園區及其周圍地區，因此能夠有效降低上、下游廠商間的交易成本，強化臺灣面板生產的競爭力。此種產業發展現象，最適合以下列哪兩個概念加以說明？
甲、垂直分工；乙、水平分工；丙、工業慣性；丁、聚集經濟。
(A) 甲乙　　　(B) 甲丁　　　(C) 乙丙　　　(D) 丙丁

7. 2013 年，臺灣經濟部曾赴美國「灣區」（The Bay Area）進行招商，邀請海外科技公司、企業到臺灣投資，強調「臺灣非常注重智慧

財產權，尤其科技業有著便捷的產業供應鏈，是研發、創新最好的地方。」臺灣經濟部招商的地點，最可能位於下列哪個都會帶內？

(A) 達拉斯－休士頓都會帶

(B) 芝加哥－匹茲堡都會帶

(C) 舊金山－聖地牙哥都會帶

(D) 波士頓－華盛頓特區都會帶

8. 美國甲公司研發的平板電腦問世後，在全球造成搶購風潮，生產線不及出貨的消息時有所聞。臺灣某消費者在甲公司的網路商店訂購了一台平板電腦，幾天後，他利用該網路商店的貨件追蹤查詢功能，得到表（二）的結果。下列哪個說法最可解釋表（二）的現象？

表（二）

運送編號：541368169　出貨日期：07 Feb 2011　目的地：臺灣臺北			
日期	時間	地點	貨件狀態
07 Feb 2011	18:20:01	中國成都	出貨
07 Feb 2011	20:23:22	中國成都	轉運中
08 Feb 2011	23:38:00	香港	轉運站收件
09 Feb 2011	03:53:21	香港	轉運中
10 Feb 2011	09:21:14	桃園-海關	等待入關檢查
10 Feb 2011	16:15:35	桃園-海關	海關檢查結束
11 Feb 2011	07:12:26	臺北	轉運中

(A) 重視產品技術研發　　　(B) 降低物流運輸成本

(C) 趨向產品的標準化　　　(D) 減少資金流通障礙

9. 中國避免油輪通過麻六甲海峽時遭受到安全威脅，因此和那個陸上鄰國合作，建立經由該國海港通往中國的油管？

(A) 緬甸　　　(B) 越南　　　(C) 寮國　　　(D) 泰國

10. 2006 年，非洲綠色革命聯盟成立，其宗旨為促進水利設施、改良土壤品質、研發適應非洲氣候的種子，並提供農民更良好的訓練，以增加糧食作物生產，解決非洲飢餓問題。該組織在非洲的農業地區推動綠色革命，需要克服下列哪項問題？

(A) 非洲境內降水量少，蒸發量大，灌溉水源不易取得

(B) 非洲農村勞力不足，無法採取精耕技術的農作方式

(C) 非洲居民大多貧窮，通常缺乏現金購買種子和肥料

(D) 跨國企業壟斷非洲農業生產，導致糧食大量地出口

11. 在歐洲人抵達美洲之前，美洲已有發展數千年的文明。下列哪個文明發源於如照片（二）所代表的自然景觀帶中？

(A) 印加文化

(B) 馬雅文化

(C) 伊努特文化

(D) 阿茲特克文化

照片（二）

12. 表（三）是中國某都市 1982-2010 年幼年人口與老年人口分別佔總人口比例的變遷。影響該都市 2000 年後老年人口比變遷的原因，與下列哪種現象關係最密切？

表（三）

	1982年	1990年	2000年	2010年
幼年人口比	18.2	18.2	12.3	8.6
老年人口比	7.4	9.4	11.5	10.1

(A) 人口政策強調晚婚與晚育　　(B) 人口成長出現少子化現象

(C) 人口戶籍受城鄉分離限制　　(D) 人口大量移入至都市地區

13. 近年來，一些國家開發生質能源以替代石化燃料。其中美國與巴西，分別以哪種作物作為產製生質能源的主要原料？
(A) 玉米、甘蔗
(B) 大豆、甘蔗
(C) 大豆、小麥
(D) 玉米、小麥

14. 圖（一）中的方塊，表示各種塊體崩壞的特性。其中哪個方塊最能夠呈現土石流的特性？
(A) 甲
(B) 乙
(C) 丙
(D) 丁

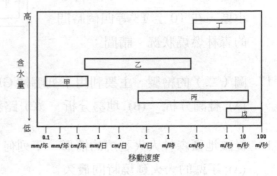

圖（一）

15. 某國家為天然氣輸出大國，2009 年冬天因與鄰國的糾紛，切斷了天然氣的供應，導致東歐和中歐十多個國家在寒冬時節無暖氣可用，該國將能源做為政治談判的工具，遭致了國際社會的嚴重批評。這個國家最可能為下列何者？
(A) 挪威
(B) 哈薩克
(C) 土耳其
(D) 俄羅斯

16. 1950-1990 年代，臺灣西南部沿海地區許多居民罹患烏腳病，此種疾病的發生與當地居民的生活環境有關。但在下列哪項措施實行後，烏腳病的發生率即顯著降低？
(A) 大量噴灑除蟲藥劑
(B) 掃除易積水的容器
(C) 提高自來水普及率
(D) 接種新型抗菌疫苗

17-18 為題組

◎ 圖（二）是透過 GIS 工具，將某地區一次森林大火事件 T0 至 T3
等四個時間的衛星影像，加以
分析繪製成的「森林大火延燒
示意圖」；圖右的資料則是該
地區的甲、乙、丙、丁、戊等
小區，在 T0 至 T3 等四個時間
的森林燃燒狀況。請問：

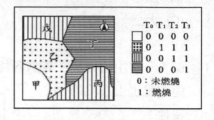

圖（二）

17. 圖（二）的繪製，主要利用下列哪種 GIS 的分析功能？
   (A) 疊圖分析　　(B) 地勢分析　　(C) 路網分析　　(D) 環域分析

18. 從該地區森林大火延燒的情形，下列何者推論最為合理？
   (A) 丁區的大火延燒時間最久
   (B) 丙區的樹種比戊區易燃
   (C) 森林大火延燒到T3時即結束
   (D) 甲區可能是湖泊或岩石裸露區

19-20 為題組

◎ 《世界是平的（The world is flat）》一書指出：「只要有寬頻，
只要有雄心，不管你在哪裡，都不會被邊緣化，競爭的立足點變
平等了。」；「小時候我常聽爸媽說：『兒子啊，乖乖把飯吃
完，因為中國跟印度的小孩沒飯吃』。現在我則說：『女兒啊，
乖乖把書唸完，因為中國跟印度的小孩正等著搶你的飯碗』」。
請問：

19. 上述書籍所提到的南亞國家，因具有下列哪兩項優越區位條件，
使得近來成為許多科技產業的外包工作地點？

甲、豐富農礦資源；乙、鄰近先進國家；丙、消費人口眾多；
丁、英語為官方語言；戊、高素質人力資源。

(A) 甲乙　　　　(B) 甲戊　　　　(C) 丙丁　　　　(D) 丁戊

20. 上述書籍所陳述的兩段內容，最能夠反映出下列哪種全球現象？

(A) 在全球經濟架構下，中國因寬頻使用有限，使經濟發展趨向
　　邊緣化

(B) 在全球環境尺度下，陸地起伏相對不明顯，所以可被視為是
　　平坦的

(C) 在全球國際分工下，各地經貿關係的密切，使個人或企業競
　　爭激烈

(D) 在全球暖化影響下，海水上升將淹沒耕地，導致各國面臨糧
　　食危機

21-22 為題組

◎ 近年來，新加坡積極招募海外的國際勞工至該國工作，至 2012 年，
　新加坡約 3.35 百萬的勞工人口中，國際勞工比例即高達 38%，這
　些國際勞工除受雇於工商企業、建築業外，亦包含一般家庭的幫
　傭。至於國際勞工的來源，除了鄰近的甲國外，主要來自下列三
　大來源區：(1) 北亞來源區：香港、澳門、韓國、臺灣；(2) 非傳
　統來源區：印度、斯里蘭卡、泰國、孟加拉、緬甸及菲律賓；
　(3) 中國。請問：

21. 新加坡國際勞工比例高達 38%，主要與該國下列的哪項特徵關係
　　最密切？

(A) 際資金流通的快速　　　　(B) 港口轉運貿易的盛行

(C) 人口自然增加的滑落　　　(D) 觀光旅遊產值的增加

22. 新加坡國際勞工來源國之一的甲國，其農業經營最可能具有下列哪項特色？
    (A) 進行大規模、專業化的單一作物耕種
    (B) 圈養牲畜，以乳製品供應鄰近大都市
    (C) 多採用機械化耕作，單位面積產量小
    (D) 日照強烈、降雨不多，相當重視灌溉

23-24 為題組

◎ 某人利用全球淹水模擬網站，並在不考慮排水系統條件下，進行海平面上升十公尺後，蘭陽平原的淹水範圍模擬。圖（三）即為截取蘭陽平原內宜蘭市一帶的淹水範圍模擬圖，深色色塊為模擬後的淹水範圍。請問：

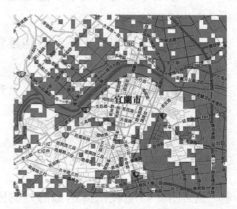

圖（三）

23. 某人在進行模擬後，發現沿著目前蘭陽平原的海岸線，會出現一條細長的未淹沒帶。這個未淹沒帶最有可能是下列何種地形景觀？
    (A) 海階　　　　(B) 沙丘　　　　(C) 海蝕平台　　(D) 濱外沙洲

24. 圖（三）展現的地理資訊，具有下列哪兩項特徵？
    甲、圖上地名與淹水範圍屬空間資料；
    乙、淹水模擬以地勢分析的方式取得；
    丙、模擬結果可以展現海拔相對高低；
    丁、圖中的淹水範圍以向量模式儲存。
    (A) 甲乙　　　　(B) 甲丁　　　　(C) 乙丙　　　　(D) 丙丁

25-26 為題組

◎ 某西非國家在法國殖民以前，主要有兩種人口：農民和游牧者。
農民居住在降水豐沛的南部，游牧者則居住在乾溼分明的北部，
以飼養牛隻為主，並從事北非和撒哈拉以南地區的商品貿易。法
國殖民後，在殖民地引進符合國際市場需求的農業活動，導致跨
越撒哈拉的貿易逐漸被人們放棄；當游牧者不再處於市場體系之
中，他們只好更集約、更頻繁地使用土地進行放牧。請問：

25. 該國在法國殖民以前，其游牧民族所進行的貿易活動，最可能將
北非的何種作物賣給南部的農民？
(A) 椰棗　　　(B) 玉米　　　(C) 稻米　　　(D) 香蕉

26. 法國殖民該國後，最可能導致該國北部出現下列哪些變化？
甲、水土資源減少；乙、氣溫上升加速；丙、生態印跡變大；
丁、雨林面積縮減。
(A) 甲乙　　　(B) 甲丙　　　(C) 乙丁　　　(D) 丙丁

27-29 為題組

◎ 表（四）是 1893-2010 年，
臺灣北、中、南、東四大
區域人口佔臺灣總人口比
例的時空變化資料表。
請問：

表（四）

區域 年代	甲	乙	丙	丁
1893	43.23	0.230	30.13	26.41
1905	35.96	1.65	30.40	32.00
1925	32.83	2.55	31.09	33.53
1965	32.85	4.12	32.91	29.82
1985	30.37	3.31	40.79	25.53
1995	29.28	2.88	42.46	25.38
2001	28.71	2.68	43.35	25.27
2010	28.01	2.49	44.46	25.04

27. 表（四）中的哪個區域，
2010 年的都市化程度最
高？
(A) 甲　　　　　(B) 乙
(C) 丙　　　　　(D) 丁

28. 乙區在 1960 年代以後呈現出的人口比例變遷過程，最適合以下列
    哪項因素來解釋其成因？
    (A) 人口高齡化 　　　　　　(B) 泡沫化經濟
    (C) 貿易自由化 　　　　　　(D) 工業化社會

29. 臺灣國家公園的標誌是根據各園區具有
    的資源特色爲主要設計理念。圖（四）
    爲某處國家公園的標誌，該國家公園位
    於表（四）中的哪個區域？
    (A) 甲 　　　　(B) 乙
    (C) 丙 　　　　(D) 丁

圖（四）

30-32 爲題組

◎ 福菜是苗栗縣公館鄉居民的傳統食物，其製作通常是在二期稻作
　 收割後，於田裏栽種芥菜，經60幾天生長後，採收醃製而成。
　 2009年，公館鄉舉辦了第一屆的福菜文化節，邀請鄉內小朋友體
　 驗採福菜、曬福菜活動，小朋友興奮地抱起一棵棵福菜，在田裡
　 鋪成臺灣的圖案。請問：

30. 若將臺灣居民分爲四大族群時，文中舉辦福菜文化節的縣份，主
    要的居住族群爲何？
    (A) 住民 　　(B) 新住民 　　(C) 閩南人 　　(D) 客家人

31. 文中採福菜、曬福菜活動的設計目的，最適合用下列哪個概念解
    釋？
    (A) 地方感 　　　　　　(B) 精緻農業
    (C) 環境倫理 　　　　　(D) 地景多樣性

32. 福茶文化節的承辦單位，最擔心遇到下列哪種天候，導致活動的舉辦受到影響？
    (A) 梅雨導致霪雨綿綿
    (B) 西南氣流引來暴風雨
    (C) 冷鋒過境夾帶細雨
    (D) 熱力對流帶來大雷雨

33-35 為題組

◎ 圖（五）是中國某都市 1961 至 1990 年的平均逐月氣候水平衡圖。圖中的可能蒸發散量，是指在給予充分的水分條件下，地表可以產生的最大蒸發散量。請問：

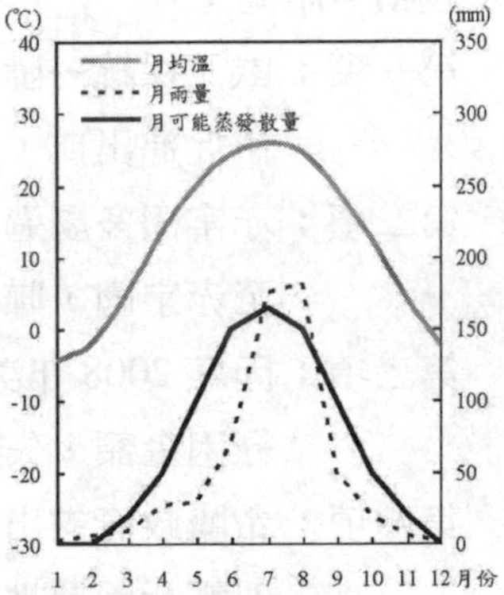

圖（五）

33. 該都市最可能是下列何者？
    (A) 廣州
    (B) 上海
    (C) 北京
    (D) 烏魯木齊

34. 依照天文季節的分法，冬季為 12-2 月，春、夏、秋三季則各依序類推 3 個月。根據圖（五），以水平衡的觀點，推論該都市在下列哪些季節的缺水現象最為嚴重？
    (A) 春秋
    (B) 夏秋
    (C) 夏冬
    (D) 冬春

35. 從圖（五）中的曲線來看，該都市逐月可能蒸發散量的變化，具有下列哪兩項特點？
    甲、月雨量愈多，可能蒸發散量愈高；
    乙、月均溫愈高，可能蒸發散量愈高；
    丙、夏季雨量充足，植物蒸發散量少；
    丁、氣溫在 0℃ 以下，可能蒸發散量為 0。
    (A) 甲丙
    (B) 甲丁
    (C) 乙丙
    (D) 乙丁

36-38為題組

◎ 歐債危機的出現，最早可追溯至 2009 年 12 月，希臘因欠下鉅額公債，導致債信被信用評等公司降級，2010-2011 年，愛爾蘭、葡萄牙、義大利與西班牙也出現類似狀況，全球各國才驚覺這是一場連鎖危機。造成各國債務飆高的原因，一般認為包括了下列幾項。請問：

第一項：歐元採統一匯率與利率，這些體質弱的赤字國無法以貶值促進出口，也無法降息來吸引投資。

第二項：赤字國多屬過度消費國，部份國家則以此契機輸入產品至赤字國，賺取外匯後，又買進赤字國公債。

第三項：因應 2008 年美國金融海嘯帶來的衝擊，各國政府提高紓困金額、失業津貼補助，加強政府支出以提振景氣。

第四項：希臘政府支出浮濫，管控不佳。愛、西、葡政府則是處理銀行因房地產市場崩盤所衍生的債務問題，導致支出大幅增加。

36. 圖（六）是綜合世界部分國家農業經營特色，所劃分而成的四種農業型態，包括亞洲型、歐洲型、非洲型、新大陸型（北美洲與大洋洲）。文中債務問題嚴重的國家，其農業經營最可能是圖（六）中的哪個型態？

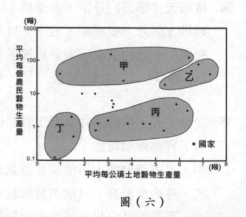

圖（六）

(A) 甲　　　　(B) 乙

(C) 丙　　　　(D) 丁

37. 這些國家債務問題嚴重的原因,主要與下列哪種現象有關?
    (A) 全球在地化　　　　　　(B) 區域專業化
    (C) 金融全球化　　　　　　(D) 社會資訊化

38. 部分學者認為臺灣也是歐債危機的間接推手之一,而臺灣也將承擔歐債危機的部分後果。其所持看法的依據,與上述引發歐債危機的哪項原因關係最為密切?
    (A) 第一項　　　(B) 第二項　　　(C) 第三項　　　(D) 第四項

貳、非選擇題(24 分)

說明: 共有三大題,每大題包含若干子題。各題應在「答案卷」所標示大題號(一、二、三)之區域內作答,並標明子題號(1、2、……),違者將酌予扣分。作答務必使用筆尖較粗之黑色墨水的筆書寫,且不得使用鉛筆。每一子題配分標於題末。

一、1976 年以後,臺灣茶葉生產發生變革,由於當時工業發展導致農村勞力不足,造成製茶成本過高,茶葉外銷數量逐漸萎縮;之後政府積極舉辦製茶比賽,將茶葉評等分級計價,部份茶農也兼營家庭式小茶廠,提升製茶技術,並以品牌化的小包裝直接銷售給消費者,促使內銷市場的成長,如位於濁水溪以南、斗六丘陵東側的南投鹿谷即為當時著名的凍頂烏龍茶產區。至 20 世紀末期,臺灣「即飲茶」產品興起,隨著市場的擴大,本土茶廠產量不足,臺灣企業遂至國外設廠生產茶葉,運回臺灣製成茶產品。請問:

1. 1960年代,因為臺灣工業進入到哪個發展階段,導致之後農村勞力不足,臺灣茶葉生產發生變革?(2 分)

2. 臺灣茶葉轉變為以內銷為主後,傳統茶業經營也逐漸「轉型」為何種農業經營類型?(2 分)

3. 凍頂烏龍茶的茶產區，主要位於臺灣五大山脈中的哪個山脈？（2 分）

4. 上述臺灣茶廠設立的區位選擇過程，最適合以何種區位空間變遷的概念解釋？（2 分）

二、 十九世紀法國作家 Jules Verne 曾撰寫一部冒險小說《環遊世界八十天》，書中主角 Phileas Fogg 由倫敦出發東行，跨越了歐、非、亞、北美各洲，最終回到倫敦，完成環遊世界一周的壯舉。圖（七）為書中主角 Fogg 行經之路線（甲～庚為都市）。請問：

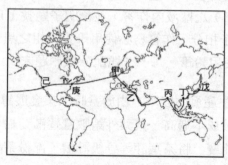

圖（七）　　　　　　　　　　　　　　圖（八）

1. 圖（八）所代表的文化景觀，在圖（七）的哪兩個都市中最常見到？（請寫代號，兩個答案全對才給分）（2 分）

2. 書中提及 Fogg 在丁戊兩地的後半段船程是順流而行，航行速度快。這丁戊兩地的後半段航程主要沿著哪股洋流行進？（2 分）

3. Fogg 在印度的旅程中，主要行經了哪兩類的自然景觀帶？（4 分）

三、表（五）為 2011 年亞洲、非洲、歐洲、美洲、大洋洲等五大洲的八種作物種植面積資料。請問：

表（五）　　　　　　　單位：千公頃

大洲代號	咖啡	玉米	馬鈴薯	稻米	小米	塊莖作物	小麥	可可豆
甲	0	16451	6140	725	838	1	59566	0
乙	56	86	43	80	38	32	13554	145
丙	5474	64501	1634	6880	143	128	35976	1602
丁	2376	34550	1883	11169	18469	940	8996	6487
戊	2570	54810	9548	145270	12442	182	102293	1769

1. 表中哪個代號所代表的大洲，其陸地範圍僅限於北半球？
（2 分）

2. 表中乙大洲的小麥，以該大洲的哪個國家境內種植面積最廣？
（2 分）

3. 表中哪個代號為非洲？（2 分）並說明你選擇該代號為非洲的一項理由？（2 分）（說明理由時，並非呈現作物種植面積的數據大小，而是指造成該種植面積數據大小的原因；另外，多寫有誤時則不給分）

102年度指定科目考試地理科試題詳解

壹：選擇題

1. **B**

   【解析】 (1) 交通革新 (B)：因時空收斂導致旅時縮短、旅費降低、易達性提高，促進都市擴張、都市郊區化。擴大了臺北、新北市與基隆市的區域生活圈。

   (2) 宜蘭：因雪隧鑿通、高速公路築成、汽車普及，交通革新縮短時空距離，故臺北、新北與基隆市的區域生活圈擴大，納入宜蘭縣。

2. **A**

   【解析】 (1) 黑鈣土分布於溫帶半乾燥大陸型氣候：(甲) 夏暖冬冷，草類秋枯、春生，提供豐富腐植質，土壤肥沃、顏色棕黑、質地鬆軟，為世界最主要農業帶。

   (2) 黑鈣土分布於年雨量約 250～500mm 地區：(丙) 雨量略少於年可能蒸發散量，淋溶較弱，腐爛草酸性不強，鹼性岩基性風化物質等於酸性有機物質，形成中性土壤。

3. **B**

   【解析】 全球衛星定位系統（GPS）：為 (1)太空 24 顆 GPS 衛星；(2) 地表的控制站；(3) 用戶的GPS接收儀三個部分組成。是以 GPS 接收儀接收 3 顆以上衛星訊號，而獲得其與衛星之距離，再計算出接收儀在地球上之三維座標值（經、緯座標及高度）。

(B) 「茂密森林」影響衛星訊號接收，星空、風雲則影響不大；GPS 接收器上方若有遮蔽物，不易接收衛星訊號。「山谷」四週山地可能阻礙衛星訊號，平原廣闊、山峰台地較易接收衛星訊號定位。

4. **D**

【解析】(1) 方法一：將本島六座國家公園座標繪圖，可判斷出甲（陽明山）、乙（墾丁）、丙（臺江）、丁（雪霸）、戊（玉山）、己（太魯閣）。

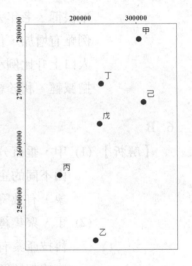

(2) 方法二：X 座標距原點最近者（距原點 163.091 公里），位置最西（丙－臺江國家公園管理處）；距原點最遠者（距原點 313.167 公里），位置最東（己－太魯閣國家公園管理處）。Y 座標距原點最近者（距原點 2427.884 公里），位置最南（乙－墾丁國家公園管理處）；距原點最遠者（距原點 2783.145 公里），位置最北（甲－陽明山國家公園管理處）。

(3) 照片 (一) 中野生動物為臺灣黑熊（學名：Ursus thibetanus formosanus、布農族語：Duma）胸前 V 字型斑紋是亞洲黑熊共有特徵，是亞洲黑熊的台灣特有亞種，現存族群不多，出沒於台灣中央山脈海拔 1000～3500 公尺的山區（丁雪霸、戊玉山、己太魯閣國家公園園區內）。

5. **D**

【解析】 晚期擴張階段（高金
字塔型）：因出生率
開始下降，故幼年人
口比例減少；而死亡
率很低，老年人口比
例雖有增加，但老年

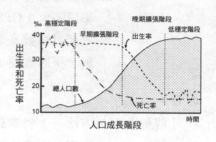

人口上升比例小於幼年人口下降的比例，青壯人口負
擔減輕，利於經濟發展，成為「人口機會窗」。

6. **B**

【解析】 (1) 甲、垂直分工：面板產業的各項製程、零件，分別
由不同的企業製造，形成上、下游廠商垂直分工現
象，有效降低成本。

(2) 丁、聚集經濟：工廠因空間聚集所產生的效益；高
科技產業有區位聚集現象（如臺灣的科學園區、印
度的邦加羅爾、美國矽谷）。臺灣面板業群聚於新
竹、中部、南部科學工業園區。

7. **C**

【解析】 (1) 臺灣強調「非常注重智慧財產權，尤其科技業有著
便捷的產業供應鏈。」可判斷招商以高科技公司為
主。

(2) 美國「灣區」（The Bay Area）：加州舊金山灣區的
矽谷地區，以史丹佛大學的技術與人才為基礎，
半導體和資訊工業崛起，為美國最重要的高科技
工業區。英特爾、蘋果、惠普（HP）、超微（AMD）
等均由此發跡。故選舊金山－聖地牙哥都會帶 (C)。

8. **B**

【解析】 全球化分工時代，美國甲公司研發的平板電腦，生產線設在中國成都，由成都工廠直接出貨給網購者，可減少庫存、降低物流運輸成本。

9. **A**

【解析】 中國為避免油輪通過麻六甲海峽時遭受到安全威脅，有經緬甸「實兌」（Sittwe）港建油管通達昆明和開鑿泰國「克拉（Kra）地峽運河」兩方案。目前已經決定要在緬甸修建輸油管通到雲南省，讓來自中東的石油經過印度洋從緬甸的實兌（Sittwe）港輸送至昆明。

10. **C**

【解析】 非洲約 10 億人口，因醫療進步死亡率下降，但出生率高，人口成長率居世界之冠，居民大多貧窮，缺乏現金購買種子和肥料 (C)。

11. **B**

【解析】 (1) 照片(二)樹冠高聳、森林高低成層，為熱帶雨林景觀。(B) 馬雅文化分布在中美洲猶加敦半島等熱帶雨林氣候區。

(2) (A) 印加文化：分布南美安地斯山區，屬熱帶高地氣候區。

(C) 伊努特文化：分布於北美極區，包括加拿大的西北地區、育空地區等寒帶氣候區。

(D) 阿茲特克文化：分布在中美墨西哥高原，屬熱帶高地氣候景觀。

12. **D**

【解析】 (1) 某都市 2000 年後老年人口比，由 11.5 減少爲 10.1
的原因，與 (D) 青壯人口大量移入都市所致。

(2) (A) 人口政策強調晚婚與晚育：1970 年代實施「晚、
稀、少政策」；而非 2000 年後實施。

(B) 人口成長出現少子化現象：中國某都市 1982-
2010 年幼年人口佔總人口的比例，由 18.2 降
爲 8.6 的原因，與 1979 年實施「一胎化政策」，
導致出生率下降相關。

(C) 人口戶籍受城鄉分離限制：1980 年代前實施
「人口城鄉分隔政策」；2000 年後已放寬。

13. **A**

【解析】 (1) 美國：研發生質能源，利用玉米轉換爲燃油，爲
全球最大玉米出口國。巴西：世界最大蔗糖出口
國；以甘蔗提煉酒精燃料技術成熟。

(2) 「第一代生質燃料」以玉米、蔗糖等糧食作物爲
原料，雖能取代化石燃料，但會影響全球糧食供應，
更因全球糧價高漲而成衆失之的。「第二代生質
燃料」利用廢棄木材或稻稈、玉米稈、回收乳品
之農業廢棄物，是現今主要研發方向。

14. **D**

【解析】 1. 土石流的特性：(1) 含水量較高：是巨石、礫、砂
等岩石碎屑與水混合的流動體。(2) 移動速度快：
沿坡迅速向下流動，破壞力大。

2. (甲) 潛移；(乙) (丙) 滑動；(戊) 落石。

15. **D**

　【解析】　俄羅斯天然氣儲量占世界 35%，居世界第一。歐洲高
　　　　　度依賴俄羅斯出口的天然氣，提升了其在世界經濟、
　　　　　能源上的影響力。2009 年 1 月俄羅斯與烏克蘭的天然
　　　　　氣費用紛爭，導致東、中歐國家寒冬無氣可用。

16. **C**

　【解析】　烏腳病（Blackfoot Disease）盛行於台灣西南沿海，特
　　　　　別是北門、學甲、布袋、義竹等鄉鎮的流行性下肢周
　　　　　邊血管疾病。台灣醫學會報告在 1954 年提出：烏腳病
　　　　　發生原因是濱海地區民眾、飲用含砷過量的深井水，
　　　　　造成的慢性砷中毒；提高自來水普及率後即顯著抑制。

17-18 為題組

17. **A**

　【解析】　GIS 的疊圖分析：圖 (二) 是將 T0 至 T3 四個時間，其
　　　　　空間位置所發生的森林燃燒狀態進行疊圖。
　　　　　(1) 方法：將比例尺、座標、投影系統相同，但不同主
　　　　　　　題的地圖加以疊合，找出符合特定需求的地區。
　　　　　(2) 功能：可準確計算不同資料間的相互關係，進行各
　　　　　　　種現象關聯性的分析。

18. **D**

　【解析】　甲區由 T0 至 T3 四個時間的衛星影像均無森林大火延
　　　　　燒，故 (D) 甲區可能是湖泊或岩石裸露區。
　　　　　(A) 乙區大火延燒時間最久，從 T1 至 T3。
　　　　　(B) 丙區與戊區圖例相同，因此易燃程度相似。
　　　　　(C) 森林延燒到 T3 時，仍有三個區在燃燒。

19-20 為題組

19. **D**

【解析】 丁、 英語為官方語言：印度憲法規定 15 種語言為主，
雅利安語系的印地語使用人數最多，曾受英國殖民，
英語教育普及。

戊、 高素質人力資源：印度積極培養優質理工人才，
科學教育成功，勞工素質高，廣設軟體科技園區，
成為許多科技產業的外包地點。

20. **C**

【解析】 在全球國際分工下，工業生產的各部門可分散至最具
優勢的國家或地區，而產生區域優勢。「只要有寬頻，
只要有雄心，不管你在哪裡，都不會被邊緣化，競爭
的立足點變平等了。」因電腦網路興起，各地間經貿
關係緊密，使個人或企業競爭激烈。

21-22 為題組

21. **C**

【解析】 (1) 新加坡：約 518.37 萬人（2011 年），因經濟高度發
展和女性就業率提高，生育率屢創新低，2012 年
僅 0.78%，人口成長率約 0.5%，15 歲以下人口佔
總居民人口 16.8%，15 至 64 歲人口佔 73.9%，65
歲以上人口佔 9.3%。人口自然增長率下滑，高齡
化趨勢拖累國家經濟，勞工明顯不足。

(2) 放寬外籍勞動人口進入（約 148 萬名外勞）：以強
　　化各級產業的勞力需求，約占總人口的 38%。

22. **A**

　　【解析】　由鄰近新加坡判斷，甲國為馬來西亞：馬國以大規模、
　　　　　　　專業化的熱帶栽培業為主。昔日種植橡膠，現種油棕
　　　　　　　櫚樹等熱帶經濟作物。

23-24 為題組

23. **B**

　　【解析】　沿著蘭陽平原海岸線的灘沙，受風力作用，堆積於海
　　　　　　　灘後方，狀似小山的帶狀沙丘。海平面上升後，可能
　　　　　　　會出露。

24. **C**

　　【解析】　甲圖地名為屬性資料、淹水範圍屬空間資料。
　　　　　　　丁圖中的淹水範圍以網格模式儲存。

25-26 為題組

25. **A**

　【解析】 椰棗：耐旱、耐熱，分布於西亞、北非等乾熱氣候區，
　　　　　西非某國在法國殖民以前，游牧者將北非的椰棗賣給
　　　　　南部的農民。

26. **B**

　【解析】 (1) 法國殖民後，在乾溼分明的北部，大規模、專業化
　　　　　　　種植可可、油棕、橡膠、香蕉等熱帶作物和採礦業。
　　　　　　　導致甲、水土資源減少；

　　　　　(2) 種植熱帶熱帶栽培業產品出口，因缺糧而進口糧
　　　　　　　食，丙、導致生態印跡變大。生態印跡（ecological
　　　　　　　footprint）是討論一個人需要多 少的土地才能滿足
　　　　　　　他的生活需求。

　　　　　(3) 乙、氣溫變化不明顯；丁、乾溼分明的北部屬莽原
　　　　　　　氣候景觀，而非雨林景觀。

27-29 為題組

27. **C**

　【解析】 (1) 都市化程度＝（都市人口/總人口數）×100%

　　　　　(2) 由資料表可判知：甲－南部（清代南部發展較早）、
　　　　　　　乙－東部（人口比例最低）、丙－北部（近代大
　　　　　　　量人口移入）、丁－中部（鄰近北部，人口被吸引）。

　　　　　(3) 2010 年都市化程度以北部區域最高（台北市、新
　　　　　　　北市、基隆市、桃園市、新竹市）。

28. **D**

【解析】 乙－東部區域，因臺灣西部工業化，吸引東部人口外
移。故東部在 1960 年代後，人口佔臺灣總人口比例降
低。

29. **A**

【解析】 台江國家公園標誌意涵：台江國家公園管理處處徽
採以河口、黑面琵鷺加上台灣船、鯤鯓（沙洲）為
設計元素，表現陸域資源特色及台江先民勇渡黑水
溝（台灣海峽）墾拓顯著歷史，象徵台江國家公園
的使命與目標。色彩上以「綠色」表現自然生態生
生不息，「藍色」寓意海洋生態資源豐沛之意象，整
體造形傳達台灣歷史足跡，更表現出獨有特色。

30-32 為題組

30. **D**

【解析】 台灣客家族群，西部主要分布在桃園縣南邊、新竹、
台中、南投、高雄及屏東，東部則在花東縱谷與宜蘭
地區。

31　**A**

【解析】 地方感：苗栗縣公館鄉舉辦了福菜文化節，邀請鄉內
友體驗，居民因接觸採福菜、曬福菜活動，而對自己
活空間產生認同感。

32 **C**

【解析】 (1) 臺灣稻作年可二穫，一期稻約在 2~7 月；二期稻則於 8~12 月。

(2) 福菜製作：二期稻作收割後（秋冬收），栽種芥菜，經 60 幾天生長後採收（冬末）醃製而成。台灣冬季常有冷鋒過境，細雨影響福菜活動。

33-35 為題組

33. **C**

【解析】 1. 根據圖(五)判知，北京屬溫帶季風氣候華北型：

(1) 月均溫：冬季（1月）介於 0℃~−10℃ 之間，夏季（7月）高溫 28℃ 上下。

(2) 月雨量：約 400~750mm，夏雨冬乾。

2. (A) 廣州為熱帶季風氣候；

(B) 上海為副熱帶季風氣候；

(D) 烏魯木齊為溫帶乾燥氣候。

34. **A**

【解析】 春季（3~5月）秋季（9~11月）：可能蒸發散量＞降雨量，為缺水現象。

35. **D**

【解析】 甲、 月雨量愈多，可能蒸發散量的高處稍延後，與雨量無直接關係。

丙、夏季雨量充足，氣溫高，植物蒸發散量大。

36-38 為題組

36. **B**

【解析】　1. 希臘、愛爾蘭、葡萄牙、義大利與西班牙債務嚴重
　　　　　　　國家，屬歐洲型農業型態。

　　　　　2. 四種農業型態：
　　　　　　　甲－新大陸型（單位勞力產量高，單位面積產量低）
　　　　　　　乙－歐洲型（單位勞力產量高，單位面積產量高）
　　　　　　　丙－亞洲型（單位勞力產量低，單位面積產量高）
　　　　　　　丁－非洲型農業型（兩者皆低）。

37. **C**

【解析】　題中「希臘因欠下鉅額公債，導致債信被信用評等公
　　　　　司降級」顯示政府欠外國大筆債務，希臘債信評級不
　　　　　斷下降，無法借到新貸款，而原有貸款即將到期無法
　　　　　償還，因金融全球化，如果沒有外來幫助，希臘破產，
　　　　　曾借給希臘錢的銀行和組織也會倒閉，產生連鎖反應，
　　　　　影響歐元區經濟，就是歐債危機。

38. **B**

【解析】　臺灣經濟以出口導向為主，產品輸至歐洲赤字國，賺
　　　　　取外匯後，又買進赤字國公債。在金融全球化下，亦
　　　　　與歐洲銀行債券相關聯。

貳、非選擇題

一、　1.【答案】　出口擴張

　　　　【解析】　1960 年代，臺灣設置加工出口區、開發農村工業
　　　　　　　　　區，使工業就業人口超越農業。

2. 【答案】 精緻農業

【解析】 強調「經營方式細膩化、生產技術科學化、產品品質高級化」、發展生態農業、提升茶葉價值。

3. 【答案】 阿里山山脈

【解析】 由「濁水溪以南、斗六丘陵東側的南投鹿谷。」為凍頂烏龍茶產區，可判斷為阿里山山脈。

4. 【答案】 區位擴散

【解析】 「隨著市場的擴大，本土茶廠產量不足，臺灣企業遂至國外設廠生產茶葉，運回臺灣製成茶產品。」顯示茶廠區位擴散，到國外設置工廠，並與臺灣茶廠進行分工。

二、 1. 【答案】 乙、丙

【解析】 圖(八)為伊斯蘭教建築；圖(七)的乙為埃及、丙為孟加拉，皆為伊斯蘭教國家。

2. 【答案】 黑潮

【解析】 圖(七)的丁為中國，戊為日本，由南向北的洋流是黑潮。

3. 【答案】 熱帶季風雨林、熱帶沙漠

【解析】 印度東方為熱帶雨林景觀帶，西北方為熱帶沙漠景觀帶。

三、 1.【答案】甲

　　　【解析】甲－歐洲陸地範圍僅限北半球緯度高於30度地
　　　　　　　　區，無熱帶氣候的咖啡、可可等熱 帶作物，
　　　　　　　　故推斷爲甲。

　　　　　　　乙－大洋洲（陸地面積相對較小，因此作物產量
　　　　　　　　較少）

　　　　　　　丙－美洲（北美洲大規模商業性穀物農業，玉
　　　　　　　　米、小麥等種植面積廣大，中南美洲巴西等
　　　　　　　　國產咖啡，故可知爲美洲）

　　　　　　　丁－非洲（熱帶栽培業爲主，糧食作物較少，多
　　　　　　　　塊莖作物）

　　　　　　　戊－亞洲（稻米面積居世界之冠）。

　　2.【答案】澳大利亞

　　　【解析】澳洲東南沿岸迎風面降水多，農業發達。引雪山
　　　　　　　大壩之水供灌溉，擴大小麥種植面積至大分水嶺
　　　　　　　山脈以西（墨累－大令盆地）。

　　3.【答案】丁

　　　【解析】非洲受殖民影響，熱帶栽培業的咖啡、可可面積
　　　　　　　廣大，糧食作物的玉米、馬鈴薯、稻米面積較少。

102年大學入學指定科目考試試題
公民與社會考科

一、單選題（占78分）

說明：第1題至第39題，每題有4個選項，其中只有一個是正確或
　　　最適當的選項，請畫記在答案卡之「選擇題答案區」。各題
　　　答對者，得2分；答錯、未作答或畫記多於一個選項者，該
　　　題以零分計算。

1. 某日新聞媒體出現下列四則事件的報導，相較而言，哪則事件最
　 合乎公民不服從的基本精神？
　 (A) 某男子因不滿司法判決不公平而引爆瓦斯抗議
　 (B) 某戶居民因政府強制徵收土地而在家絕食抗議
　 (C) 某民間團體為反對課徵新稅而向議會陳情請願
　 (D) 某市市民為抗議議會立法自肥而集體拒絕繳稅

2. 某民間團體向政府提出以下公開要求：
　 甲、反對開徵證券交易所得稅；乙、調降遺產稅率，由50% 降至
　 10%；丙、調降營利事業所得稅率，由25% 降至17%。根據上述
　 資訊，該民間團體最可能是下列何者？
　 (A) 民營事業機構受薪員工組成的工會
　 (B) 專門職業工作者組成的專門職業公會
　 (C) 財團與企業經營者組成的工商團體
　 (D) 外國企業經營者在臺灣所合組的商會

3. 有學者主張將「公共領域」（public sphere）定義為既不屬於政府，
　 亦不營利的溝通空間，以公開、公平為原則，維護參與者的言論
　 自由與平等，藉以形成與公共利益有關的輿論或行動。根據上述，
　 下列何者最接近公共領域的理想？

(A) 某電視政論節目製作人，不邀請與自己政治立場相左的來賓出席討論議題

(B) 某報社的記者與編輯合組工會，推動新聞專業自主、自律，拒絕雇主干預

(C) 某地方政府爲興建垃圾焚化爐而舉行公聽會，但拒絕外縣市環保人士發言

(D) 某議會在通過法案時，由各政黨授權其代表秘密協商法案內容並達成協議

4. 圖一是某市議員候選人的競選傳單。傳單的競選政見中，何者屬於社會保險的範疇？

(A) 甲乙

(B) 甲丁

(C) 乙丙

(D) 丁戊

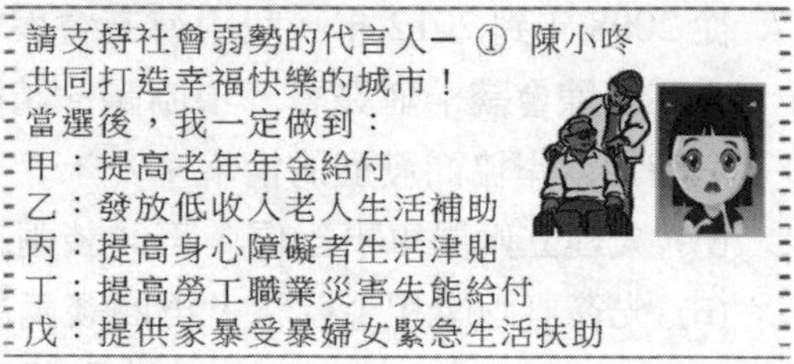

> 請支持社會弱勢的代言人─ ① 陳小咚
> 共同打造幸福快樂的城市！
> 當選後，我一定做到：
> 甲：提高老年年金給付
> 乙：發放低收入老人生活補助
> 丙：提高身心障礙者生活津貼
> 丁：提高勞工職業災害失能給付
> 戊：提供家暴受暴婦女緊急生活扶助

圖一

5. 某校推動「友善校園」，向全校同學徵求提案，希望達到「體現生命價值、建構安全和諧及相互關懷的溫馨校園」等目的。如果從培養理想「公民資質」的觀點來評量，以下由同學所提出的方案何者理應獲選爲最佳提案？

(A) 爲培養學生身體自主管理的能力，學校應該要放寬有關服裝儀容的規定

(B) 爲讓學生能獲得到充分的睡眠，學校應該將早上到校時間延後至八點鐘

(C) 爲學生的安全與校園環境衛生，學校應和環保局合作捕捉校內的流浪狗

(D) 爲加強學生環境意識，學校應鼓勵同學自組團隊認養校園的綠地與老樹

6. 在中國大陸一般人並無法直接閱聽臺灣的媒體或新聞網站。晚近某官辦雜誌的主編力邀臺灣十數名作家撰述臺灣民主轉型經驗的專刊，封面主題定為「臺灣之足」。但在出刊前夕其上級主管突然宣佈雜誌改版，並停止刊出該專號，負責主編在抗議後也被迫離職。根據上述，判斷以下何者應為中共官方舉措的理由？
   (A) 為了維護國家利益，對於新聞言論進行嚴格的事後審查
   (B) 認為臺灣民主發展經驗，對中國體制改革並無參考價值
   (C) 對公開宣揚臺灣從黨國體制轉型民主的經驗，感到不安
   (D) 擔心此舉將會破壞兩岸關係和諧氣氛，因此不允許出版

7. 從 2008 年到 2012 年，我國海基會與中國大陸海協會舉行了多次「江、陳會談」並簽署多項協議。請問下列敘述何者最能說明此一時期兩岸協商發展的情境？
   (A) 先建立兩岸軍事互信，再商談兩岸經貿與社會交流協議
   (B) 先簽訂兩岸和平協議，再商談兩岸經貿與社會交流協議
   (C) 先擱置兩岸政治爭議，由文教議題開始再商談經貿議題
   (D) 先擱置兩岸政治爭議，由經濟及容易議題開始進行協商

8. 中國大陸黨政體制與民主國家並不相同，有關其政治運作方式，下列敘述何者正確？
   (A) 中共南京市委書記接受南京市長的領導
   (B) 國家主席由全國人民代表大會選舉產生
   (C) 中國共產黨為執政黨而其他所有黨派為在野黨
   (D) 國務院總理由全國人民政治協商會議選舉產生

9. 冷戰時期的國際關係除了「東西對抗」外，也存在「南北對抗」的情勢。以下關於「南北對抗」的敘述何者正確？
   (A) 南方國家和北方國家的最主要區別是依據經濟發展的程度來決定

(B) 南方國家多半是屬於富裕國家而北方國家則多半是屬於貧窮國家

(C) 南北對抗的主要場域是世界貿易組織，很少在聯合國內產生衝突

(D) 南北對抗的主要因素仍然是冷戰，因為南方國家大多屬蘇聯盟國

10. 沉默螺旋是指當一個人發現自己的意見與周遭多數意見不同時，因為害怕孤立而選擇緘默。以下事例何者最能說明「沉默螺旋」的意涵？

(A) 爸媽都不喜歡我的新髮型，不斷批評我的審美觀，我選擇沉默以對

(B) 爸媽的政治立場和我們小孩不同，為了和諧我們在家都不討論政治

(C) 同學們因畢業旅行地點爭執不下，我感覺爭執沒有意義而不表意見

(D) 同學都說某歌手的新專輯是最好的，我雖不同意但寧可選擇不發言

11. 我們常在生活中利用表決方式來解決問題，若依民主政治的多數決精神，下列哪種情形最適合使用多數決？

(A) 社區有花圃因所有權不明而引發部分住戶互爭，管理委員會採取全體住戶投票解決

(B) 甲的遊戲機不見了，他懷疑被乙私自取走，老師於班會時請大家表決乙是不是小偷

(C) 網路店家取消購物免運費優惠，網友號召大家在網路上投票，欲以絕對多數要求店家恢復

(D) 大學生認為學校管制網路使用時間的規定太嚴格，校方讓同學用投票方式決定是否要放寬

12. 關於我國核四電廠是否續建的爭議，政府擬交付全民公投，受到社會高度關注。根據我國《公民投票法》的相關規定，下列敘述何者正確？
    (A) 人民提案通過門檻即可成案不須審議
    (B) 行政院沒有全國性公民投票的提案權
    (C) 提案前提須是「核四續建」政策已經遭到國會否決
    (D) 只要有效投票數超過全國總投票人數的半數即通過

13. 現代民主政治體制的運作應具備某些基本的特徵及要求，下列何者為民主政治體制運作的必要條件？
    (A) 國家最高行政首長透過公平、公開的公民直選過程而產生
    (B) 確保人民能獲得政府作為相關資訊，使政治權力運作透明
    (C) 國會議員有連任限制，促使多元民意獲得公平展現的機會
    (D) 國家的根本大法須為成文憲法，以保障人民基本權利義務

14. 民國 103 年底我國將舉行首次七合一選舉，屆時所有的地方政府民選公職，包括直轄市市長、市議員，縣市長、議員，鄉鎮市長、代表，以及村里長等，將一併改選。關於此次選舉的方式，下列敘述何者正確？
    (A) 所有的選舉皆採取「單一選區相對多數制」
    (B) 所有的候選人只要年滿 23 歲就都有參選資格
    (C) 所有縣市長選舉時必須同時提出副首長人選
    (D) 所有縣市長任期皆為四年並得連選連任一次

15. 某位家境清寒人士，求職時個人資料遭詐騙集團盜用於銀行開人頭戶而成為詐欺罪被告，該人士應該向哪個單位尋求法律協助最為適當？
    (A) 行政院消費者保護委員會
    (B) 行政院金融監督管理委員會

(C) 財團法人法律扶助基金會

(D) 財團法人犯罪被害人保護協會

16. 大明與小美結婚多年，一直無法懷孕生子。請問如果兩人想要擁有小孩、建立「親子」關係，下列何種方式可以獲得我國現行法律的保障？

　　(A) 大明與小美可認朋友女兒作乾女兒來當成自己小孩

　　(B) 大明與小美可採用意思表示來認領共同朋友的小孩

　　(C) 大明與小美可進行不孕治療，以試管方式進行人工生殖

　　(D) 大明與小美可委託小美姊姊，由她來代替小美懷孕生子

17. 民事法律上「侵權行為」訂有行為人須出於故意或過失始須負賠償責任的一般性原則；但有些情形即使無過失仍須負責。下列何種情形屬無過失但亦須負賠償責任？

　　(A) 無故遭追打，不得已打破窗戶躲進他人家中避難

　　(B) 與好朋友鬧翻，心神不寧又被後車追撞傷及路人

　　(C) 遭他人言語挑釁而辱罵對方，造成對方心靈受創

　　(D) 學校福利社販售鮮奶，學生購買飲用後食物中毒

18. 一對年輕情侶，男 19 歲，女 17 歲，兩人因為戀情不被家人接受，被迫在外租屋同居。日前女生在租屋處生下一名男嬰，兩人因無力扶養，便聯合將嬰兒棄置公園草叢，導致嬰兒死亡。關於此事，兩人所涉及的刑責，下列敘述何者正確？

　　(A) 男生尚未成年，無刑事責任

　　(B) 女生未滿 18 歲，無刑事責任

　　(C) 女生處境堪憐，但仍屬犯罪

　　(D) 男生滿 18 歲，量刑無須考慮其處境

19. 司法院釋字第 684 號解釋認為，如果大學侵害學生的基本權利，學生應可向行政法院提起訴訟，請求救濟。下列有關權利主張的

事例，何者屬正確且符合上述解釋？

(A) 李生在寢室賭博而被沒收牌具，主張隱私權受到侵害

(B) 王生參與街頭抗議活動被記過，主張結社權受到侵害

(C) 陳生申請成立社團被學校否決，主張集會權受到侵害

(D) 張生因學校未開必修課而延畢，主張受教育權受侵害

20. 某夜店違法使用易燃裝潢材料致生大火並造成多人死亡。為亡羊補牢，市政府全面清查營業場所，只要查出店內有任何可能導致公共危險的物品，一律勒令停業。以下關於市政府行為是否合法的判斷與陳述，何者屬正確？

(A) 行為不合法；因市政府勒令停業的措施會損害店家的生存權

(B) 行為不合法；因市政府未考慮違法情節的輕重，皆勒令停業

(C) 行為合法；因停止營業是法律規定得採取不同手段中的一種

(D) 行為合法；因市政府命令店家停止營業具有公共安全的考量

21. 甲補習班於報紙廣告中宣稱「本班學測英文科滿級分人數，大幅超越本縣其他乙、丙、丁補習班的總和」。但因其所述並非事實，引發其他補習班不滿。請問其他補習班可如何主張甲補習班的行為違法？

(A) 不實廣告影響學生權益，違反《消費者保護法》

(B) 不實廣告將影響交易秩序，違反《公平交易法》

(C) 擅自用乙、丙、丁補習班名號，違反《商標法》

(D) 因不實招生廣告缺乏原創性，違反《著作權法》

22. 王老先生與妻生有二女一男，並依法收養一女。王妻早逝，長女已嫁，次女與收養之三女均未嫁。兒子娶媳婦後，王老先生一家的生活起居均由媳婦負責照顧。未料，某日王老先生與兒子一同外出時遭逢車禍同時去世，王老先生並未留下遺囑。以我國現行《民法》規定，下列關於王老先生繼承關係的敘述，何者正確？

(A) 次女爲王老先生女兒，得以第一順位之血親繼承人繼承其遺產

(B) 長女出嫁未照顧娘家，僅能繼承夫家財產，無法繼承其父遺產

(C) 媳婦嫁入王家多年，辛苦照料王老先生一家之生活，可繼承其遺產

(D) 三女因無血緣關係，僅能受王老先生之生前扶養，無法繼承其遺產

23. 某公立學校學生於假日到校打球，被高空自然落下的大王椰子枯葉砸到導致腦震盪，該同學因此向學校請求國家賠償。下列何者**不是**本案成立要件？

(A) 校工執行職務有違法情形

(B) 校園植栽管理維護有缺失

(C) 同學的身體受到具體損害

(D) 傷害確實是校園植栽造成

24. 某法律教科書舉出兩則法律被宣告違憲的事例，藉以說明各國違憲審查時運用某項憲法基本原則的情況。例一：過去日本刑法規定，殺害直系血親尊親屬與殺害一般人不同，刑度應較重，只能在死刑或無期徒刑間擇一處罰。例二：過去我國《社會秩序維護法》關於性交易應處罰鍰的規定，僅處罰意圖得利的一方，而不處罰支付對價的相對人。根據上述，此項基本原則最可能是以下何者？

(A) 誠信原則　　　　　　　(B) 平等原則

(C) 適當性原則　　　　　　(D) 明確性原則

25. 所有經濟問題均與資源稀少性有關。下列有關「稀少性」的敘述，何者正確？

(A) 若資源不具稀少性，我們就不需要買那麼多衣服

(B) 若資源不具稀少性，我們就可以生產各種想要的商品

(C) 因為資源具稀少性，你在吃到飽的火鍋店會不停地吃

(D) 因為資源具稀少性，世界首富也可能買不到棒球賽門票

26. 商店街上某家商店整修及裝飾店面後，吸引許多消費者前來購買，同時也為附近店家帶來人潮並獲得好處。請問下列有關前述外部性的敘述，何者正確？

(A) 外部性對社會產生的效益或成本，市場機制會自動加以消除

(B) 必須所有店家平均分攤外部性的影響，才能提高資源使用效率

(C) 外部性與公共財的共享性質相似，但只有前者才會發生市場失靈

(D) 透過補貼店家整修店面，可解決正面外部性所導致的市場失靈問題

27. 國與國間簽訂的自由貿易協定，主要目的在消除各種貿易障礙，其中以免除進口關稅最為普遍。假如臺灣與其他國家簽訂自由貿易協定時，允諾兩國同時降低農產品進口關稅，則下列關於臺灣農產品市場的敘述何者正確？

(A) 市場價格上升　　　　(B) 消費者將受害

(C) 生產者將受益　　　　(D) 進出口皆增加

28. 民國 98 年我國財政支出超過財政收入約新臺幣 1648 億元，請問當年度政府可透過下列何種方法來降低財政赤字？

(A) 發行消費券　　　　　(B) 開徵新稅賦

(C) 增加政府投資　　　　(D) 提高利率水準

29. 近二十年來，臺商採取「臺灣接單，中國大陸製造」或是「臺灣研發，中國大陸製造」再轉銷世界各國的貿易模式，對我國經濟

產生重大的影響。表一是我國對中國大陸及美國的進出口貿易總值、其占我國貿易總額之比重及出超資料。請問下列敘述何者正確？

表一　　　　　　　　　　單位：億美元

年度	對中國大陸			對美國		
	貿易總值	比重 (%)	出超	貿易總值	比重 (%)	出超
1996	324	14.7	229	468	21.5	69
2001	419	17.9	259	465	19.9	97
2006	1161	27.2	628	550	12.9	97
2011	1696	28.8	790	621	10.5	106

(A) 對中國大陸及美國都有出超，表示只有我國由雙邊貿易獲得利益

(B) 臺商貿易模式讓我國得到分工利益，因此對中國大陸的出超金額增加

(C) 對中國大陸及美國的出超都呈增加趨勢，故對他們的貿易依賴程度都上升

(D) 臺商大舉投資中國大陸再轉銷美國，使我國對中國大陸及美國的貿易比重都提高

30. 民國 102 年春節中央銀行為因應民間習俗，除印製新鈔指定七大行庫及中華郵政開放提領，並要求各金融機構備妥年節需求資金，從平日約 300 億元增加至 1200 億元，也派員監看各金融機構跨行資金流動的狀況。這些措施反應了中央銀行的哪些職能？

甲、發行貨幣　　　　　　　　乙、控制貨幣數量
丙、促進金融穩定　　　　　　丁、商業銀行的資金融通者

(A) 甲乙丙　　(B) 乙丙丁　　(C) 甲乙丁　　(D) 甲丙丁

31. 表二為某國近五年之消費者物價指數及物價膨脹率，請根據表中資料選出正確選項？

表二　　　　　　　　基期：2011年

	2008	2009	2010	2011	2012
消費者物價指數	98.5	97.6	98.5	100.0	101.9
物價膨脹率 (%)	3.5	–0.9	0.9	1.5	1.9

(A) 根據 2008 年的資料，2007 年消費者物價指數應爲 95

(B) 若近五年存款利率均爲 1%，透過存款會增加實質財富

(C) 若物價指數基期改爲 2010 年，則各年物價膨脹率均下降

(D) 是同樣一筆錢，則消費者在 2009 年可購買最多商品數量

32-33 爲題組

表三是甲、乙、丙、丁四個國家 1990 年至 2000 年間的四項社會統計平均值，請依據表中資料回答下列問題：

表三

項目 國家	低教育程度者的 勞動參與率 (%)	所得最高 10% 之所得 爲最低 10% 之倍數	勞工移民移入 增加率 (%)	代間的職業 流動率 (%)
甲	61.6	27.0	5.8	14.5
乙	55.1	7.1	3.4	48.6
丙	45.1	15.1	16.8	19.2
丁	34.9	10.3	9.1	60.3

32. 哪個國家的社會階級複製情形相對最高？

(A) 甲　　　　　(B) 乙　　　　　(C) 丙　　　　　(D) 丁

33. 從表三資料判斷各國的社會與經濟發展狀況，下列推論何者最可能爲正確？

(A) 甲國的勞工教育水準比其他國家低

(B) 乙國的國民所得成長比其他國家低

(C) 丙國新移民勞動權問題相對較迫切

(D) 丁國的職業世代相傳情形最爲普遍

34-35 為題組

立法機關為修改某法律而舉行公聽會,以下是參與公聽會四個民眾的發言主張。

甲、為保障奉公守法的公民,危害社會秩序的人應沒有資格受到這項法律的保護

乙、法律制訂和修改應以維護社會整體福利為前提,以免被濫用而喪失立法原意

丙、憲法明文保障此項基本權利,即使須以法律限制時仍要符合憲法規範的要件

丁、法律保障「小我」也保障「大我」,個人固然要自由但國家更要完全的自由

34. 根據上述,哪位民眾的發言最符合人權與法治的精神?
   (B) 甲　　　　(B) 乙　　　　(C) 丙　　　　(D) 丁

35. 該立法機關所欲修改的法律,最可能涉及下列哪種議題?
   (A) 集會遊行　(B) 食品衛生　(C) 智慧財產　(D) 全民健保

36-37 為題組

圖二是某個內閣制國家歷屆國會大選的席次比例分布,請回答下列問題:

36. 下列有關甲乙丙三黨的敘述何者正確?
   (A) 甲丙兩個政黨的意識型態立場很相近

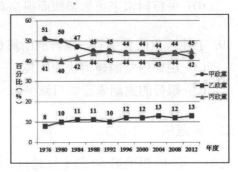

圖二

   (B) 丙政黨很可能在 2016 年選舉單獨執政
   (C) 1980 年以前甲政黨可以單獨執政,但是之後則三黨不過半
   (D) 1984 年以後丙政黨實力日益增強,但始終無法超越甲政黨

37. 假定該國選舉制度是採取比例代表制，請問下列哪項描述最符合 2012 年的選舉結果？
    (A) 在各個選區都是甲丙兩大黨的對決
    (B) 只有票數最多的甲政黨可單獨組閣
    (C) 乙政黨實力足以成為關鍵性的少數政黨
    (D) 乙黨的得票比例可能低於獲得的席次比例

38-39 為題組

一個國家若發生大量的投機活動，將會使得該國之資產價值超過實際經濟價值。在投機活動發展到一定程度後，因缺乏實質面支撐，該國之資產價值將會迅速下跌。例如：2000 年臺灣股票指數上升至 10393 的高點後，一路反轉下跌至 2001 年的 3411 點。

38. 上述經濟現象發生的成因，**最不可能**為下列何者？
    (A) 人們對未來景氣樂觀而增加不動產投資
    (B) 廠商對未來景氣樂觀而相繼地擴大產能
    (C) 外資對未來景氣樂觀而將資金匯入臺灣
    (D) 央行對未來景氣樂觀而提高存款準備率

39. 上述現象的發生對一國經濟所造成之影響，下列何者正確？
    (A) 短期內整體經濟快速成長　　(B) 投資與消費大幅減少
    (C) 銀行的逾期未還帳目減少　　(D) 房地產價格持續上漲

二、多選題（22 分）

說明：第 40 題至第 50 題，每題有 5 個選項，其中至少有一個是正確的選項，請將正確選項畫記在答案卡之「選擇題答案區」。各題之選項獨立判定，所有選項均答對者，得 2 分；答錯 1 個選項者，得 1.2 分；答錯 2 個選項者，得 0.4 分：答錯多於 2 個選項或所有選項均未作答者，該題以零分計算。

40. 公司主管對某位下屬表示特別好感，經常藉口出差，邀其同行。主管除答應將來要調升其職務，並表達發展親密關係的暗示，但為該員工拒絕。未料該員工隨即被降調，不久後又被公司無理由解雇。上述案例中，該員工可以援引哪些法律進行權利救濟？
    (A) 《訴願法》　　　　　　　(B) 《勞動基準法》
    (C) 《性騷擾防治法》　　　　(D) 《性別工作平等法》
    (E) 《性侵害犯罪防治法》

41. 將我國所有家戶依照其所得的高低均分為五組，其中所得最低的 20% 家戶，具有以下人口特色：戶內的老年人口、需要長期照護人口、中老年失業人口的比率均高，且平均每戶有薪資所得的人數較低。根據上述資訊，如要減緩貧富差距擴大的速度，下列哪些政策在短期內即能獲得效果？
    (A) 補助民營企業增聘中高齡員工，擴大就業機會
    (B) 推動簽訂自由貿易協定，擴大進出口貿易總額
    (C) 增加失業救助，提高各類社會保險的年金給付
    (D) 擴大引進國際專業人才，提升產業的創新能力
    (E) 擴大家務勞動以及長期照護的補助範圍與金額

42. 某校的「公民與社會」課程進行課堂討論，主題為「媒體的性質與功能」。下列是同學們討論時提出的見解，哪些正確？
    (A) 媒體為第四權，表示媒體受到憲法保障，屬於制衡政府的第四個公權力
    (B) 為有效達到監督政府的目的，應該立法禁止政府規範媒體的經營與報導
    (C) 記者報導特定事件時，不應未求證直接使用網路流傳的照片及影音資料
    (D) 政府為救災封鎖重大災害現場且禁止記者進入，未必構成侵害新聞自由

(E) 為了充分保障社會大衆的媒體近用權，記者有權報導公衆人物的私生活

43. 針對以下公務員涉及選舉活動的一些行爲，哪些**違背了**行政中立原則？
    (A) 下班後穿有政黨標記的服飾與家人外出用餐
    (B) 促使其部屬購買某候選人之募款餐會的餐券
    (C) 公開舉辦業務說明會，並爲某政黨政見背書
    (D) 宣佈自己將接受某黨徵召參加下屆民代選舉
    (E) 擔任某候選人競選總部政策顧問之正式職務

44. 由於經濟全球化的發展，各國政府常因經貿、環保、人權、貧窮等問題而摩擦，「反全球化」論述與社會運動也隨之興起。下列敘述何者屬於「反全球化」的主張？
    (A) 跨國公司爲追求更大利潤，常利用所擁有的政治及經濟影響力逃避其對環境與生態應盡的維護責任
    (B) 跨國公司在低度開發國家所進行的投資雖帶來就業機會，但也出現剝削當地勞工基本權益的問題
    (C) 如果擴大世界銀行、國際貨幣基金（IMF）等組織的影響力，能緩和窮國與富國間的財富分配不公問題
    (D) 爲加速經濟成長並提高國民所得，低度開發國家應對外資開放並減少行政干預，落實自由經濟政策
    (E) 爲保護本土產業、防止外國商品的傾銷，低度開發國家應加強執行維護智慧財產權的相關法令

45. 臺北某私立高中學生甲，經常嘲笑講話會翹蓮花指的男同學乙是個「娘娘腔」。乙不滿，向學校性別平等教育委員會提出言語性

霸凌案的調查申請。學校據該會調查報告，依《性別平等教育法》規定將甲退學。甲不服此退學處分，請求救濟。下列甲可運用的法律主張或可採取的救濟途徑何者正確？

(A) 本案退學處分違反信賴保護原則

(B) 甲的退學處分違反法律保留原則

(C) 得向學生申訴評議委員會提申訴

(D) 得向學校教育主管機關提出訴願

(E) 得向臺北地方法院提起民事訴訟

46. 道德與法律皆屬社會規範之一種，雖然其產生與制裁方式不同，但亦會相互影響。下列《民法》中規定，何者源自於我國固有道德觀念？

(A) 滿 20 歲為成年　　　　　(B) 子女應孝敬父母

(C) 禁止直系姻親間的近親結婚

(D) 夫妻住所應由雙方共同協議

(E) 繼承人所負清償責任，以其所繼承遺產為上限

47. 「法治國家中，行政機關干預人民權利的行為須有法律明文授權，但私人間之往來交易，原則上均可自由約定，不以法律有明文規定為限」。前述內容包含下列哪些原則？

(A) 法律優位　　　　　　　(B) 法律保留

(C) 罪刑法定　　　　　　　(D) 私法自治

(E) 信賴保護

48. 當經濟高度成長時，社會大眾的福祉反而減少，這是因為以支出面衡量國內生產毛額時，遺漏掉一些重要因素。請問下列哪些是<u>沒有</u>被考慮進去而使社會福祉減少的因素？

(A) 薪資所得　　　　　　　(B) 中間產品的價值

(C) 環境汙染成本　　　　　(D) 所得分配不均

(E) 最終產品市場價值

49. 當我們與他人同住一棟公寓時，我們的各種行為或舉動，有些會產生外部效果，有些則不會。請問以下哪些行為或舉動會產生外部效果？

(A) 起床後整理自己的床舖

(B) 自己準備碗筷吃晚飯

(C) 深夜在屋內練習彈鋼琴

(D) 在房間認真寫作業

(E) 打掃公寓樓梯間

50. 目前我國規定中國大陸資金來臺灣購置房地產，貸款不得超過 5 成，每年居留時間不超過 4 個月，3 年內不得轉賣；並計畫進行「總量管制」，打算規定陸資買房每戶面積最多 80 坪，全國每年配額 200 戶。請問在這些限制下，以下敘述何者正確？

(A) 陸客除了向我國商業銀行借貸，無法經由其他管道取得資金

(B) 貸款比例愈高，和貸款利率下降一樣，都能吸引陸資來臺灣投資

(C) 即使陸客來臺灣投資意願提高，我國房地產市場的價格也不一定會上升

(D) 陸客攜帶人民幣來臺灣從事經濟活動，必須接受我國中央銀行的監督和管理

(E) 「總量管制」將使每人購買數量降低，但管制下的成交數量可能高於市場均衡數量

102年度指定科目考試公民與社會考科試題詳解

一：單擇題

1. **D**

　　【解析】　公民不服從是指公開、非暴力且基於良知的違法行為，
　　　　　　　其目的在於促使政府改變不正義的政策與作為。
　　　　　　　(A) 引爆瓦斯抗議（為暴力行為）
　　　　　　　(B) 在家絕食抗議（不符合『公開』及『違法行為』）
　　　　　　　(C) 向議會陳情請願（陳情為合法行為）。

2. **C**

　　【解析】　由『乙、調降遺產稅率』（對資產較高的企業經營者，
　　　　　　　而言稅率調降可減少負擔）及『丙、調降營利事業所
　　　　　　　得稅率』（對財團，而言調降營所稅可減輕公司的稅賦
　　　　　　　負擔），因此推斷該團體應該為 (C)。

3. **B**

　　【解析】　(A)(C) 皆限制不同意見者的發言機會，
　　　　　　　(D)『秘密協商』違反「公共領域」公開的原則。

4. **B**

　　【解析】　甲：屬社會保險，乙、戊：屬社會救助，丙：屬社會
　　　　　　　津貼，丁：屬勞工保險。

5. **D**

　　【解析】　依題意，提案的目標必須符合「體現生命價值、建構

安全和諧及相互關懷的溫馨校園」，而只有 (D) 並非以維護『自身權益』為目的，符合題意。

6. **C**

【解析】 (A) 中國的新聞審查為『事前』審查 (C) 該新聞內容，將可能提供給中國人民，推動民主學習仿效的對象，此舉將使中國官方感到不安。

7. **D**

【解析】 『2008年到2012年』馬總統主政時期，極力與中國修好，馬總統主張兩岸間應「擱置爭議、共創雙贏」，在經濟方面提升兩岸間的合作。

8. **B**

【解析】 (A) 中國政體『以黨領政』，因此應為市長受『市委書記』（黨職）的領導

(C) 中國共產黨為執政黨，但並無其他『實質』的反對黨

(B) (D) 國家主席：類似虛位元首，代表國家出席國際場合；國務院總理：國務院為中央行政機關，向全國人大負責，兩者皆由全國人民代表大會選舉產生。

9. **A**

【解析】 (A) (B) 第二次世界大戰以後，因為經濟與資源所產生的國際衝突，以開發中國家與已開發之工業國家間的衝突及對抗為代表，稱為「南（窮國）、北（富國）衝突」或「南、北對抗」。

(C) 由南方國家成立的「七七集團」，也利用聯合國大
　　會爭取各項權利

(D) 與冷戰無直接關係。

10. **D**

【解析】 (A) (B) 並非屬多數意見，(C) 沉默螺旋指本身的意見與
周遭多數意見不同時，選擇緘默，而(C) 為『因大家意
見紛歧，選擇不表意見』，兩者並不相同。

11. **D**

【解析】 (A) 社區大樓每戶持有『比例』不同，換言之，持有比
例高的與持有比例低的居民，投票權相同時，會出
現不公平的現象，因此不適合以『多數決』決定

(B) 犯罪事件應查明真相，『多數決』無法取代真相

(C) 商業活動若不違法，應依據市場法則自由競爭，
而非以『多數決』來施以壓力

(D) 校方讓同學用投票決定，以『多數決』方式來徵
詢多數意見。

12. **B**

【解析】 (A) 人民提案通過後，還須送『公投審議委員會』審查

(C) 並沒有議題必須先經『國會否決』的規定

(D) 應為投票人數達投票權人總數二分之一以上，且有
效投票數超過二分之一同意者，即為通過。

13. **B**

【解析】 (A) 最高行政首長是否為人民『直選』產生，並非必要
條件，如內閣制

    (C) 國會議員主要任務在於監督施政，於行政機關掌
    有行政權（資源較多，決策權較大）不同，因此
    不需有『連任限制』

    (D) 憲法主要價值在於，維護人民權利，並能發揮制
    衡效果，至於為成文或不成文憲法並非關鍵。

14. **D**

【解析】 (A) 首長選舉才是採取「單一選區相對多數制」，民意
    代表，則採『複數選區相對多數制』

    (B) 參選年齡，直轄市市長、縣市長：年滿 30 歲，鄉
    鎮市長：年滿 26 歲，民代：年滿 23 歲

    (C) 我國只有總統選舉，需同時提出副首長人選。

15. **C**

【解析】 司法院成立「<u>財團法人法律扶助基金會</u>」，目的在於讓
經濟上弱勢的當事人也可獲得律師的協助，維護其訴
訟權。

16. **C**

【解析】 想要擁有小孩，依現行法律可分兩方面：

  1. 可採取『收養』建立法定血親關係，故 (A) 乾女兒
    不屬之 (B) 認領：指非婚生子女經生父認領及撫育
    之情形。

  2. 人工生殖，但我國目前不允許『代理孕母』。

17. **D**

【解析】 (A)屬緊急避難行為
    (B) (C) 為侵權行為

(D) 我國<u>消費者保護法</u>，為防止企業經營者以不正當的手段來獲取利益，對民眾權益造成侵害，採取『無過失責任原則』，意即不問企業經營者有無過失，只要商品造成消費者損害,就應負擔損害賠償責任。

18. **C**

【解析】 兩人遺棄嬰兒的行為，可能涉及刑法的『遺棄罪』甚至是『殺人罪』，而我國刑法無行為能力人為未滿十四歲之人，因此兩人都需負起刑責。

19. **D**

【解析】 (A) 『沒收牌具』，為『財產權』受到侵害

(B) 街頭抗議活動被記過，並非限制其遊行，且遊行屬『集會權』

(C) 申請成立社團，屬『結社權』。

20. **B**

【解析】 依題意『…，一律勒令停業』，若不分輕重都以相同的方式處分，有違平等原則及比例原則，因此行為不合法，縱有公共安全的考量，仍須遵循『程序正義』。

21. **B**

【解析】 本案違反『公平交易法』中的『不公平競爭行為』，妨礙競爭以不正當方法奪取交易機會。

22. **A**

【解析】 依民法 1138 條，**繼承順位為配偶及直系血親卑親屬→父母→兄弟姊妹→祖父母**，因王老先生與兒子同時死

亡，因此依民法『推定同死，互不繼承』，是以王老先
生的繼承人為長女（出嫁女兒亦可繼承）、二女、及三
女（被收養子女之繼承權與親生子女相同），媳婦無繼
承權。

23. **A**

【解析】 依題意傷者遭『自然落下的大王椰子枯葉砸到』，校園
植栽應屬「公有公共設施」，因此植栽傷人，符合
《國家賠償法》第三條之規定：『公有公共設施因設
置或管理有欠缺，致人民生命、身體或財產受損害者，
國家應負損害賠償責任。』(A) 校工執行職務有違法情
形，則是指公務員（工友）積極作為（故意）導致人
民受有傷害，與題意不合。

24. **B**

【解析】 依題意上開兩則例子，皆被宣告違憲，綜觀兩者有一
共同特性，即『法律之規定，皆有差別對待』，依此違
反 (B) 平等原則。

25. **D**

【解析】 『稀少性』並非指資源數量稀少，而是只要人們的欲
求多於實際所擁有的，就會相對地使這些資源讓人感
到稀少。因此 (D) 因為心中的『慾望』使得縱使是世
界首富，也無法完全滿足心中所有的欲求。

26. **D**

【解析】 **外部性**：指某些人的消費或生產行為影響到其他人，其
中包括外部成本及外部效益，而只要市場存在外部性，

就無法達到社會福利最大的狀態，稱爲『市場失靈』。

(A) 外部性的出現，市場機制無法自動消除，必須由政府介入

(C) 外部性與公共財，都會發生市場失靈

(D) (B) 依題意『某家商店整修店面』後帶來當地的繁榮，爲『外部效益』，因此若可補貼店家整修店面，將可鼓勵店家提高整修的意願，解決『外部效益』供給過少的市場失靈問題。而其他店家很難有效的『平均分攤』外部性。

27. D

【解析】 (A) (D) 若『臺灣與他國簽訂自由貿易協定，允諾兩國同時降低農產品進口關稅』，將使台灣自國外進口農產品的成本的下降，市場價格下降，因此進口增加（台灣消費者受惠，生產者受損）；相對台灣出口的農產品也會減少在當地關稅的負擔，售價可下降，因此會增加出口（台灣生產者將受益，消費者將受害）。

28. B

【解析】『財政支出超過財政收入』將出現財政赤字，因此

(B) 開徵新稅賦，可增加政府收入。

(A) (C) 皆會增加政府支出

(D) 提高利率水準，資金成本上升，可能影響市場投資活動，間接降低政府稅收。

29. B

【解析】 (A) 對中國大陸及美國都有出超，僅代表我國對於兩國出口大於進口，但國際貿易對於貿易國都會獲益，因此並非只有我國獲益。

(C) 對美國的出超都呈『下降』趨勢，反之，對於中國的貿易依賴程度上升

(D) 依表一顯示，我國對美國的貿易比重下滑。

30. **A**

【解析】 由上述內容『印製新鈔（甲、發行貨幣）…』，也派員監看各金融機構跨行資金流動的狀況（乙、控制貨幣數量；丙、促進金融穩定），其中(丁) 也是央行的職能，但在題目中並未表現。

31. **D**

【解析】 (A) 物價膨脹率計算方式：以 2012 年通貨膨脹率為例，公式即為：通貨膨脹率 $_{2012}$ ＝（ CPI_{2012} － CPI_{2011} ）÷ CPI_{2011} X 100%，故以 (A) 而言，假設 2007 年的消費者物價指數為 95，則依公式計算 2008 年的物價膨脹率應為 3.68%。

(B) 整體而言，2008～2012 的物價膨脹率皆大於 1%，因此實質利率應為『負利率』（實質利率計算方式：實質利率＝名目利率－通貨膨脹率），存款反而會使財富減少。

(C) 若物價指數基期改為 2010 年，則各年物價膨脹率將會依比例的變動，但並不會『均下降』

(D) 因 2009 年物價指數最低，代表物價下降，表示消費者實質購買力上升。

32-33 為題組

32. **A**

【解析】 比較四個國家的『代間流動』（指個人的社會階層，與

　　　　父母的社會階層之間的改變。）比率，其中甲國最
　　　　低，意謂階級複製情況較高。

33. **C**

【解析】 (A) 表三只能觀察到甲國的『低教育程度者的勞動參與
　　　　　　 率較高』，但無法判斷『勞工教育水準』是否較低
　　　　 (B) 無法觀察
　　　　 (C) 丙國新移民勞動人口最多，因此勞動權問題的確
　　　　　　 相對較迫切
　　　　 (D) 承上題，甲國的『代間流動』比率最低，因此職
　　　　　　 業世代相傳（階級複製）情形最爲普遍。

34-35 爲題組

34. **C**

【解析】 甲：縱爲『危害社會秩序的人』，仍應受到『基本權
　　　　 利』的保障；乙、法律制訂和修改應以維護『人民基
　　　　 本權利』爲前提；丙、丁：依據憲法第 23 條，國家限
　　　　 制人民自由的條件包括：
　　　　 (1) 限制人民自由的理由，必須基於保護公共利益之
　　　　　　 需要。
　　　　 (2) 限制人民自由的方式，必須符合法律保留原則與
　　　　　　 比例原則。換言之，即使須以法律限制人民自由，
　　　　　　 仍要符合憲法規範的要件；因此，國家的自由仍
　　　　　　 應維護個人自由。

35. **A**

【解析】 上述四種法律，唯獨 (A) 集會遊行，涉及人民基本權
　　　　 利（自由權）的限制。

36-37 為題組

36. **C**

【解析】(A) 甲丙席次比率相近，但不代表意識型態相近，若兩
個政黨的意識型態立場相近，反而會互相競爭。

(B) 丙政黨雖席次漸增，但民意如流水，無法就此推論
2016 年必能獲得過半席次。

(D) 1984 年以後丙政黨實力日益增強，但於 2012 年則
超越甲政黨。

37. **C**

【解析】(A) 比例代表制，是以各政黨的政黨票的得票率來分配
席次，因此並無『各選區』的問題

(B) 2012 甲政黨席次並未過半

(C) 因總席次為 100 席，因此乙政黨與甲或丙合作都可
過半，因此為具有關鍵角色的少數政黨

(D) 因總席次為 100 席，而採比例代表制之下，乙黨的
得票比例會等於其獲得的席次。

38-39 為題組

38. **D**

【解析】(A) (B) (C) 皆為市場對於未來景氣感到樂觀，而增加
投資，若過度投資則可能出現『泡沫經濟』

(D) 央行若對未來景氣樂觀，為穩定金融，避免出現
『泡沫經濟』，會設法減少市場流動資金，因此會
提高存款準備率，促使市場流動的資金減少。

39. **B**

【解析】依題意若經濟反轉泡沫破裂，將會出現 (B) 投資與消費

大幅減少，(A) 經濟停滯或下滑 (C) 銀行的逾期未還帳目增加 (D) 房地產價格下跌。

二、多選題

40. **BCD**

【解析】(A)《訴願法》適用於不服行政機關之行政處分時提出『訴願』

(E) 依題意主管並未達到性侵害的程度。

41. **ACE**

【解析】(B) 推動簽訂自由貿易協定，國外優勢產品將可以更低廉的價格進如台灣，可能使台灣弱勢產業面臨高度競爭，失業率可能上升

(D) 擴大引進國際專業人才，將使國內就業市場面臨高度競爭，國內弱勢就業者可能會失業。

42. **CD**

【解析】(A) 媒體為『第四權』的說法，只在彰顯媒體的價值，但並未具有『公權力』

(B) 媒體應享有新聞自由，但對於不當或違背新聞倫理、甚至是法律的行為，仍應立法規範

(E) 公眾人物的私生活，應與公眾利益相關，否則仍可受到限制（如隱私權）。

43. **BCE**

【解析】行政中立：指公務人員所為之行政行為須依照法律之規定，並且於處理公務時，應以同一標準公平對待任何個人、團體或政黨。(A) 屬私人行為 (D) 若只是「宣布」參選，而尚未展開競選活動，因此還無法判斷是否違背行政中立的情況。

44. **AB**

【解析】(A)(B) 「反全球化」，主張全球化是一種西方化、美國化，認為西方強國藉由其所擁有的政治及經濟影響力，來維護自身利益。

(C) 反全球化人士認為，世界銀行、國際貨幣基金，仍由西方強國主導，仍以西方利益優先

(D) 低度開發國家，若完全的對外資開放，將可能使經濟受到西方強國的主導

(E) 對於『低度開發國家』，而言智慧財產權，並非其本土產業的強項（因產業較為落後），因此無助於保護本土產業。

45. **CD**

【解析】(A)(B) 依題意學校依法進行懲處，並無違反信賴保護原則或違反法律保留原則

(C)(D)(E) 依大法官釋字 382 號解釋：『各級學校依有關學籍規則或懲處規定，對學生所為退學或類此之處分行為，足以改變其學生身分並損及其受教育之機會，…此種處分行為應為訴願法及行政訴訟法上之行政處分。』，依題意學生甲遭到退學處分，除適用校內申訴管道外，尚可提起訴願及行政訴訟。

46. **BC**

【解析】(A) 成年年齡之規定，為立法者的考量

(D) 過去男尊女卑的觀念下，妻需以夫的居所為居所，在男女平權的新觀念之下，才修改為『夫妻住所應由雙方共同協議』

(E) 限定繼承觀念，也不符合舊時代『父債子還』的規定。

47. **BD**

【解析】 行政機關干預人民權利的行為須有法律明文授權：為法律保留原則；私人間之往來交易，原則上均可自由約定，不以法律有明文規定為限：為私法自治，契約自由的精神。

48. **CD**

【解析】 GDP 計算時未考慮 (C) 環境汙染成本，無法看出 (D) 所得分配不均的情況，(A) (E) 則有計入，(B) 為避免重覆計算，中間產品不計入。

49. **CE**

【解析】 **外部性**：指某些人的消費或生產行為影響到其他人，其中包括外部成本及外部效益；外部成本，指人們的經濟行為有一部分的成本自己毋須負擔；外部效益，指人們的經濟行為有一部分的利益不能歸自己享受。因此 (A) (B) (D) 都只影響自己。(C) 外部效益；(E) 外部成本。

50. **BCD**

【解析】 (A) 陸客除了向我國商業銀行借貸，還可由海外資金匯入

(B) 貸款比例愈高（自備款就越低），和貸款利率下降（成本下降），都能吸引陸資來臺灣投資

(C) 陸客來臺灣投資意願提高，會使需求增加，但若供給也同時增加，房地產價格可能會下降，而題目並未提供該訊息，因此無法判斷

(E) 「總量管制」將使每人購買數量降低，若政府能有效管制交易數量，並不會發生『成交數量高於市場均衡數量』的現象。

102 年大學入學指定科目考試試題
物理考科

第壹部分：選擇題（占 80 分）

一、單選題（占 60 分）

說明： 第 1 題至第 20 題，每題有 5 個選項，其中只有一個是正確或
最適當的選項，請畫記在答案卡之「選擇題答案區」。各題答
對者，得 3 分；答錯、未作答或畫記多於一個選項者，該題
以零分計算。

1. 下列的現象或應用，何者的主因是波的繞射性質造成的？
 (A) 琴弦振動產生駐波 　　　 (B) 波浪進入淺水區波速變慢
 (C) 以 X 射線拍攝胸腔照片 (D) 以 X 射線觀察晶體結構
 (E) 陰極射線實驗中螢幕的亮點位置會隨外加磁場改變

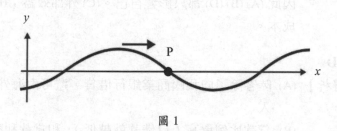

圖 1

2. 一彈性繩上的小振幅週期波由左向右方傳播，某一瞬間其振動位
 移 y 與位置 x 的關係如圖 1 所示，繩上質點 P 恰在 x 軸上，則質
 點 P 在這一瞬間的運動方向最接近下列何者？
 (A) ↑（向上）
 (B) ↓（向下） 　　　　　　　(C) ←（向左）
 (D) →（向右） 　　　　　　　(E) 沒有確定的方向，因其速度為零

3. 某樂器以開管空氣柱原理發聲，若其基音頻率爲 390Hz，則其對
   應的空氣柱長度約爲幾公分？假設已知音速爲 340m/s。
   (A) 44cm　　(B) 58cm　　(C) 66cm　　(D) 80cm　　(E) 88cm

4. 下列關於體積固定之密閉容器內理想氣體的性質敘述，何者正確？
   (A) 壓力和分子平均動量的平方成正比
   (B) 壓力和所有氣體分子之移動動能的和成正比
   (C) 溫度升高時，每一個氣體分子的動能都會增加
   (D) 溫度下降時，密閉容器內理想氣體的壓力升高
   (E)_氣體分子和容器壁的碰撞是否爲彈性碰撞，並不會影響壓力
      的量値

5. 密閉汽缸內定量理想氣體原來的壓力爲 2 大氣壓，當汽缸的體積
   被活塞從 10m^3 壓縮至 5m^3，同時把汽缸內氣體的溫度從 313℃
   降溫至20℃，則熱平衡後汽缸內氣體的壓力最接近下列何者？
   (A) 8 大氣壓　　　　　　　(B) 4 大氣壓
   (C) 2 大氣壓　　　　　　　(D) 1 大氣壓
   (E) 0.25 大氣壓

6. 雷射光以一入射角 θ 自空氣入射雙層薄膜再進入空氣，其中各層
   薄膜厚度皆爲 d 而折射率各爲 n_1 及 n_2，光路徑如圖 2 所示。今
   以折射率爲 n 且厚度爲 2d 的薄膜
   取代原雙層薄膜，若光線射入與
   射出的位置、角度皆與圖 2 相同，
   則 n_1、n_2 與 n 的大小關係爲下列
   何者？
   (A) $n > n_1 > n_2$　　　(B) $n_1 > n_2 > n$
   (C) $n > n_2 > n_1$　　　(D) $n_2 > n > n_1$
   (E) $n_1 > n > n_2$

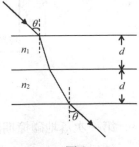

圖 2

7. 某生使用波長為 λ 的光源進行雙狹縫干涉實驗，若兩狹縫間的距離 $d = 9\lambda$，則第 5 暗紋所在位置至雙狹縫中點之連線與中央線的夾角約為幾度？

   (A) 30°　　(B) 45°　　(C) 53°　　(D) 60°　　(E) 75°

8. 一質點在一直線上運動，圖 3 為此質點所受的外力與位置的關係，質點的起始位置為 $x = 0$，起始速度沿著 $+x$ 方向，則此質點在何處的速率最大？

   (A) 甲　　(B) 乙　　(C) 丙
   (D) 丁　　(E) 戊

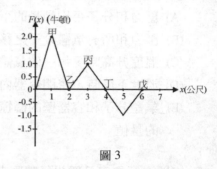

圖 3

9-10 為題組

如圖 4 所示，一質量為 m 可視為質點的小球從離地 H 處水平射出，第一次落地時的水平位移為 $\dfrac{4H}{3}$，反彈高度為 $\dfrac{9H}{16}$。若地板為光滑，且空氣阻力可以忽略，而小球與地板接觸的時間為 t，重力加速度為 g。

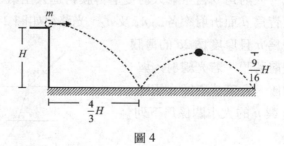

圖 4

9. 第一次落地碰撞期間，小球在鉛直方向所受到的平均作用力之量值為何？

(A) $\dfrac{m\sqrt{2gH}}{4t}$ 　　(B) $\dfrac{7m\sqrt{2gH}}{16t}$ 　　(C) $\dfrac{25m\sqrt{2gH}}{16t}$

(D) $\dfrac{5m\sqrt{2gH}}{4t}$ 　　(E) $\dfrac{7m\sqrt{2gH}}{4t}$

10. 小球第一次落地點到第二次落地點的水平距離為何？

(A) H 　　(B) $\dfrac{4H}{3}$ 　　(C) $\dfrac{3H}{2}$ 　　(D) $2H$ 　　(E) $\dfrac{8H}{3}$

11. 已知火星的平均半徑約為地球的 0.5 倍，火星表面的重力加速度約為地球的 0.4 倍，則火星表面上的脫離速率（不計阻力下，使物體可脫離其重力場所需的最小初速率）約為地球上的多少倍？

(A) $\sqrt{\dfrac{1}{5}}$ 　　(B) $\sqrt{\dfrac{1}{3}}$ 　　(C) $\sqrt{\dfrac{4}{5}}$ 　　(D) $\sqrt{3}$ 　　(E) $\sqrt{6}$

12. 由一對完全相同的強力理想彈簧所構成可垂直彈射之投射裝置，如圖 5 所示，設 g 為重力加速度，彈簧的力常數為 k。若質量為 m 的物體置於質量可忽略的彈射底盤上，欲將物體以 $5g$ 的起始加速度垂直射向空中，此時兩彈簧與鉛垂線的夾角皆為 $\theta = 60°$，則每個彈簧的伸長量為下列何者？

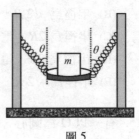

圖 5

(A) $\dfrac{5mg}{2k}$ 　　(B) $\dfrac{3mg}{k}$ 　　(C) $\dfrac{4mg}{k}$ 　　(D) $\dfrac{5mg}{k}$ 　　(E) $\dfrac{6mg}{k}$

13. 考慮以 P 點為圓心、半徑為 R 的部份或整個圓周上的四種電荷分佈情形，如圖 6 所示：（甲）電荷 q 均勻分佈在四分之一的圓周；

（乙）電荷 $2q$ 均勻分佈在半圓周；（丙）電荷 $3q$ 均勻分佈在四分之三的圓周；（丁）電荷 $4q$ 均勻分佈在整個圓周。試問這四種情形在 P 點所造成的電場，依其量值大小排列的次序爲何？

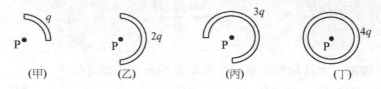

圖6

(A) 甲 > 乙 > 丙 > 丁　　　(B) 丁 > 丙 > 乙 > 甲

(C) 乙 > 甲 = 丙 > 丁　　　(D) 丁 > 乙 > 甲 = 丙

(E) 甲 = 乙 = 丙 = 丁

14. 一個半徑爲 R 的圓形線圈通有順時針方向的電流 I，其圓心的磁場爲 B。今在同一平面上加上一個同心的圓形線圈，若欲使其圓心處的磁場爲零，則所加上圓形線圈的條件爲下列何者？

(A) 半徑爲 $2R$，電流爲 $\sqrt{2}I$，方向爲順時針方向

(B) 半徑爲 $\sqrt{2}R$，電流爲 $2I$，方向爲順時針方向

(C) 半徑爲 $2R$，電流爲 $2I$，方向爲順時針方向

(D) 半徑爲 $2R$，電流爲 $2I$，方向爲逆時針方向

(E) 半徑爲 $\sqrt{2}R$，電流爲 $2I$，方向爲逆時針方向

15. 有一以 O 爲圓心、L 爲半徑的 OMN 扇形電路置於均勻磁場 B 中如圖 7 所示，磁場垂直穿入紙面，半徑 OM 之間有電阻 R，電路中其他電阻可忽略不計。OM 與 MP 弧固定不動，而長度爲 L 的 ON 以 O 爲軸心作順時針往 P 方向旋轉，角速率爲 ω，則電路中電流爲下列何者？

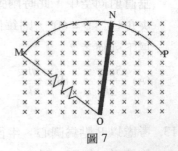

圖7

(A) $\dfrac{\omega BL^2}{2R}$　　　(B) $\dfrac{\omega BL^2}{R}$　　　(C) $\dfrac{\omega BL}{R}$

(D) $\dfrac{\omega^2 BL^2}{2R}$　　　(E) $\dfrac{\omega^2 BL^2}{R^2}$

16. 地球繞太陽運動軌道的平均半徑定義爲一個天文單位，某行星繞太陽之平均半徑約爲 10 個天文單位，則該行星公轉的週期約爲地球上的多少年？

(A) 1　　　(B) 5　　　(C) 15　　　(D) 32　　　(E) 100

17. 在靜力平衡實驗中，甲、乙、丙三力與一輕圓環以及一個插栓，在力桌上達成平衡時小圓環緊靠著插栓，如圖 8 所示。圓環與插栓間的摩擦力可忽略，若只調整其中兩力的量值，欲移動圓環使插栓位於圓環正中央，則下列有關施力過程的敘述何者正確？

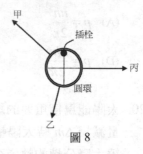

圖 8

(A) 增加甲、乙兩力的量值，且甲力的量值增加較多
(B) 增加甲、丙兩力的量值，且甲力的量值增加較多
(C) 增加乙、丙兩力的量值，且乙力的量值增加較多
(D) 增加乙、丙兩力的量值，且丙力的量值增加較多
(E) 增加甲、丙兩力的量值，且丙力的量值增加較多

18. 下列爲五種電磁波源：

氫氣放電管：爲不連續的光譜線

鎢絲電燈泡：其光譜與溫度有關且爲連續光譜

藍光雷射：波長約介於 360nm 到 480nm 之間的雷射光

FM 調頻廣播：其波長介於 2.8m 到 3.4m 之間

X 射線：其波長介於 0.01nm 到 1nm 之間

以上何者之光譜最接近黑體輻射？

(A) 氫氣放電管　　　　　(B) 鎢絲電燈泡

(C) 藍光雷射　　　　　　(D) FM 調頻廣播

(E) X 射線

19. 在波耳的氫原子模型中，電子可視爲以質子爲中心做半徑爲 r 的等速圓周運動。考量物質波模型，當電子處於容許的穩定狀態時，軌道的周長必須符合圓周駐波條件。軌道半徑也隨著主量子數 n 而愈來愈大。設普朗克常數爲 h，當電子處於主量子數爲 n 的穩定軌道的情形之下，電子的動量 p 量值爲何？

(A) $p = \dfrac{nh}{2r}$　　　(B) $p = \dfrac{nh}{2\pi}$　　　(C) $p = \dfrac{nh}{2\pi r}$

(D) $p = \dfrac{nhr}{2\pi}$　　　(E) $p = \dfrac{h}{2nr}$

20. 太陽能爲極重要的綠色能源，在太陽進行核融合的過程中，當質量減損 Δm 時太陽輻射的能量 $\Delta E = \Delta m \times c^2$（ c 爲光速）。地球繞太陽公轉的軌道平均半徑約爲 1.5×10^{11}m，鄰近地球表面正對太陽處測得太陽能的強度約爲 1.4×10^3W/m^2，已知光速爲 3.0×10^8m/s，則太陽因輻射而減損的質量，每秒鐘約爲多少公斤？（球的表面積爲 $4\pi r^2$，其中 r 爲球的半徑）

(A) 1.5×10^{-2}　　　(B) 1.5×10^3　　　(C) 3.3×10^5

(D) 1.1×10^7　　　(E) 4.4×10^9

二、多選題（占 20 分）

說明：第 21 題至第 24 題，每題有 5 個選項，其中至少有一個是正確的選項，請將正確選項畫記在答案卡之「選擇題答案區」。各題之選項獨立判定，所有選項均答對者，得 5 分；答錯 1 個選項者，得 3 分；答錯 2 個選項者，得 1 分；答錯多於 2 個選項或所有選項均未作答者，該題以零分計算。

21. 圖 9 中一光滑水平面上有三物體，甲、乙的質量均為 m，丙的質量為 $2m$。開始時，乙和丙均為靜止而甲以等速度 v 向右行進。設該三物體間的碰撞皆為一維彈性碰撞，則在所有碰撞都結束後，各物體運動速度的敘述哪些正確？

    (A) 甲靜止不動

    (B) 乙靜止不動

    (C) 甲以等速度 $\dfrac{1}{3}v$ 向左行進

    (D) 乙以等速度 $\dfrac{1}{3}v$ 向右行進

    (E) 丙以等速度 $\dfrac{2}{3}v$ 向右行進

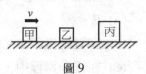

圖 9

22. 圖 10 為單狹縫繞射實驗裝置示意圖，其中狹縫寬度為 d。今以波長為 λ 的平行光，垂直入射單狹縫，屏幕邊緣 Q 點與狹縫中垂線的夾角為 θ_m。若在屏幕上未觀察到繞射形成的暗紋，下列哪些選項是可能的原因？

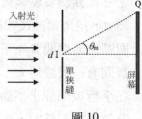

圖 10

    (A) $d \gg \lambda$

    (B) $d\sin\theta_m < \lambda$

    (C) 入射光太亮

    (D) 入射光不具有同調性

    (E) 入射光為單色光

23. 如圖 11 所示，一質量為 m、帶正電荷 q 的小球以一端固定的細繩懸掛著，繩長為 ℓ，系統置於均勻的磁場中，磁場 B 的方向垂直

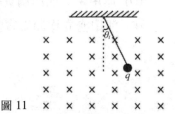

圖 11

穿入紙面。開始時靜止的小球擺角與鉛直線夾 θ_i，釋放後帶電小球向左擺動，設其左側最大擺角與鉛直線夾 θ_f。若摩擦力與空氣阻力均可忽略，重力加速度為 g 而小球在最低點的速率為 v，則下列關於小球受力與運動狀態的關係式或敘述，哪些正確？

(A) $\theta_i < \theta_f$

(B) 在擺動過程中，磁力不對小球作功

(C) 在擺動過程中，重力對小球永遠作正功

(D) 小球在第一次通過最低點時，繩子的張力
$$T = mg + qvB + \frac{mv^2}{\ell}$$

(E) 小球在運動過程中所受的重力及磁力均為定值

24. 密立坎油滴實驗裝置中，兩平行板之間距為 d，接上電源後如圖 12 所示，S 為電路開關。若開關 S 壓下接通後，發現平行板間有一質量為 m，帶電量為 q 之小油滴在平行板間靜止不動，設 g 為重力加速度。若忽略空氣浮力，則下列敘述哪些正確？

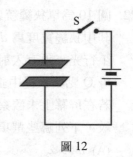

圖 12

(A) 小油滴帶正電

(E) 直流電源提供之電動勢為 $\dfrac{mgd}{q}$

(C) 將平行板間距加大時，該小油滴仍將停留不動

(D) 運用密立坎油滴實驗可測量光子的質量

(E) 運用密立坎油滴實驗可測量基本電荷的電量

第貳部分：非選擇題（佔 20 分）

說明：本部分共有二大題，答案必須寫在「答案卷」上，並於題號
　　　欄標明大題號（一、二）與子題號（1、2、……）。作答時
　　　不必抄題，但必須寫出計算過程或理由，否則將酌予扣分。
　　　作答務必使用筆尖較粗之黑色墨水的筆書寫，且不得使用鉛
　　　筆。每一子題配分標於題末。

一、以一顆電池、一台安培計和一個可變電阻 P 串聯所組成的簡易
　　電阻測量器，可用來測量電阻，即相當於使用三用電表的歐姆
　　檔位。如圖 13 所示，電池的電動勢為 1.5V 且其內電阻可忽略；
　　安培計的讀數範圍從 0 至 1mA，每隔 0.1mA 有一個刻度，其內
　　電阻為 20Ω；可變電阻 P 的範圍為 100Ω 至 2500Ω。

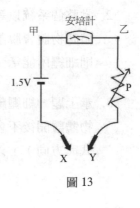

圖 13

1. 為了配合安培計的最大讀數，此電
阻測量器在測量電阻之前必須先調
整可變電阻，此步驟稱為歸零。試
說明如何將此簡易電阻測量器歸零。
（2 分）

2. 承第 1 小題歸零後，將一待測物體
的兩端分別連至 X 及 Y，若安培計
的讀數為 0.5mA，則該物體的電阻
為幾歐姆？（2 分）

3. 承第 1 小題歸零後，將安培計讀數範圍限制在 0.1mA 到
0.9mA 之間，試求該電阻器可量測的電阻範圍。（2 分）

4. 如果在甲、乙兩點間與安培計並聯一個小的電阻 $r = 20\Omega$，並重新歸零，若與第 3 小題的結果比較，可量測的電阻範圍將如何變化？試說明原因。（4分）

二、 如圖 14 所示，水平地面上有一斜角為 θ 的光滑 斜面，在其頂端以質輕之細線平行於斜面懸掛一質量為 m 的小體積物體，開始時斜面靜止且物體底部離地面之垂直高度為 h，設重力加速度為 g。

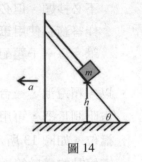

圖 14

1. 當斜面靜止時，細繩上張力與物體所受斜面的正向力之比值為何？（3分）

2. 當整個系統以等加速度 a 向左運動時，則加速度 a 最低為何值時物體會脫離斜面？若物體脫離斜面時，細繩也恰好斷裂，則細繩所能承受之最大張力為何？（4分）

3. 承上題，細繩斷裂後，斜面繼續以加速度 a 向左運動，已知物體離開後不會再撞到斜面，簡述物體會如何運動（包含形式與方向），以及何時會撞擊地面？（3分）

102年度指定科目考試物理科試題詳解

第壹部分：選擇題

一、單選題

1. **D**

　　【解析】 (A) 駐波

　　　　　　(B) 折射

　　　　　　(C) X 光穿透性

　　　　　　(D) 布拉格繞射

　　　　　　(E) 電子受磁場改變運動方向

2. **A**

　　【解析】
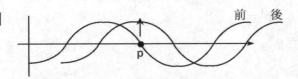

3. **A**

　　【解析】 開管 $\rightarrow f = \dfrac{hv}{2L}$

　　　　　　$390 = \dfrac{1 \times 3401}{2 \times L}$

　　　　　　$L = \dfrac{340}{2} \times \dfrac{1}{390} = \dfrac{34}{78} = \dfrac{17}{39} \approx 0.44\text{m}$

4. **B**

【解析】 (A) 平均動量 = 0

(B) $\frac{3}{2}PV = \frac{3}{2}nRT = NE_k$

(C) 有些上升有些下降但總能上升

(D) $PV = nRT$，$p \propto T$

(E) 如為非彈，壓力下降 $F = \dfrac{\Delta mv}{\Delta t}$

5. **C**

【解析】 $pv = nRT$，$pv \propto T$

$2 \times 10 : p^1 \times 5 = 586 : 293$

$20 : 5p^1 = 2 : 1$

$10p^1 = 20$

$p^1 = 2$

6. **E**

【解析】

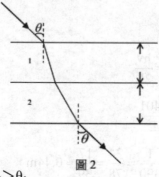

圖 2

$\theta_2 > \theta_3 > \theta_1$

$n_1 > n > n_2$

7. **A**

　　【解析】　雙狹縫 $d\sin\theta = m\lambda$，第五暗 $m = \dfrac{9}{2}$

$$9\lambda\sin\theta = \dfrac{9}{2}\lambda$$

$$\sin\theta = \dfrac{1}{2} \qquad \theta = 30^{\circ}$$

8. **D**

　　【解析】　$Fs = \dfrac{1}{2}mv^2$，在丁點作最多正功

9-10 為題組

9. **E**

　　【解析】　落地速度 $\sqrt{2gh}$

反彈速度 $-\sqrt{2g\dfrac{9}{16}H}$

$F \quad t = \quad mv$

$$F = \dfrac{mv}{t} = \dfrac{m(-\dfrac{3}{4}\sqrt{2gh} - \sqrt{2gh})}{t} = -\dfrac{7}{4}\dfrac{m}{t}\sqrt{2gh}$$

10. **D**

　　【解析】　地面光滑→無摩擦→水平速度不變

$$V_{水平} \times \sqrt{\dfrac{2H}{g}} = \dfrac{4}{3}H$$

$$V_{水平} \times 2 \times \sqrt{\dfrac{2 \times \dfrac{9}{16}H}{g}} = 2H$$

11. **A**

【解析】 $R_火 = 0.5R_地$ $\quad g = \dfrac{GM}{R^2}$

$g_火 = 0.4g_地$ $\quad GM = gR^2$

脫離速率

力學能守恆：$\dfrac{-GMm}{R} + \dfrac{1}{2}mv^2 = 0 + 0$

$\dfrac{1}{2}mv^2 = \dfrac{GMm}{R}$ $\quad V \propto \sqrt{\dfrac{GM}{R}}$

$\dfrac{V_火}{V_地} = \sqrt{0.5 \times 0.4} = \sqrt{0.2} = \sqrt{\dfrac{1}{5}}$

12. **E**

【解析】 外力和 $= m \times 5g = 5mg$

外力 → 重力 + 拉力

$5mg = -mg + F$ $\quad F = 6mg$ 向上

彈簧力為 $6mg$ $\quad$ 伸長量為 $\dfrac{6mg}{k}$

13. **C**

【解析】

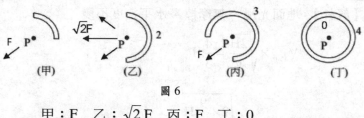

圖 6

甲：F 乙：$\sqrt{2}F$ 丙：F 丁：0

乙＞甲＝丙＞丁

14. **D**

　　【解析】　$B = \dfrac{\mu_0 i}{2r}$

15. **A**

　　【解析】　$\varepsilon = \dfrac{\Delta \phi_B}{\Delta t} = \dfrac{\dfrac{1}{2} wtl^2 \times B}{t} = \dfrac{1}{2} wl^2 B$

　　　　　　$\varepsilon = IR \quad I = \dfrac{\varepsilon}{R} = \dfrac{wl^2 B}{2R}$

16. **D**

　　【解析】　$\dfrac{R^3}{T^2} = \dfrac{1}{1} = \dfrac{10^3}{T^2} \Rightarrow \dfrac{10^3}{T^2} = 1 \Rightarrow T^2 = 10^3 \Rightarrow T = 10^{\frac{3}{2}} \approx 32$

17. **B**

　　【解析】　插栓無摩擦表正向力上接觸面→故圓杯需要受力向上
　　　　　　水平力 $F_{甲} \cos \theta + F_{乙} \cos \theta_{乙} = F_{丙}$
　　　　　　$\Delta F_{甲} > \Delta F_{丙}$

18. **B**

　　【解析】　黑體輻射光譜為受溫度改變

19. **C**

　　【解析】　$mvr = \dfrac{n\mu}{2\pi} = p$

20. **E**

　　【解析】　$4\pi \times 1.4 \times 10^3 \times (1.5 \times 10^{11})^2 = \Delta m \times (3 \times 10^8)^2$

　　　　　　$\Delta m \approx 4.4 \times 10^9$

二、多選題

21. **BCE**

【解析】

22. **ABD**

【解析】 $d\sin\theta = m\lambda$　　$y = \dfrac{m\lambda r}{d}$

(A) $y \to 0$

(B) 第一暗 $d\sin\theta = m\lambda$，$d\sin\theta_n < \lambda$ 無法出現

(C) 無關

(D) 不同色光造成亮紋覆蓋其餘色光之暗紋

(E) 無關

23. **BD**

【解析】 (A) 摩擦力作功 $\theta_f < \theta_i$

(C) 運動至左側，重力作負功

(D)

$$T - mg - F_B = m\frac{v^2}{\ell}$$

$$T = mg + F_B + m\frac{v^2}{\ell}$$

(E) 施力 $F = qvB$，v 非定值

24. **BE**

【解析】 (A) 負電

(B) $mg = qE = q\dfrac{v}{d}$ ，$v = \dfrac{mgd}{q}$

(C) $d\uparrow qE\downarrow$

(D) 光子無質量

第貳部分：非選擇題

一、1.【解法一】以文字說明

將 X 和 Y 兩端相接後，調整可變電阻 P，使安培計的讀數為最大值 1mA，即可將此簡易電阻測量器歸零。

【解法二】以計算方式表達

因為安培計的讀值最大為 1.0mA

$$\therefore \frac{1.5V}{1.0 \times 10^{-3} A} = 1500\Omega$$

又因為安培計內電阻為，20Ω

故需將可變電阻調至 $1500\Omega - 20\Omega = 1480\Omega$ 。

2. 【解法一】計算電路中的總電阻，再利用歐姆定律求解

先求歸零時的可變電阻值R_P，

$$\frac{1.5V}{R_P + 20\Omega} = 1mA \Rightarrow R_P = 1480\Omega$$

再求待測物之電阻值$R_{待測}$，

$$\frac{1.5V}{R_{待測} + R_P + 20\Omega} = 0.5mA \Rightarrow R_{待測} = 1500\Omega$$

【解法二】由各元件兩端的電位差之總和等於總電壓求解

先求歸零時的可變電阻值R_P，

$$1.5V = R_P \times 1.0mA + 20\Omega \times 1.0mA \Rightarrow R_P = 1480\Omega$$

再求待測物之電阻值$R_{待測}$，

$$1.5V = R_0 \times 0.5mA + R_{待測} \times 0.5mA$$

$$= (1480 + 20) \times 0.5mA + R_{待測} \times 0.5mA$$

其中R_0為歸零時的總電阻值，$R_{待測}$為待測物之電阻值

故 $R_{待測} = \dfrac{0.75V}{0.5mA} = 1500\Omega$ 。

3. 【解法一】計算電路中的總電阻，再利用歐姆定律求解

當通過安培計電流為 0.1mA：

$$\frac{1.5V}{R_{待測} + 1480\Omega + 20\Omega} = 0.1mA \Rightarrow R_{待測} = 13500\Omega$$

當通過安培計電流為 0.9mA：

$$\frac{1.5V}{R_{待測} + 1480\Omega + 20\Omega} = 0.9mA \Rightarrow R_{待測} = \frac{500}{3}\Omega \approx 167\Omega$$

∴可測量電阻的範圍：167Ω到13500Ω

【解法二】由各元件兩端的電位差之總和等於總電壓求解

當通過安培計電流為 0.1mA：

$$1.5V = R_0 \times 0.1mA + R_{待測} \times 0.1mA \Rightarrow R_{待測} = \frac{1.35V}{0.1mA} = 13500\Omega$$

當通過安培計電流為 0.9mA：

$$1.5V = R_0 \times 0.9mA + R_{待測} \times 0.9mA \Rightarrow R_{待測} = \frac{0.15V}{0.9mA}$$

$$= \frac{500}{3}\Omega \approx 167\Omega$$

∴可測量電阻的範圍：167Ω到13500Ω

備註：因計算或有效數字而使求出的數值在可容許的範圍
　　　之內，仍為可給全部分數之答案。例如取兩位有效
　　　數字，則可測量電阻的範圍為170Ω到14000Ω。

4. 【解法一】以文字說明

可測量的電阻範圍會變小，因為在安培計兩端並聯一個與
安培計內電阻值相同的小電阻，電路中的總電流（即通過
待測物的電流）變為原來的 2 倍，由於電池的電動勢仍
為 1.5V，可測量的電阻範圍因而變小。

【解法二】以計算方式表達

20Ω // 20Ω = 10Ω

歸零時通過安培計的電流 = 1.0mA，則通過 R_P 的電流
= 2×1.0mA = 2.0mA

$$\therefore \frac{1.5V}{R_P + 10\Omega} = 2.0mA \Rightarrow R_P = 740\Omega$$

並聯 r 的電路，安培計電流 = 0.1mA，則通過 $R_{待測}$ 的電
流 = 0.2mA：

$$\frac{1.5V}{R_{待測} + 740\Omega + 10\Omega} = 0.2\text{mA} \Rightarrow R_{待測} = 6750\Omega$$

並聯 r 的電路，安培計電流 = 0.9mA，則通過 $R_{待測}$ 的電流 = 1.8mA：

$$\frac{1.5V}{R_{待測} + 740\Omega + 10\Omega} = 1.8\text{mA} \Rightarrow R_{待測} = 83\Omega$$

並聯 r 的電路可測量電阻的範圍：83Ω 到 6750Ω。

與第 3 題結果相比，可測量電阻的範圍變小。

二、1.【解法一】將物體受力分解為水平與鉛直方向的分量

水平方向：$T\cos\theta - N\sin\theta = 0$ (1)

鉛直方向：$T\sin\theta + N\cos\theta = mg$ (2)

解 (1), (2) 式得

$N = mg\cos\theta$ $T = mg\sin\theta$

$T/N = \tan\theta$

【解法二】將物體受力分解為平行斜面與垂直斜面方向的分量

平行斜面方向：$T - mg\sin\theta = 0$

垂直斜面方向：$N - mg\cos\theta = 0$

移項後，兩式相除，求得 $T/N = \tan\theta$。

【解法三】畫出力圖表達力的平衡

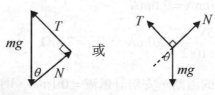

$N\tan\theta = T$ $T/N = \tan\theta$

【解法四】畫出力圖，並利用拉密定理求解

拉密定理：$\dfrac{T}{\sin(180^\circ - \theta)} = \dfrac{N}{\sin(90^\circ + \theta)} = \dfrac{mg}{\sin 90^\circ}$

$\therefore \dfrac{T}{N} = \tan \theta$

2. 【解法一】將物體受力分解為水平與鉛直方向的分量

水平方向：$T\cos\theta - N\sin\theta = ma$　　(3)

鉛直方向：$T\sin\theta + N\cos\theta = mg$　　(4)

有加速度 a 時，當 N = 0 物體則脫離

解 (3), (4) 式得

$N = mg\cos\theta - ma\sin\theta = 0$

$\Rightarrow a \geq g\cot\theta$

$\Rightarrow T = ma\cos\theta + mg\sin\theta$

而 $a = g\cot\theta \Rightarrow T = \dfrac{mg}{\sin\theta}(= mg\csc\theta)$

【解法二】將物體受力分解為平行斜面與垂直斜面方向的分量

垂直斜面方向：$N = ma\sin\theta - mg\cos\theta$　　(5)

平行斜面方向：$T = ma\cos\theta + mg\sin\theta$　　(6)

當 N = 0 時，物體恰可脫離斜面，故式 (5) 為

$ma\sin\theta = mg\cos\theta \Rightarrow a$ 最小值為 $g\cot\theta$

則式 (6) 為 $T = \dfrac{mg}{\sin\theta}$

3. 【解法一】物體的水平初速度爲零

若在瞬間加速，斜面一獲得加速度 a 時，繩子便斷裂，而物體未獲得水平方向的初速度，因此物體會作自由落體運動。

由 $h = gt^2/2$，可知落地時間 $t = \sqrt{\dfrac{2h}{g}}$。

【解法二】物體的水平初速度不爲零

若是逐漸加速，在細繩斷裂之後，斜面會繼續以等加速度 a 向左運動，且物體會獲得一向左的水平初速度。此時物體已脫離斜面，故物體在水平方向作等速運動，而在鉛直方向作加速度爲 g 的等加速運動，即物體作向左之水平拋體運動。

由 $h = gt^2/2$，可知落地時間 $t = \sqrt{\dfrac{2h}{g}}$。

102 年大學入學指定科目考試試題
化學考科

說明：下列資料，可供回答問題之參考

一、 元素週期表（1～36 號元素）

1 H 1.0																	2 He 4.0
3 Li 6.9	4 Be 9.0											5 B 10.8	6 C 12.0	7 N 14.0	8 O 16.0	9 F 19.0	10 Ne 20.2
11 Na 23.0	12 Mg 24.3											13 Al 27.0	14 Si 28.1	15 P 31.0	16 S 32.1	17 Cl 35.5	18 Ar 40.0
19 K 39.1	20 Ca 40.1	21 Sc 45.0	22 Ti 47.9	23 V 50.9	24 Cr 52.0	25 Mn 54.9	26 Fe 55.8	27 Co 58.9	28 Ni 58.7	29 Cu 63.5	30 Zn 65.4	31 Ga 69.7	32 Ge 72.6	33 As 74.9	34 Se 79.0	35 Br 79.9	36 Kr 83.8

二、 理想氣體常數 $R = 0.08205$ L atm $K^{-1}mol^{-1} = 8.31$ J $K^{-1}mol^{-1}$
　　 莫耳體積 = 22.4 升（STP）

二、 甲基紅的變色範圍：pH4.2～pH6.3

二、 AgCl　$K_{sp} = 1.8 \times 10^{-10}$　　　　Hg_2Cl_2　$K_{sp} = 1.4 \times 10^{-18}$

二、 $Ag^+_{(aq)} + 2NH_{3(aq)} \rightleftharpoons Ag(NH_3)^+_{2(aq)}$　　$K = 1.7 \times 10^{-7}$

第壹部分：選擇題（占 84 分）

一、單選題（占 36 分）

說明：第 1 題至第 12 題，每題有 5 個選項，其中只有一個是正確或最適當的選項，請畫記在答案卡之「選擇題答案區」。各題答對者，得 3 分，答錯、未作答或畫記多於一個選項者，該題以零分計算。

1. 電解水時，若在陰極產生 1 克的氫氣，則理論上在陽極可得多少升的氧氣（在標準狀況）？
   (A) 1.1　　(B) 2.2　　(C) 2.8　　(D) 5.6　　(E) 11.2

2. 下列有關實驗安全的行為，何者正確？
   (A) 取高揮發性液體時，應於通風櫥中進行
   (B) 加熱試管時，須使用試管夾，並固定在管底加熱
   (C) 被強酸潑到時要立刻以鹼中和，並以消毒過的紗布擦乾
   (D) 實驗時，應專注於實驗過程，若有藥品溢出，要待實驗結束後再清潔
   (E) 剛加熱過的玻璃試管，可用自來水沖洗其外部，使其迅速冷卻，以利實驗進行

3. 苯的路易斯結構 ⬡ 有時以 ⬡ 來表示 π 電子共振的概念，圖 1 為化合物蒎的結構，若以路易斯結構表示時，則蒎的結構總共會出現幾個 π 鍵？
   (A) 6　　(B) 7　　(C) 8
   (D) 9　　(E) 12

圖 1

4. 已知不穩定的原子核可能經由一系列的衰變過程而逐漸變成穩定的原子核，碘-131 的原子核不穩定，因此具有放射性，其反應如下：

$$^{131}_{53}I \longrightarrow \ ^{131}_{54}Xe + x\beta + \gamma$$

已知碘-131 衰變為氙的半生期約為 8 天，下列有關含放射性碘-131 化合物的敘述，哪個正確？

(A) 用液態氮凍結後，其放射性即可消失

(B) 該核反應式中，β 的係數 x 為 2

(C) 已知此反應的速率常數為 8.7×10^{-2} 天$^{-1}$，則碘-131 衰變為氙屬於一級反應

(D) 將其還原成固態的碘後，再將碘加熱昇華就可去除其放射性

(E) 用強酸溶解後，加入鉛離子產生難溶的碘化鉛，就可去除其放射性

5. 下列有關處理實驗室廢棄物的敘述，哪一項錯誤？

(A) 拋棄式的乳膠手套，用後為避免污染，不可直接丟入一般垃圾桶

(B) 含碘之廢棄溶液，酸化後要以過氧化氫處理

(C) 用過的 KSCN 溶液貯存於無機鹽類廢液桶中

(D) 實驗剩餘的斐林試液，應倒入重金屬廢液桶中，再交予環保單位統一處理

(E) 剩餘的鹽酸溶液以氫氧化鈉中和，並以大量水稀釋後排入水槽

6. 下列有關 $[Ag(NH_3)_2]Cl$ 的敘述，哪一項錯誤？

(A) 此化合物的 Ag^+ 配位數為 2

(B) NH_3 與 Ag^+ 以配位鍵結合

(C) [Ag(NH₃)₂]Cl 中 Cl⁻ 的價電子組態為 $3s^23p^6$

(D) [Ag(NH₃)₂]Cl 溶於水後會解離成 [Ag(NH₃)₂]⁺ 和Cl⁻

(E) [Ag(NH₃)₂]Cl 中的 Cl⁻ 具有孤電子對，故也以配位鍵方式與 Ag+ 結合

7. 氮氣與氧氣反應時可生成 X、Y 與 Z 三種常見的氮氧化合物，其中各化合物的氮含量如圖 2 所示。根據此圖，試問下列敘述，哪一項正確？

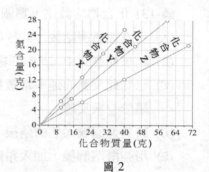

圖 2

(A) 化合物 X 在低溫時為無色，在高溫為紅棕色

(B) 化合物 Y 中各原子均符合八隅體結構

(C) 銅離子與濃硝酸反應時可生成化合物 Y

(D) 化合物 Y 與 O₃ 反應可生成 Z

(E) 化合物 Z 中氮的氧化數是 +5

8. 在裝有觸媒的反應器中，灌入氣體 X 與 Y 各 1 莫耳。在反應進行中的某一時刻，測得混合氣體的總莫耳數為 1.8 莫耳，且 X、Y、Z 三種氣體的分壓比為 7:9:2。已知該反應的化學反應式為 aX + bY → cZ，則反應式中的係數 a、b、c 是下列哪一組數字？

(A) 1、2、3　　　　(B) 3、2、1　　　　(C) 7、9、2

(D) 3、1、8　　　　(E) 3、1、2

9. 實驗桌上有三瓶試藥，只知其為氯化鈉、氯化銀及氯化亞汞，但因標籤脫落，難以辨識。陳同學從三瓶中各取出少許，分別置入甲、乙、丙三支試管，再以蒸餾水及濃氨水進行檢驗，所得結果

如下表所示：

試劑	試管甲	試管乙	試管丙
蒸餾水	溶解	不溶	不溶
濃氨水	溶解	溶解	灰色沉澱

根據其檢驗結果，試問甲、乙、丙三試管所含的物質依序各為何？

(A) 氯化鈉、氯化亞汞、氯化銀

(B) 氯化銀、氯化鈉、氯化亞汞

(C) 氯化亞汞、氯化鈉、氯化銀

(D) 氯化鈉、氯化銀、氯化亞汞

(E) 氯化銀、氯化亞汞、氯化鈉

10. 以 0.10M 的 NaOH 溶液滴定某單質子弱酸的滴定曲線如圖 3 所示。橫軸為加入 NaOH 的毫升數，縱軸為溶液的 pH 值。試問下列何者正確？

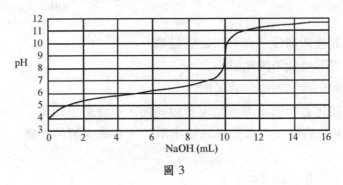

圖 3

(A) 在滴定過程中，當加入 0.10M 的 NaOH 溶液 2mL 時，所得的溶液具有最佳的緩衝能力

(B) 此單質子弱酸的解離常數（ Ka ）約為 1.0×10^{-6}

(C) 此弱酸的濃度為 10^{-4}M

(D) 此實驗最好選用甲基紅做指示劑

(E) 此滴定反應為吸熱反應

11. 丙烯醯胺在常溫下為白色結晶，易溶於水，且可能致癌。油炸含碳水化合物的食物，溫度高於 130℃ 就會出現丙烯醯胺。試問丙烯醯胺的化學式為下列何者？

    (A) $CH_2CHCH_2NH_2$ (B) $CH_3COCH_2NH_2$

    (C) $CH_3CH_2CONH_2$ (D) $CH_3CH_2CH_2CONH_2$

    (E) $CH_2CHCONH_2$

12. 為了增加豬肉中的瘦肉，有些養豬戶會在豬的飼料中，添加禁藥「瘦肉精」。瘦肉精可以促進蛋白質合成，增加瘦肉。圖 4 為某一瘦肉精的結構式。下列有關此化合物的敘述，何者錯誤？

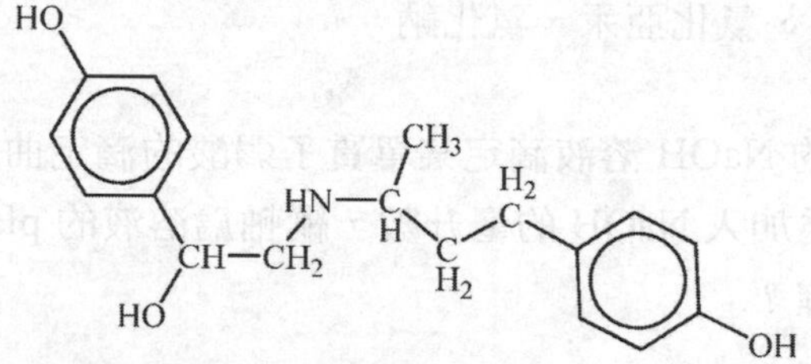

圖 4

    (A) 此瘦肉精分子含有二級醇結構
    (B) 可形成分子間氫鍵
    (C) 此化合物的水溶液呈酸性
    (D) 此化合物的水溶液加入多侖試劑，不會產生銀鏡
    (E) 此化合物加入氯化鐵酒精水溶液，會造成顏色改變

二、多選題（佔 48 分）

說明：第 13 題至第 24 題，每題有 5 個選項，其中至少有一個是正確的選項，請將正確選項畫記在答案卡之「選擇題答案區」。各題之選項獨立判定，所有選項均答對者，得 4 分；答錯 1 個選項者，得 2.4 分；答錯 2 個選項者，得 0.8 分；答錯多於 2 個選項或所有選項均未作答者，該題以零分計算。

13. 已知石墨和金剛石（鑽石）的莫耳燃燒熱分別是 $-394kJ$ 及 $-396kJ$。下列敘述，哪些正確？
   (A) 石墨既不導電也不導熱
   (B) 金剛石是碳元素的最穩定結構
   (C) 從石墨製造金剛石是放熱反應
   (D) 從石墨製造金剛石的反應熱為 +2kJ mol
   (E) 石墨（$C_{(s)}$）的莫耳燃燒熱相當於 $CO_{2(g)}$ 的莫耳生成熱

14. 下列物質：銅、水、食鹽、醋酸酐、石英等，受其鍵結與作用力的影響，具有明顯的形態和性質的差異。下列有關這些物質的敘述，哪些正確？
   (A) 銅金屬可視為銅陽離子浸於電子海中
   (B) 石英屬於共價網狀固體，是由共價鍵結合而成
   (C) 食鹽屬於離子化合物，是由陰、陽離子間的靜電吸引力結合而成
   (D) 水分子內有共價鍵，分子間有氫鍵但無凡得瓦力
   (E) 醋酸酐分子內有共價鍵，分子間有氫鍵及凡得瓦力

15. 常見的強酸有鹽酸、硝酸、硫酸、過氯酸，但只有濃硫酸常作為下列反應中強酸的來源。

$$CH_3CH_2OH \xrightarrow[170\text{-}180℃]{濃硫酸} H_2C = CH_2 + H_2O$$

   試問下列哪些應為選用濃硫酸較合理的原因？
   (A) 濃硫酸的酸性最強
   (B) 濃硫酸具有較強的還原力
   (C) 濃硫酸具有較強的脫水性
   (D) 濃硫酸為有機酸，有利於有機反應
   (E) 濃硫酸有利該反應的平衡往右進行

16. 將含有酚酞、碘化鉀與澱粉的混合液加入 U 型管，再把接於電池兩端的石墨棒，放入 U 型管中，形成電解電池如圖 5。下列有關此電解電池的敘述，哪些正確？

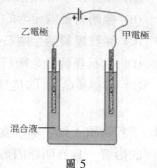

(A) 電解時水被氧化
(B) 乙電極附近有氧氣生成
(C) 乙電極附近溶液變藍色
(D) 甲電極端發生氧化反應
(E) 甲電極附近溶液的 pH 值上升

圖 5

17. 在實驗室通常使用電石和水來製備乙炔。下列有關此一實驗的敘述，哪些正確？

(A) 電石的化學式為 CaC
(B) 實驗過程中除了乙炔生成外，還會產生氫氧化鈣
(C) 將乙炔通入溴的四氯化碳溶液會褪色並進行取代反應
(D) 將乙炔通入微鹼性的過錳酸鉀溶液，會產生二氧化錳
(E) 製備乙炔時，應將水逐滴加到電石，以避免反應過於劇烈而發生危險

18. 硫代硫酸鈉 ($Na_2S_2O_3$) 可有效去除水中殘餘的氯，其化學反應如下所示：

$$Na_2S_2O_3 + x\,Cl_2 + y\,H_2O \rightarrow 2NaHSO_4 + z\,HCl$$

式中 x、y 與 z 為該反應式經平衡後的係數。下列哪些敘述正確？

(A) $z = 2x$
(B) $x + y > z$
(C) Cl_2 被氧化
(D) S 的氧化數由 +2 變成 +4
(E) 此反應為自身氧化還原反應

19. 若硫代硫酸鈉與鹽酸在含有少量界面活性劑的水溶液中進行反應，則下列有關敘述，哪些正確？
    (A) 反應物恰好完全作用後溶液為酸性
    (B) 界面活性劑的作用為維持反應容器的清潔
    (C) 產物中可能會有氧化數為零的奈米硫粒子
    (D) 由於廷得耳效應，照光後可以觀察到產物所造成的光折射現象
    (E) 產物中含硫物質之總氧化數較反應物中含硫物質之總氧化數減少

20. 五個錯合物如下：

    $[Co(H_2O)_4Cl_2]Cl$　　　　　$K_2[Fe(EDTA)]$　　　　$[Co(en)_x]Cl_3$
    　　　甲　　　　　　　　　　　　乙　　　　　　　　　　丙

    $[Cr(NH_3)_6]Cl_3$　　　　　$[Pd(NH_3)_4]Cl_2$
    　　丁　　　　　　　　　　戊

    其中，EDTA（乙二胺四醋酸根）為六牙基，en（乙二胺）為雙牙基。下列有關此五個錯合物的敘述，哪些正確？
    (A) 甲錯合物，Co 的配位數為 7，Co 的氧化數為 +2
    (B) 乙錯合物，Fe 的氧化數為 +4
    (C) 丙錯合物，x 為 3
    (D) 各取 10^{-3} 莫耳的丙與丁分別溶於 1000 克水中，丁溶液的沸點高於丙溶液的沸點
    (E) 取等莫耳的丙與戊分別溶於等量的水中，加入過量的硝酸銀溶液至完全沉澱，則沉澱量丙大於戊

21. 下列哪些聚合物較易被生物分解？

(A)

(B)

(C)

(D)

(E)

22. 下列有關乙烯和乙炔的敘述，哪些正確？

(A) 乙炔不會進行聚合反應

(B) 乙炔加水反應可以得到乙醇

(C) 可用含氯化亞銅的氨水溶液來分辨乙烯和乙炔

(D) 乙烯可與溴分子溶液反應產生 1,2-二溴乙烷

(E) 在低溫下，乙烯可與鹼性過錳酸鉀溶液反應得到 1,2-乙二醇

23. 構成生物體的主要胺基酸有 20 種。試問下列有關胺基酸的敘述，哪些正確？

(A) 不溶於水

(B) 含有胺基與羧基兩種官能基

(C) 是組成植物纖維素的結構單元

(D) 是組成許多天然酵素的結構單元

(E) 是組成動物毛髮主要成分的結構單元

24. 某生分析某聚合物，發現有下列重複的結構：

$$\cdots\cdots - [CH_2 - CH = CH - CH_2]_x - [CH_2 - CH(CN)]_y -$$
$$[CH_2 - CH(C_6H_5)]_z - \cdots\cdots$$

試問下列敘述，哪些正確？

(A) 合成 $\text{+CH}_2 - \text{CH} = \text{CH} - \text{CH}_2\text{+}_x$ 的單體是具有單鍵與雙鍵交錯的結構

(B) 此聚合物的單體均無幾何異構物

(C) 此聚合物是經由縮合反應而產生的共聚物

(D) 單獨使用 $\text{CH}_2 = \text{CH} - \text{CH} = \text{CH}_2$ 為單體，也可製造此聚合物

(E) 合成此聚合物的三種單體，分別稱為 1,3-丁二烯、丙烯腈、苯乙烯

第貳部分：非選擇題（佔 16 分）

說明：本部分共有二大題，答案必須寫在「答案卷」上，並於題號欄標明大題號（一、二）及子題號（1、2、……），作答時不必抄題。計算題必須寫出計算過程，最後答案應連同單位劃線標出。作答務必使用筆尖較粗之黑色墨水的筆書寫，且不得使用鉛筆。每一子題配分標於題末。

一、 在 25.0℃ 時，鎂帶與鹽酸反應產生氫氣，可利用排水集氣法將生成的氫氣完全收集於集氣管中。某生測得集氣管內氣體體積為 29.80mL，集氣管內水柱比管外水面高出 6.80cm，如圖 6 所示。（已知實驗當時的大氣壓力為 75.88cm-Hg、飽和蒸氣壓 32.37gw/cm^2、水銀密度 = 13.6g/cm^3，水密度 = 1.00g/cm^3）

試回答下列各題（每一子題 2 分，共 8 分）：

1. 寫出鎂帶與鹽酸作用產生氫氣的平衡化學反應式。

2. 集氣管中的氣體壓力為幾cm-Hg？

3. 集氣管中氫氣的分壓為幾cm-Hg？

4. 參與反應的鎂有多少公克？

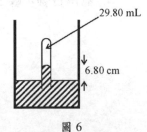

圖 6

二、 有兩種無機物粉末,甲爲暗灰色金屬,乙爲白色的無水化合物。
　　王同學爲了要探究其爲何種物質,做了下列實驗:
　　步驟 1: 分別稱取適量的甲與乙,混合後置入燒杯再加入蒸餾
　　　　　　水,即見溶液呈藍色。在攪拌混合物溶液的過程中,
　　　　　　溶液的藍色漸漸變淺,最終呈現淺綠色,並見杯底有
　　　　　　沉澱。
　　步驟 2: 過濾得濾液丙,將沉澱先以稀鹽酸沖洗後,再以蒸餾
　　　　　　水沖洗,得到紅棕色沉澱丁,經測試知其爲金屬。將
　　　　　　0.1M 氯化銀溶液滴入濾液丙,立見白色沉澱。
　　步驟 3: 將丁與 12M 的硫酸共熱,會放出難聞氣體。繼續加熱,
　　　　　　將溶液濃縮後靜置,得藍色晶體戊。
　　步驟 4: 晶體戊經反覆數次的磨碎與加熱後,終得白色粉末乙。
　　　　　　實驗後王同學想不出答案,就請教張老師。老師取少許
　　　　　　甲的粉末放在紙上,並將磁鐵棒放在紙下,則見粉末會
　　　　　　隨磁鐵的移動而移動。最後,老師還暗示王同學:甲原
　　　　　　子的基態,其電子組態中有 d^6。

　　試回答下列問題(每一子題 2 分,共 8 分):

1. 寫出甲的化學式。

2. 寫出乙的化學式。

3. 寫出戊的化學式。

4. 寫出實驗步驟 3 中,丁與硫酸共熱的平衡化學反應式。

102年度指定科目考試化學科試題詳解

第壹部分：選擇題

一、單選題

1. **D**

   【解析】　電解水⇒陰極生成 H_2 mol 數：陽極生成 O_2

   mol 數 = 2:1　⇒ $\dfrac{1}{2}:n_{O_2}=2:1\Rightarrow n_{O_2}=0.25$mol

   又在 STP 下 1mol O_2 $V=22.4(\ell)\Rightarrow 0.25\times 22.4=5.6(\ell)$

2. **A**

   【解析】　(B) 非固定在管底加熱（會受熱不均）

   (C) 應以水中和非用鹼

   (D) 應立刻清潔

   (E) 此操作易使玻璃試管因溫度下降太快而碎裂

3. **C**

   【解析】

   ⇒ 8 個 π 鍵

4. **C**

   【解析】　解：$^{131}_{53}I\rightarrow\,^{131}_{54}Xe+1^{\;0}_{-1}\beta+\gamma$

   (A) 放射性仍存在　　　　(B) β 係數為 1

   (C) 正確　　　　　　　　(D) 加熱無法去除放射性

   (E) 形成沉澱並無法去除放射性

5. **B**

【解析】 (B) 應加還原劑或加鹼

6. **E**

【解析】 (E) 以離子鍵方式

7. **D**

【解析】 $X : \dfrac{13}{14} : \dfrac{7}{16} \approx 2 : 1 \Rightarrow N_2O$

$Y : \dfrac{28}{14} : \dfrac{32}{16} = 1 : 1 \Rightarrow NO$

$Z : \dfrac{6}{14} : \dfrac{14}{16} \approx 1 : 2 \Rightarrow NO_2$

(A) N_2O 為無色 gas

(B) N 未符合八隅體

(C) 銅與稀硝酸反應生成 Y

(D) Z 中氮氧化數為 4

8. **E**

【解析】 分壓比 = mol 數比 = 7：9：2 ⇒ X、Y、Z

mol 數分別為 0.7、0.9、0.2 mol

$$aX + by \rightarrow cZ$$

$$
\begin{array}{ccc}
1 & 1 & \\
-a & -b & +c \\
\hline
0.7 & 0.9 & 0.2
\end{array}
\Rightarrow a : b : c = 3 : 1 : 2
$$

9. **D**

【解析】 NaCl 可溶於蒸餾水與濃氨水；AgCl 不溶於水但溶於濃氨水，Hg_2Cl_2 不溶於水和濃氨水

10. **B**

【解析】(A) 半當量點有最佳緩衝 $\Rightarrow$ 5ml 時

(B) 半當量點時 pH = pKa = 6 $\Rightarrow$ Ka = 1.0×10^{-6}

(C) $\sqrt{CKa} = \sqrt{C \times 10^{-6}} = 10^{-4} \Rightarrow C = 10^{-2}\,M$

(D) 當量點為弱鹼性應用酚酞

(E) 酸鹼中和為放熱反應

11. **E**

【解析】丙烯醯胺 $\Rightarrow$ $C = C - \underset{\underset{O}{\|}}{C} - NH_2 \Rightarrow CH_2CHCONH_2$

12. **C**

【解析】(A) 由結構

(B) 有羥基，可行成分子間氫鍵

(C) 鹼性　　　　　　　(D) 正確

(E) Fe^{3+} 和 的結構產生顏色

二、多選題

13. **DE**

【解析】(A) 石墨會導電　　(B) 最穩定的是石墨

(C) (D) $C_{石墨} \rightarrow C_{金剛石}$，$\Delta H =$ 反應物燃燒熱 $-$ 生成物

燃燒熱 $= -394-(-396) = 2 > 0$，吸熱

(E) $C + O_2 \rightarrow CO_2$

14. ABC

【解析】(D) 有凡得瓦力

(E) 　　　　　　　　沒有氫鍵

15. CE

【解析】(E) 由勒沙特列，濃硫酸的脫水性會造成反應右移

16. CE

【解析】(A) I^- 被氧化

(B) 產生 I_2、I_3^-

(C) I_2 與澱粉呈藍色

(D) 還原反應

(E) $2H_2O + 2e^- \rightarrow H_2 + 2OH^-$，產生 OH^-，pH 上升

17. BDE

【解析】(A) CaC_2

(B) $CaC_2 + 2H_2O \rightarrow Ca(OH)_2 + C_2H_2$

(C) 加成反應

(D) $KMnO_4$ 在微鹼環境中會產生 MnO_2

(E) 正確

18. **AB**

【解析】 $Na_2S_2O_3 + 4Cl_2 + 5H_2O \rightarrow 2NaHSO_4 + 8HCl \Rightarrow x = 4, y = 5, z = 8$

(C) Cl_2 被還原

(D) $+2 \rightarrow +6$

19. **AC**

【解析】 (A) $S_2O_3{}^{2-} + 2H^+ \rightarrow S + H_2SO_3$

(B) 減緩硫沉澱速度

(D) 反射

20. **CE**

【解析】 (A) 配位數：6，氧化數：+3

(B) +2

(C) $3 \times 2 = 6$，$6 \div 2 = 3$

(D) 丙的 $i = 4$，丁的 $i = 4$，沸點相等

21. **AE**

【解析】 (A) 醣類

(E) 胺基酸聚合物

22. **CDE**

【解析】 (A) C_2H_2 可進行聚合反應

(B) 乙醛

23. **BDE**

【解析】 (A) 可溶於水

(C) 構成蛋白質的結構單元

(D) 天然酵素多為蛋白質

24. **ABE**

【解析】 (A) 單體：$CH_2 = CH - CH = CH_2$

(B) $CH_2 = CH - CH = CH_2$，$CH_2 = CH$，$CH_2 = CH$
$\quad\quad\quad\quad\quad\quad\quad\quad\quad\quad\quad\quad CN$

(C) 加成反應

(D) 不行

(E) 由 (B)，正確

第貳部分：非選擇題

一、【解析】

1. $Mg_{(s)} + 2HCl_{(aq)} \rightarrow MgCl_{2(aq)} + H_{2(g)}$

$Mg_{(s)} + 2H^+_{(aq)} \rightarrow Mg^{2+}_{(aq)} + H_{2(g)}$

說明：反應物與生成物須正確，平衡係數亦須正確。

2. $75.88cm - Hg - \dfrac{6.8cm \times 1.00g/cm^3}{13.6g/cm^3 \times 1cm - Hg} cm - Hg$

$= 75.38cm - Hg$

說明：須列式正確，並計算正確。

3. $\dfrac{32.37\text{gw}/\text{cm}^2}{13.6\text{gw}/\text{cm}^3 \times 1\text{cm}-\text{Hg}} = 2.38\text{cm}-\text{Hg}$

$75.38\text{cm}-\text{Hg} - \dfrac{32.37\text{gw}/\text{cm}^2}{13.6\text{gw}/\text{cm}^3 \times 1\text{cm}-\text{Hg}} (= 2.38\text{cm}-\text{Hg})$

$= 73.00\text{cm}-\text{Hg}$

說明：須列式正確，並計算正確，計算的結果容許有些
微的誤差。

4. 由 $PV = nRT$

$\dfrac{73}{76} \times 29.8 \times 10^{-3} = n \times 0.082 \times 298$

$n = 1.17 \times 10^{-3}\,(\text{mol})$

鎂的克數 $= 1.17 \times 10^{-3} \times 24.3 = 0.0284$（克）

說明：須列式正確，並計算正確，計算的結果容
許有些微的誤差。

二、【解析】

1. Fe

2. $CuSO_4$

3. $CuSO_4 \cdot 5H_2O$

$Cu(H_2O)_5SO_4$

說明：$CuSO_4 \cdot nH_2O$（n 不為 5）給 1 分

4. $Cu_{(s)} + 2H_2SO_{4(conc)} \rightarrow CuSO_{4(aq)} + SO_{2(g)} + 2H_2O_{(l)}$

$Cu_{(s)} + H_2SO_{4(conc)} + 2H^+_{(aq)} \rightarrow Cu^{2+}_{(aq)} + SO_{2(g)} + 2H_2O_{(l)}$

102 年大學入學指定科目考試試題
生物考科

第壹部分：選擇題（占 71 分）

一、單選題（占 20 分）

說明：第 1 題至第 20 題，每題有 4 個選項，其中只有一個是正確或最適當的選項，請畫記在答案卡之「選擇題答案區」。各題答對者，得 1 分；答錯、未作答或畫記多於一個選項者，該題以零分計算。

1. 下列何者是葡萄糖從腸腔進入消化道上皮細胞的吸收方式？
   (A) 主動運輸　　　　　　(B) 簡單擴散
   (C) 胞吞作用　　　　　　(D) 與脂肪酸共同運輸

2. 下列有關 ABO 血型之敘述，何者正確？
   (A) 依血清中含有的抗體來區分
   (B) 細胞免疫造成血型的不同
   (C) 依紅血球細胞膜上的抗原來區分
   (D) 後天性免疫導致血型的不同

3. 下列何種臟器能分泌分解醣、蛋白質及脂質的酵素（酶）到消化道？
   (A) 腎臟　　　(B) 肝臟　　　(C) 脾臟　　　(D) 胰臟

4. 下列何種腺體會釋放抗利尿激素？
   (A) 腦垂腺後葉　　　　　(B) 甲狀腺
   (C) 腎上腺皮質　　　　　(D) 副甲狀腺

5. 下列何種激素的功能與血中鈉離子濃度恆定有關？
   (A) 鹽（礦物性）皮質素（如醛固酮）
   (B) 糖皮質素　　　　　　　　(C) 甲狀腺素
   (D) 副甲狀腺素

6. 蛋白質分子中的肽鍵是由哪兩種元素形成？
   (A) C-H　　　　(B) C-O　　　　(C) C-S　　　　(D) C-N

7. 在進行聚合酶連鎖反應（PCR）時，下列哪一個因子會直接影響
   DNA 聚合酶作用的速率？
   (A) 四種去氧核苷三磷酸的比例
   (B) 重複複製 DNA 片段的次數
   (C) 作為模版的 DNA 片段　　(D) 反應溫度

8. 人體尿液的形成，從過濾到再吸收的順序，下列何者正確？
   (A) 腎小球→遠曲小管→亨耳氏套（亨耳環管）→近曲小管→
       集尿管
   (B) 腎小球→近曲小管→亨耳氏套（亨耳環管）→遠曲小管→
       集尿管
   (C) 腎小球→亨耳氏套（亨耳環管）→近曲小管→遠曲小管→
       集尿管
   (D) 腎小球→近曲小管→遠曲小管→亨耳氏套（亨耳環管）→
       集尿管

9. 激素的調控有正回饋、負回饋及拮抗等機制。下列哪一組激素的
   調控關係與胰島素和升糖素相似？
   (A) 雄性素和雌性素　　　　　　(B) 副甲狀腺素和降鈣素
   (C) 腎上腺素和去甲基（正）腎上腺素
   (D) 濾泡刺激素（促濾泡成熟激素）和黃體素

10. 若某一極地生態系最主要的食物網是：浮游生物→魚→海獅→北極熊，則下列敘述何者正確？
    (A) 海獅能提供北極熊的能量比魚多
    (B) 該生態系浮游生物的能量總和比海獅少
    (C) 北極熊可能累積最高量的脂溶性毒性物質
    (D) 該生態系海獅的數量會比魚多

11. 下列有關氣孔的敘述，何者正確？
    (A) 氣孔愈多的植物體愈適合生長於乾旱的環境
    (B) 氣孔的關閉機制是保衛細胞內的鈉離子流出所造成
    (C) 氣孔打開時若以離層素（酸）處理則氣孔會關閉
    (D) 調控氣孔開閉的保衛細胞之細胞壁厚度不均，外側壁較厚

12. 局部感染引起發炎時，皮下組織血管擴張的主要原因為何？
    (A) 乙醯膽鹼的作用   (B) 組織胺的作用
    (C) 去甲基（正）腎上腺素的作用
    (D) 免疫球蛋白的作用

13. 下列哪一項是植物對抗感染之病原體或害蟲的化學防禦方式？
    (A) 組織細胞含有某種分子以毒殺啃食其組織的昆蟲
    (B) 植物表面一些特殊結構可以減少草食性生物啃食
    (C) 完整的木栓層構造可用以防止病原體進入
    (D) 藉由生長於其上的其他生物以擊退啃食組織的昆蟲

14. 下列有關後天性免疫反應的敘述，何者正確？
    (A) 吞噬細胞都會呈現病原體的抗體
    (B) 輔助 T 細胞（T_H）釋出物質使受病毒感染的細胞死亡
    (C) 記憶性 B 細胞在相同病原體入侵時會快速活化
    (D) 記憶性 T 細胞不能辨識相同的抗原

15. 植物體因頂芽優勢而抑制側芽生長，下列何種激素與頂芽優勢有
　　關？
　　(A) 生長素　　　　　　　　　(B) 吉貝素
　　(C) 細胞分裂素　　　　　　　(D) 離層素（酸）

16. 下列何組生物之間的關係與『寄生蜂幼蟲寄生在蝴蝶幼蟲體內生
　　活』最接近？
　　(A) 蒼蠅被捕蠅草葉片夾住
　　(B) 榕果小蜂棲息在榕果內
　　(C) 蘭花著生在榕樹的樹幹上
　　(D) 菟絲子纏繞著生在牽牛花的莖上

<u>17-18為題組</u>

圖 1 為真核細胞基因轉錄示意圖，試據
此回答第 17-18 題。

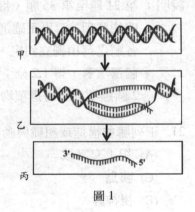

圖 1

17. 下列有關真核細胞進行基因轉錄的
　　相關敘述，何者正確？
　　(A) 轉錄發生在細胞質中
　　(B) 甲為雙股 DNA 分子的一小段
　　(C) 乙具三股 DNA 的構造
　　(D) 丙的 3' 端會加上端帽

18. 將「乙」置於試管中，加入含有各種核酸酶的消化液，經充分作
　　用後，最多可產生幾種核苷酸？
　　(A) 4 種　　　　(B) 6 種　　　　(C) 8 種　　　　(D) 64 種

19-20為題組

圖 2 為某種植物葉片的橫切面，
試據此回答第 19-20 題。

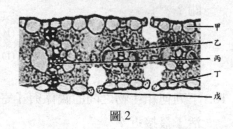

圖 2

19. 圖中哪些組織或細胞可以行
    光合作用？
    (A) 甲乙　　　(B) 丙丁
    (C) 甲丁　　　(D) 乙戊

20. 此種植物可能為下列何者？
    (A) 水稻　　　(B) 玉米　　　(C) 榕樹　　　(D) 鳳梨

二、多選題（占 30 分）

說明：第 21 題至第 35 題，每題有 5 個選項，其中至少有一個是正
　　　確的選項，選出正確選項畫記在答案卡之「選擇題答案區」。
　　　各題之選項獨立判定，所有選項均答對者，得 2 分；答錯 1
　　　個選項者，得 1.2 分；答錯 2 個選項者，得 0.4 分；答錯多於
　　　2 個選項或所有選項均未作答者，該題以零分計算。

21. 下列哪些構造或組織與動物光週期行為的關係密切？
    (A) 視上交叉核　　　　　　(B) 松果腺
    (C) 胰島　　　　　　　　　(D) 腎上腺皮質
    (E) 視神經

22. 對實驗動物注射腎上腺素與升糖素之混合針劑，稍後可觀察到以
    下哪些變化？
    (A) 血糖降低、心跳加速　　(B) 血糖增加、心跳降低
    (C) 血糖不變、血鈣降低　　(D) 血糖增加、血鈣不變
    (E) 血鈣不變、心跳加速

23. 下列有關木本雙子葉植物莖部橫切面的敘述，哪些正確？
    (A) 邊材在維管束外側、心材在維管束內側
    (B) 早材與晚材交替形成年輪
    (C) 維管束散生在基本組織中
    (D) 維管束中常可觀察到纖維細胞
    (E) 切面中央的髓多為小而厚的細胞

24. 一個處於哈溫平衡的族群，其控制某性狀的不同基因型及個體數目分別是 AA = 77，Aa = 94，aa = 29。以下哪些敘述正確？
    (A) A 等位基因的頻率是 0.62
    (B) 下一代的 A 等位基因頻率是 0.31
    (C) a 等位基因的頻率是 0.26
    (D) 若下一代有 1000 個體，則 Aa 基因型的個體約有 470 個
    (E) 當族群大小驟減時，A 等位基因在下一代遺失的機率小於 a 等位基因

25. 人體肝臟細胞的細胞膜含有下列哪些成份？
    (A) 膽固醇　　(B) 磷脂　　(C) 核酸　　(D) 醣蛋白　　(E) 肝醣

26. 下列有關人體感覺與其受器之配對，哪些正確？
    (A) 聽覺：毛細胞　　　　　(B) 味覺：桿細胞
    (C) 視覺：錐細胞　　　　　(D) 平衡覺：支持細胞
    (E) 觸覺：感覺神經末稍

27. 下列有關植物激素的敘述，哪些正確？
    (A) 一般產生和作用的位置可能不同
    (B) 吉貝素參與日照長短變化誘導開花
    (C) 吲哚乙酸（IAA）含量高時會誘發種子休眠

(D) 同一種激素可能促進莖的生長卻抑制根的生長

(E) 細胞分裂素可促進側芽的生長

28. 下列有關脊椎動物處理含氮廢物的方式，哪些正確？
   (A) 尿素在腎臟中形成　　　　　(B) 硬骨魚由鰓部排除尿素
   (C) 兩生類成體以排除氨爲主　　(D) 鳥類以排除尿酸爲主
   (E) 哺乳類以排除尿素爲主

29. 下列有關大腸桿菌的敘述，哪些正確？
   (A) 具有細胞壁
   (B) 細胞質內具有膜狀構造
   (C) 在粒線體中經由電子傳遞鏈產生 ATP
   (D) 缺乏乳糖時會開啓乳糖操縱組
   (E) 乳糖操縱組基因在細胞質中轉錄 mRNA

30. 下列哪些因素會促使心跳加快？
   (A) 交感神經活性增強　　　　　(B) 副交感神經活性增強
   (C) 去甲基（正）腎上腺素釋出增多
   (D) 乙醯膽鹼釋出增多　　　　　(E) 劇烈運動

31. 若全球持續暖化，預期對臺灣的生物造成下列哪些影響？
   (A) 櫻花鉤吻鮭的分布將擴展到整個大甲溪流域
   (B) 臺灣山椒魚分布的最低海拔將比目前還高
   (C) 高山草原的分布範圍將擴及目前闊葉林區域
   (D) 沿海紅樹林的分布範圍將僅見於臺灣南部
   (E) 每年冬至前後，烏魚的洄游南界將向北移動

32. 有關一般神經細胞產生動作電位的敘述，下列哪些正確？
   (A) 膜電位高於閾值時會啓動動作電位

(B) 去極化是因鉀離子通道的開啓

(C) 只要鈉離子在細胞內外分布不均就會造成靜止膜電位

(D) 過極化是因爲鈉鉀離子幫浦啓動所造成

(E) 再極化時鉀離子會流出神經細胞

33. 下列有關綠色植物進行碳反應的敘述，哪些正確？

(A) 二氧化碳被固定　　　　　(B) 消耗 ATP 與 NADPH

(C) 發生在類囊體的膜上　　　(D) 僅發生在黑暗中

(E) 會有三碳物質暫時產生

34. 果蠅的白眼性狀爲一性聯遺傳，下列相關敘述哪些正確？

(A) 白眼性狀僅見於雄果蠅

(B) 白眼性狀在某一性別較常見

(C) 白眼等位基因可由任一親代傳給子代

(D) 白眼等位基因可由親代雄果蠅傳給子代雄果蠅

(E) 白眼等位基因可由親代雌果蠅傳給子代雌果蠅

35. 比較 B 淋巴細胞與胞毒 T 細胞（T_C）的防禦特性，下列哪些描述是正確的？

(A) 兩種淋巴細胞表面都具有能辨識抗原的專一性受體分子

(B) 兩種淋巴細胞的抗原專一性受體都能直接與任一病原體上的抗原結合

(C) 兩種淋巴細胞都能被輔助 T 細胞（T_H）產生的細胞激素刺激而增強活性

(D) 病毒感染時，只有 T_C 會被活化而殺死被病毒感染的細胞

(E) B 細胞活化後會分化爲漿細胞產生抗體，抗體和抗原結合後可使病原體失去致病力

三、閱讀題（占 22 分）

說明： 第 36 題至第 44 題，包含單選題與多選題，單選題有 4 個選
項，多選題有 5 個選項，每題選出最適當的選項，標示在答
案卡之「選擇題答案區」。單選題各題答對得 2 分，答錯、
未作答或畫記多於 1 個選項者，該題以零分計算。多選題所
有選項均答對者，得 3 分；答錯 1 個選項者，得 1.8 分；答
錯 2 個選項者，得 0.6 分；答錯多於 2 個選項或所有選項均
未作答者，該題以零分計算。

閱讀一：

麻瘋分支桿菌（*Mycobacterium leprae*）是麻瘋病（leprosy）的病
原菌，它會侵入並存活在巨噬細胞的吞噬小體，並經由特殊代謝獲得
能量而進行繁殖。2001 年，Cole S. 等人於自然雜誌發表麻瘋分支桿菌
的基因體序列，並與肺結核分支桿菌（*Mycobacterium tuberculosis*）
的基因體序列作比較，對麻瘋分支桿菌特有的代謝方式及特殊的縮減
式演化（reductive evolution）提出合理的解釋。麻瘋分支桿菌約有 330
萬個鹼基，其中有 1600 個功能基因，而肺結核分支桿菌有 440 萬個鹼
基，其中有 4000 個功能基因；肺結核分支桿菌中有許多的功能基因，
在麻瘋分支桿菌因結構不完整而以無功能性的假基因方式存在。後來
的研究發現，麻瘋分支桿菌失去許多分支桿菌屬致病性細菌代謝宿主
脂類的相關基因。推測麻瘋分支桿菌可能是經由不同於其他分枝桿菌
的代謝途徑，才得以在巨噬細胞中生長與繁殖。

相較於其非寄生性的始祖，麻瘋分支桿菌有一半以上的基因，因
為不再是生存所需而逐漸丟失，且丟失比例遠高於目前所有研究過的
生物。唯這種基因丟失並不影響其致病能力，反而因為基因組成簡單，
有利於科學家定位重要致病基因群，進而發展麻瘋病的新疫苗及診斷
試劑。依本文所述及相關知識，回答下列問題：

36. 下列關於麻瘋分支桿菌縮減式演化的敘述，哪些正確？
　　(A) 逐漸失去部份基因　　　　　(B) 導致體積變小
　　(C) 有助於找出致病基因群　　　(D) 導致致病力降低
　　(E) 導致基因體縮小

37. 下列關於麻瘋分支桿菌特徵的敘述，哪些正確？
　　(A) 與肺結核分支桿菌使用相同的代謝途徑
　　(B) 體積較小故生長緩慢
　　(C) 丟失許多代謝宿主脂類的相關基因
　　(D) 功能性基因數明顯少於肺結核分支桿菌
　　(E) 是目前研究過已知基因丟失比例最高的生物

38. 推測麻瘋分支桿菌最可能利用下列何種方式在巨噬細胞中生長與
　　繁殖？
　　(A) 暫時停止生長　　　　　　　(B) 抑制巨噬細胞的生理活性
　　(C) 利用巨噬細胞提供的物質　　(D) 促進吞噬小體與溶體的融合

閱讀二：

　　巴金森氏症是一種常見的神經退化性疾病，65 歲以上的人約有
1% 有此疾病。巴金森氏症的致病因子除了環境因素外，近年來的研
究顯示，粒線體功能正常與否，和此疾病的發生密切相關。家族性
巴金森氏症患者的基因研究顯示，眾多的巴金森氏症致病基因中，
PINK1 基因的產物為一種位在粒線體上具有磷酸酶活性的酵素。在
正常情況下，粒線體的內膜兩側氫離子分布不均，形成電位差，將
PINK1 酵素運送至內膜而快速分解。但當粒線體膜電位受到破壞時，
PINK1 酵素留在粒線體外膜上，並自體磷酸化而累積，導致細胞質
中的 Parkin 蛋白轉移到粒線體上，進而促使某些粒線體外膜蛋白被
泛素化（ubiquitination）修飾，最終誘發受損的粒線體經由細胞自噬

途徑分解。因此 PINK1 或 Parkin 基因突變失去功能時，都可能造成細胞無法有效清除受損的粒線體，使細胞失去活性走向死亡。依本文所述及相關知識，回答下列問題：

39. PINK1 酵素的哪一種活性有助於 Parkin 蛋白轉移到粒線體上？
    (A) 醣化　　　(B) 磷酸化　　　(C) 泛素化　　　(D) 蛋白質分解

40. 下列何種情況會促使 Parkin 蛋白轉移到粒線體？
    (A) PINK1 酵素被分解
    (B) PINK1 酵素留在粒線體外膜上
    (C) PINK1 酵素被泛素化修飾
    (D) Parkin 蛋白被泛素化修飾

41. 粒線體內膜電位差是因為下列何者在內膜兩側移動所造成？
    (A) 電子　　　(B) 氧離子　　　(C) 氫離子　　　(D) 鈉離子

閱讀三：

在臺灣發現的紅火蟻主要是 *Solenopsis invicta*，它是 *Solenopsis* 中 280 個物種之一，原產於南美洲，但最直接的來源指向美國加州。1930 年代，紅火蟻在美國的南方沿海各州被發現，並引人注意。經追查，此物種最先出現在阿拉巴馬州，與貨船的泊靠有關。為防止紅火蟻在臺灣造成嚴重危害，2004 年各方力促成立專責機構，採取積極行動，以降低其對人體健康、社會擾動、經濟損失以及生態變遷等的危害。

紅火蟻是絕佳的掠食者，其獵物包括甘蔗的害蟲白斑擬蝶蛾，及水稻的害蟲稻褐蝽等。但是牠也殺害傳粉昆蟲，如蜜蜂等諸多物種。控制紅火蟻並不容易，物理方法是對蟻巢用火燒或噴熱蒸氣來

消滅蟻塚，但卻是危險的行動；化學方法如用毒劑混入食餌中毒殺之。在南美洲，蚤蠅（*Pseudacteon tricupis*）會產卵並寄生在紅火蟻的頭胸部，且具有物種專一性。蚤蠅的幼蟲會逐步啃食紅火蟻的頭部，以其外骨骼的成份作爲蛹殼。科學家也發現 20% 的紅火蟻帶有 SINV-1 病毒，造成蟻群慢慢死亡。依本文所述及相關知識，回答下列問題：

42. 下列有關紅火蟻的敘述，何者正確？
    (A) 學名必爲 *Solenopsis invicta*
    (B) 出現在美國是由於其族群自然遷徙所致
    (C) 引入臺灣的目的是控制稻褐蝽的危害
    (D) 掠食的優勢會傷害本地生態平衡

43. 在一個紅火蟻巢內數量最多，對人威脅最大的是下列何種蟻？
    (A) 工蟻　　　(B) 兵蟻　　　(C) 雄蟻　　　(D) 蟻后

44. 下列有關臺灣防治紅火蟻的敘述，哪些正確？
    (A) 物理方法有效且值得推廣
    (B) 引進蚤蠅是一項可以嘗試的作法
    (C) 用化學毒劑毒殺時應注意其副作用
    (D) 紅火蟻可控制部分農業疫情，但控制紅火蟻並不容易
    (E) 引入 SINV-1 病毒是快速有效的方法

第貳部分：非選擇題（占 29 分）

說明：本部分共有四大題，答案必須寫在「答案卷」上，並於題號欄標明大題號（一、二、……）與子題號（1、2、……），作答時不必抄題。作答務必使用筆尖較粗之黑色墨水的筆書寫，且不得使用鉛筆。每一子題配分標於題末。

一、 細胞中很多的有機物質皆含有氮，因此氮為植物之必需營養元素，試回答下列有關植物和氮的問題。

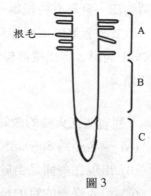

圖3

1. 醣、蛋白質、脂肪、核酸等有機物，哪些以氮為其主要構成元素之一？（2分）
2. 圖3為根的示意圖，哪一區域對含氮物質的吸收最為活躍？其名稱為何？（2分）
3. 微生物與豆科植物共生而進行固氮作用的構造為何？（2分）
4. 承上題，所固定的氮源為何？（2分）

二、 酵素的活性會受到實驗條件如溫度、酸鹼值以及受質濃度改變的影響，當它與受質結合時，會催化受質進行化學反應。圖4中的實線甲代表某種酵素在某溫度與某酸鹼值下，進行催化作用所得之反應速率與受質濃度的關係。

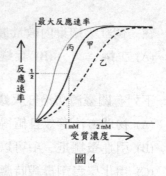

圖4

當達最大反應速率一半時（圖中的 1/2），所需的受質濃度為 1 mM，而達最大反應速率所需的受質濃度是 2 mM。請回答下列各小題。

1. 在此酵素與受質的反應系統中加入某化學物質，使反應曲線向右移動如虛線乙所示。試問所加化學物質對此反應速率的作用為何？（2分）
2. 承上題，試由圖形虛線乙推論達到最大反應速率的一半時，所需受質濃度是多少 mM？（取小數點一位）（2分）

3. 如果該酵素是唾液澱粉酶，那麼改變何種因素，可以使圖中實線甲向左移動至細線丙？（2分）

三、紅樹林是熱帶亞熱帶海岸特有的生態系統，也是許多遷移性鳥類的渡冬地點。臺灣招潮蟹、水筆仔、海生疫病菌、小白鷺、雙殼貝以及巢鼠等都是淡水紅樹林一帶常見的生物。試根據以上描述及相關知識，回答下列各小題。

1. 可將物質由無機轉換至有機世界的生物為何？（2分）
2. 胎生生物有哪些？（2分）
3. 哪些真核生物每天直接面臨環境中鹽分（度）劇烈變化的挑戰？（3分）

四、圖5為蛋白質合成時 tRNA 分子的反密碼子與 mRNA 上密碼子配對的情形，請回答下列相關問題。

1. tRNA 甲端攜帶的X 分子為何？（2分）

2. 與此 tRNA 的反密碼子配對之密碼子為何？（2分）

3. 此合成作用在細胞內的哪一種構造上進行？（2分）

4. 此 mRNA 上之丙和丁的方向性為何？（2分）

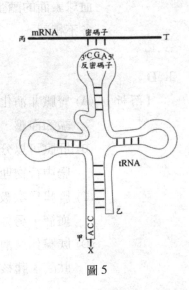

圖 5

102年度指定科目考試生物科試題詳解

第壹部分：選擇題

一、單選題

1. **A**

【解析】 小腸吸收葡萄糖爲次級主動運輸，先利用鈉鉀幫浦耗能使絨毛細胞和腸腔形成鈉離子的濃度差，再利用此濃度差造成的電位能將腸腔中的葡萄糖及鈉離子以同向運輸的方式送入絨毛細胞，藉以吸收葡萄糖。

2. **C**

【解析】 ABO 血型是由血球表面上的抗原來區分，血型抗原爲血球表面的醣蛋白，每一種血型其血球表面的醣蛋白各不相同。

3. **D**

【解析】
(A) 腎臟非消化系統的組成器官，其主要功能爲排泄、調節血壓、維持血液恆定。
(B) 肝臟可以分泌膽汁，膽汁儲存在膽囊，可排放至小腸中行物理消化乳化脂肪。
(C) 脾臟爲次級淋巴器官，內含淋巴組織，並可以儲存血液，另外會破壞衰老的紅血球。
(D) 胰臟作爲消化腺可分泌胰澱粉酶、胰脂肪酶、胰多肽酶、胰核酸酶，可以分解多種營養成分。

4. **A**

【解析】 抗利尿激素（ADH）由下視丘神經內分泌細胞分泌，
儲存在腦下腺後葉，需要時由後葉釋放。

5. **A**

【解析】 (A) 礦物性皮質素如醛固酮，可以使遠曲小管、集尿
管再吸收鈉離子、水，並排出鉀離子。

(B) 醣皮質素可以刺激肝臟糖質新生，抑制部分的免
疫反應。

(C) 甲狀腺素和人體的產熱作用及幼年時期神經、骨
骼發育有關。

(D) 副甲狀腺素為升鈣素，作用在於提高血鈣濃度。

6. **D**

【解析】 蛋白質中的肽鍵（C—N）由相鄰兩胺基酸的<u>羧基</u>
（—COOH）和<u>氨基</u>（—NH$_2$）脫水形成。

7. **D**

【解析】 聚合酶連鎖反應（PCR）中的 DNA 聚合酶為 Taq DNA
聚合酶，其作用的溫度約 70℃。因此溫度為最主要影
響其活性的因子。

8. **B**

【解析】 尿液形成的過程：腎小球行濾過作用→近曲小管行再
吸收作用→亨耳氏套進一步減少尿液→遠曲小管受到
激素調控行再吸收作用→集尿管受到激素調控行再吸
收作用，並且濃縮尿液。

9. **B**

【解析】 題幹中胰島素和升糖素為拮抗作用。選項中只有 (B) 副甲狀素負責升高血鈣，而降鈣素會降低血鈣濃度，兩者拮抗。

10. **C**

【解析】 食物鏈中，能量傳遞每一次只能傳遞給下一階層消費者 10% 的能量，且能量塔不會成倒金字塔型。

(A) 魚能提供給北極熊的能量比海獅可以提供給北極熊的能量多。

(B) 浮游生物所含的總能量在此生態系中為最大。

(C) 脂溶性毒物時常因為不易代謝而累積，隨著食物鏈造成生物放大作用，因此北極熊可能有最高量的脂溶性毒物。

(D) 此環境中魚的數量應比海獅數量多。

11. **C**

【解析】 (A) 氣孔越多，氣孔開啟時蒸散作用旺盛，水分散失越快，越不易生存在乾旱環境。

(B) 氣孔開關受到保衛細胞中鉀離子濃度的影響，若鉀離子濃度越高則氣孔開啟；若鉀離子濃度越低則氣孔關閉。

(D) 保衛細胞內側壁較厚、外側壁較薄。

12. **B**

【解析】 組織胺為發炎介質，可引起血管通透性增加，使組織液流出量較正常時多。

13. **A**

　　【解析】　四個選項皆為植物防禦的機制，但題目問化學防禦的
　　　　　　　方式，則 (A) 選項為答案

14. **C**

　　【解析】　(A) 吞噬細胞會呈現病原體的抗原。樹突細胞、巨噬細
　　　　　　　　　胞可以轉變為抗原呈現細胞，利用 MHCII 呈現抗
　　　　　　　　　原；含有細胞核的細胞則在被感染後以 MHCI 呈現
　　　　　　　　　抗原。
　　　　　　　(B) 胞毒性 T 細胞才可以釋出物質使受病毒感染的細胞
　　　　　　　　　穿孔死亡。
　　　　　　　(C) 記憶性的淋巴球參與續發性的免疫反應，作用速度
　　　　　　　　　較第一次接觸病原體時快速。
　　　　　　　(D) 記憶性 T 細胞要參與續發性的免疫反應，當辨識到
　　　　　　　　　相同的抗原時會快速的活化。

15. **A**

　　【解析】　生長素造成植物的頂芽優勢；細胞分裂素造成植物的
　　　　　　　側芽優勢。兩者拮抗。

16. **D**

　　【解析】　(A) 蒼蠅被捕蠅草夾住為掠食的關係。
　　　　　　　(B) 榕果小蜂可以幫助榕屬植物傳粉，兩者關係為互利
　　　　　　　　　共生。
　　　　　　　(C) 蘭花在榕樹的樹幹上著生，以取得陽光來源，但不
　　　　　　　　　會影響榕樹正常生長，此為片利共生。
　　　　　　　(D) 菟絲子寄生在牽牛花的莖，兩者為寄生關係，和題
　　　　　　　　　目中寄生蜂和蝴蝶幼蟲的關係相同。

17-18 題爲題組

17. **B**

【解析】 (A) 轉錄作用發生在細胞核及細胞質中的粒線體、葉綠體基質中。

(B) 甲圖爲要表現的基因片段，爲雙股 DNA 的一小段。

(C) 乙圖中的三股，分別爲轉錄中的 DNA 模板股和密碼股，及轉錄出的 RNA 分子。

(D) 丙圖爲轉錄出的 RNA 分子，在眞核細胞中 RNA 分子要在 5' 端加端帽、3' 端加多聚腺苷酸尾。

18. **C**

【解析】 乙圖含有 DNA 和 RNA 分子，兩種核酸經分解後會產生其組成單元，其中 DNA 組成單元爲 dAMP、dTMP、dCMP、dGMP；RNA 組成單元爲 AMP、UMP、CMP、GMP。故共有 8 種核苷酸。

19-20 題爲題組

　　圖中葉片的葉肉細胞沒有區分出柵狀組織、海綿組織，皆爲葉肉細胞，由此可判讀此植物爲 C4 植物。圖中甲爲上表皮、乙爲維管束鞘細胞、丙爲維管束、丁爲下表皮、戊爲保衛細胞。

19. **D**

【解析】 C4 植物可以行光合作用的部位包括維管束鞘細胞 (乙) 及保衛細胞 (戊)。

20. **B**

【解析】 玉米爲 C4 植物。水稻和榕樹爲 C3 植物、鳳梨爲 CAM 植物。

二、多選題

21. **ABE**

【解析】 松果腺藉由感光細胞及眼部神經連接等作用來調節人
體晝夜的節律；另外視交叉上核位於下視丘，可以接
收視網膜的神經節細胞受光刺激而傳遞訊息，調節人
體的生理時鐘。

22. **DE**

【解析】 腎上腺素和升糖素皆可以升高血糖，但對血鈣濃度沒
有影響。此外，腎上腺素還可以加速心跳，使血液循
環加快。

23. **BD**

【解析】 (A) 邊材和心材皆爲雙子葉木本植物維管束內側木質部
的構造。

(C) 單子葉植物的莖，維管束才是散生。雙子葉植物維
管束屬於環狀排列的形式。

(E) 切面中央爲木質部的心材，不爲薄壁細胞組成的髓。

24. **ADE**

【解析】 題幹說明此爲一個符合哈溫平衡的族群，依照題意，
先計算兩個等位基因分別在此等位基因總數中所佔的
頻率：

① A 所佔的頻率爲：$(77 \times 2 + 94) \div [(77 + 94 + 29) \times 2]$
$= 0.62$

② a 所佔的頻率爲：$1 - 0.62 = 0.38$

(A) A 所佔頻率爲 0.62

(B) 因爲符合哈溫定律,故下一子代其等位基因頻率不
變。A 所佔頻率仍爲 0.62。

(C) a 所佔頻率爲 0.38

(D) 根據哈溫平衡的公式,可知在 1000 個個體中,Aa
基因型所佔個體數爲:$1000 \times (2 \times 0.62 \times 0.38) =$
471.2,約爲 470 人。

(E) 因爲在族群中擁有 a 基因的人較少,較容易受到遺
傳漂變的影響,故 A 基因在下一代消失的機率較小

（註）此題 (E) 選項若用哈溫平衡的觀念來看會產生爭
議,是一個有爭議的選項。

25. **ABD**

【解析】 此題即問細胞膜上有那些成分,包括了磷脂質、膽固
醇、醣蛋白、周邊蛋白、嵌入蛋白、醣脂等。

26. **ACE**

【解析】 (B) 味覺的感覺受器爲味蕾中的毛細胞。

(D) 平衡覺的靜平衡感覺受器爲前庭中橢圓囊、球囊的
味覺斑;動平衡感覺受器爲半規管壺腹中的頂蓋、
毛細胞。

27. **ADE**

【解析】 (B) 吉貝素沒有參與日照長短變化而誘導植物開花的功
能。主要功能爲打破種子休眠、刺激細胞分裂和生
長,使莖拉長、矮種植物長高,另外也可以促進葡
萄的產生無籽葡萄。

(C) 在離素含量過高時才會誘導種子休眠。

28. **DE**

　　【解析】(A) 尿素在肝臟的粒線體合成。

　　　　　　(B) 硬骨魚由鰓部排除氨。

　　　　　　(C) 兩生類成體以排除尿素為主。

29. **AE**

　　【解析】(B) 原核生物細胞質中沒有膜狀胞器，其唯一的胞器為核醣體。

　　　　　　(C) 原核生物沒有膜狀胞器，不會有粒線體存在細胞中。

　　　　　　(D) 有乳糖存在時會開啟乳糖操作組，再由葡萄糖量的多少來調節基因表現的速度。

30. **ACE**

　　【解析】使心跳加速的因素有：交感神經興奮、腎上腺素、正腎上腺素增加、體溫上升等。

　　　　　　使心跳減緩的因素有：副交感神經興奮、體溫下降等。

　　　　　　由於副交感神經的神經傳遞物質為乙醯膽鹼，故乙醯膽鹼釋出量增加時，也會使心跳減緩。

31. **BE**

　　【解析】(A) 因為溫度上升，會使適合低溫的櫻花鉤吻鮭的分布越來越往上游發展。

　　　　　　(C) 闊葉林分布在高溫的低海拔地區，高山草原則較適合低溫環境所以應會遠離闊葉林才對。

　　　　　　(D) 因為溫度上升，所以原僅分布在南部的紅樹林品種，也可以向北部發展，因此應該會分布全台才對。

32. **AE**

【解析】 (B) 應該為鈉離子。

(C) 靜止電位的形成與鈉離子、鉀離子、磷酸根、蛋白質…等因素都有關。

(D) 為鉀離子的通道關閉較緩慢所致,與幫浦無關。

33. **ABE**

【解析】 (C) 碳反應發生在葉綠體的基質。

(D) 碳反應需要許多酵素參與反應,其中許多酵素需要光活化才可作用。

34. **BCE**

【解析】 (A) 雌果蠅若有兩個帶有白眼基因的 X 染色體,也會表現出白眼性狀。

(D) 雄果蠅傳給下一代雄果蠅為 Y 染色體,而白眼性狀在 X 染色體上,所以白眼基因不可能由雄性親代傳給雄性子代。

35. **ACE**

【解析】 (B) 專一性的受體和病原體抗原的結合有專一性,並非可以和所有抗原結合。

(D) 病毒感染時,Tc 細胞和 B 細胞皆會活化,不是只有 Tc 細胞活化而已。

（註） 此題 (D) 選項若以題幹而言,只問 Tc 細胞和 B 細胞的特性比較,則因為只有 Tc 細胞可以殺死受病毒感染細胞,所以會產生爭議,是一個有爭議的選項。

三、閱讀題

36. **ACE**

【解析】 (B) 並非體積減小，而是 DNA 鹼基數減少、功能基因數目減少。

(D) 文中有提及，基因的丟失並不影響其致病能力。

37. **CDE**

【解析】 (A) 文中有提及，痲瘋分支桿菌與肺結核分支桿菌的代謝途徑已不相同。

(B) 文中並無提及體積變小、生長減緩的敘述。

38. **C**

【解析】 文中有提及，痲瘋分支桿菌可以存在巨噬細胞的吞噬小體，並經由特殊代謝獲得能量進行繁殖。由選項判斷最合理的是利用巨噬細胞提供的物質進行生長、繁殖。

39. **B**

【解析】 Parkin 要轉移到粒線體上需要先由 PINK1 自體磷酸化。

40. **B**

【解析】 當 PINK1 留在粒線體的外膜上時，才會自體磷酸化而累積，促使 Parkin 轉移到粒線體上。

41. **C**

【解析】 造成內膜電位差是因氫離子移動造成。

42. **D**

【解析】 (A) Solenopsis invicta 是主要在台灣發現的紅火蟻的學名，而非所有紅火蟻的學名。

(B) 和貨船的泊靠有關，並非自然遷移。

(C) 並無引入台灣，最主要原因可能為貨船的泊靠。

43. **A**

【解析】 一窩螞蟻中最主要在外工作且數量最多者為工蟻。

44. **BCD**

【解析】 (A) 物理方法是一危險的行動，因此不值得推廣。

(E) SINV-1 造成蟻群慢慢死亡，並非一個快速有效的方法。

第貳部分：非選擇題

一、【解答】 1. 蛋白質、核酸。

兩者中有 N 元素組成。

2. A；成熟部。

圖中 A 為成熟部、B 為延長部、C 為頂端分生組織和根冠。只有在成熟部的細胞才會完整分化出細胞的功能。

3. 根瘤。

4. 氮（N_2）。

根瘤菌固定的是空氣中的氮氣。

二、【解答】　1. 反應速率減慢。

可在圖中，固定一受質濃度來判斷。

2. 1.5mM。

由圖形可知。

3. 調整到適當的酸鹼度（pH6.8）；在一定的範圍下提升溫度。

此題考的是要如何增加酵素的活性，每一種酵素都有各自適合的環境，包括溫度、酸鹼度。

三、【解答】　1. 水筆仔。

可將物質由無機轉至有機世界的為生產者。

2. 巢鼠。

（註）水筆仔為胎生植物，本題問的是胎生生物，因此答案寫「水筆仔、巢鼠」也應該得分。是一題爭議題。

3. 水筆仔、雙殼貝、台灣招潮蟹。

三者生存環境較為固定，在紅樹林的範圍。另外海生疫病菌為原核生物。

四、【解答】　1. 胺基酸。

甲端為 3' 端，連接胺基酸。

2. 5'-GCU-3'。

由反密碼子核苷酸配對可推得。

3. 核醣體。

核醣體為細胞中蛋白質合成的場所。

4. 丙 5' → 丁 3'。

可由對應的反密碼子推得。

102 年大學入學指定科目考試試題
國文考科

第壹部分：選擇題（占 55 分）

一、單選題（占 34 分）

說明： 第 1 題至第 17 題，每題有 4 個選項，其中只有一個是正確或最適當的選項，請畫記在答案卡之「選擇題答案區」。各題答對者，得 2 分；答錯、未作答或畫記多於一個選項者，該題以零分計算。

1. 下列各組「 」內的字音，前後**不同**的選項是：
   (A) 若「埞」若穴／「喋」血山河
   (B) 交「戟」之衛士／王俱與「稽」首
   (C) 西方有木焉，名曰「射」干／每公卿入言，賓客上「謁」
   (D) 不知軍之不可以退而謂之退，是謂「縻」軍／侶魚蝦而友「麋」鹿

2. 新聞標題與新聞內容理應一致，然而有時並非如此。下列各「標題」與「內容」**不一致**的選項是：
   (A) 標題：烏有大學，重金吸菁英／內容：學測成績出爐，烏有大學設立績優獎學金，提供給學測成績優秀來申請入學的學生
   (B) 標題：租屋無認證，烏有大學將抵制房東／內容：烏有大學為保障學生校外租屋的安全，將抵制不參加安全防火認證的房東
   (C) 標題：世界語言，烏有大學校長看好華語／內容：烏有大學校長昨天表示，未來五到十年，世界上主要流通的語言可能是華語

(D) 標題：有大學首位文學院院長，是老外／內容：日本籍的大
村直人教授，這學年成為烏有大學文學院成立五十年來首位
外國籍院長

3. 下列文句，依文意選出排列順序最適當的選項：
「我懷想著故鄉的雷聲和雨聲。
甲、使它簇生油綠的枝葉而開出紅色的花
乙、細草樣柔的雨聲又以溫存之手撫摩它
丙、這些懷想如鄉愁一樣縈繞得使我憂鬱了
丁、那隆隆的有力的搏擊，從山谷返響到山谷
戊、彷彿春之芽就從凍土裡震動，驚醒，而怒茁出來
我心裡的氣候也和這北方大陸一樣缺少雨量，一滴溫柔的淚在我
枯澀的眼裡，如遲疑在這陰沉的天空裡的雨點，久不落下。」
（何其芳〈雨前〉）
(A) 丙乙甲丁戊　　　　　　　(B) 丙乙戊丁甲
(C) 丁戊乙甲丙　　　　　　　(D) 丁甲戊乙丙

4. 「關城樹色催寒近」、「亂花漸欲迷人眼」、「滄海客歸珠迸淚」、
「翠華想像空山裡」分別為四首詩中對仗句的上句，選出其下句
依序對應正確的選項：
(A) 玉殿虛無野寺中／章臺人去骨遺香／御苑砧聲向晚多／
淺草纔能沒馬蹄
(B) 章臺人去骨遺香／玉殿虛無野寺中／淺草纔能沒馬蹄／
御苑砧聲向晚多
(C) 淺草纔能沒馬蹄／御苑砧聲向晚多／玉殿虛無野寺中／
章臺人去骨遺香
(D) 御苑砧聲向晚多／淺草纔能沒馬蹄／章臺人去骨遺香／
玉殿虛無野寺中

5. 古文中的詞語解釋，有的可以從上下文意直接判斷，有的可從文
   化傳統中尋思其長期累積的意義。下列屬於後者的選項是：
   (A) 將〈燭之武退秦師〉：「子犯請擊之，公曰：不可。微夫人
       之力不及此」的「夫人」解釋爲「秦伯」
   (B) 將范仲淹〈岳陽樓記〉：「遷客騷人，多會於此，覽物之情，
       得無異乎」的「騷人」解釋爲「失意文人」
   (C) 將王羲之〈蘭亭集序〉：「故列敘時人，錄其所述，雖世殊
       事異，所以興懷，其致一也」的「時人」解釋爲「參加蘭亭
       修禊的人」
   (D) 將蒲松齡〈勞山道士〉：「乃以箸擲月中。見一美人，自光
       中出，初不盈尺，至地，遂與人等。纖腰秀項，翩翩作霓裳
       舞」的「美人」解釋爲「嫦娥」

6. 《論語》中「君子」與「小人」之對比，有時指上位者與下民，
   有時指有德者與無德者。下列與「君子學道則愛人，小人學道則
   易使也」中，「君子」、「小人」所指相同的選項是：
   (A) 君子喻於義，小人喻於利
   (B) 君子周而不比，小人比而不周
   (C) 君子泰而不驕，小人驕而不泰
   (D) 君子有勇而無義爲亂，小人有勇而無義爲盜

7. 古人常有手書前人名句的習慣，下列**不可能**發生的選項是：
   (A) 劉基手書「諮諏善道，察納雅言」
   (B) 韓愈手書「蓋文章，經國之大業，不朽之盛事」
   (C) 陶淵明手書「山不在高，有仙則名；水不在深，有龍則靈」
   (E) 王安石手書「滄浪之水清兮，可以濯吾纓；滄浪之水濁兮，
       可以濯吾足」

8. 下列文字所描繪的人物，其時代先後順序正確的選項是：
   甲、何處招魂，香草還生三戶地；當年呵壁，湘流應識九歌心
   乙、王業不偏安，兩表於今懸日月；臣言當盡瘁，六軍長此駐風雲

丙、氣備四時，與天地日月鬼神合其德；教垂萬世，繼堯舜禹湯
　　文武作之師

丁、你原本是一朵好看的青蓮，腳在泥中，頭頂藍天，無需潁川
　　之水，一身紅塵已被酒精洗淨

(A) 甲丙乙丁　　　(B) 乙丁丙甲　　　(C) 丙甲乙丁　　　(D) 丁乙甲丙

9. 列關於現代文學的敘述，**錯誤**的選項是：

(A) 吳晟擅寫臺灣鄉村風貌，詩作內容多與土地及生活息息相關

(B) 陳列作品以散文為主，創作題材包含山水與自然，抒發生命
　　感懷

(C) 龍應台作品多為小說，兼及雜文、文學評論與戲劇等文類的
　　創作

(D) 賴和被尊稱為「臺灣新文學之父」，其作品總是站在人民的
　　立場書寫

10. 下列是一則摘自報紙上的謝啟，根據謝啟的內容，□□依序應是：

遺　澤　綿　延　無　盡　感　恩

　　□□張公　諱光明府君
慟於民國一〇〇年六月五日壽終正寢
已擇日完成奉安
並於八月十九日假懷恩堂舉行追思紀念會
辱蒙　縣長與各級長官前輩至親好友親臨懷思
隆情厚誼　歿榮存感　節孝在身未克踵府叩謝
高誼雲情　謹申謝悃　伏祈
□□

　　　　　　　　　大華
　　　　棘人　　　　　叩謝
　　　　　　　　　大年
中　華　民　國　一　〇　〇　年　八　月　二　十　日

(A) 先妣／矜鑒　　　　　　(B) 先嚴／鈞鑒

(C) 先慈／鈞鑒　　　　　　(D) 先君／矜鑒

11. 閱讀下文，選出最適合填入＿＿＿＿中的選項：

　　　齊桓公之時，晉客至，有司請禮，桓公曰「告仲父」者三。而優笑曰：「易哉爲君！一曰『仲父』，二曰『仲父』。」桓公曰：「吾聞＿＿＿＿＿。吾得仲父已難矣，得仲父之後，何爲不易乎哉？（《韓非子・難二》）

> 仲父：指管仲

(A) 我無爲，而民自化

(B) 君人者勞於索人，佚於使人

(C) 爲政以德，譬如北辰，居其所而眾星共之

(D) 君尊則令行，官修則有常事，法制明則民畏刑

12. 閱讀下文，根據墨子的看法，飾攻戰者所犯錯誤最可能是：

　　　飾攻戰者言曰：「南則荊、吳之王，北則齊、晉之君，始封於天下之時，其土城之方，未至有數百里也；人徒之眾，未至有數十萬人也。以攻戰之故，土地之博，至有數千里也；人徒之眾，至有數百萬人。故當攻戰而不可爲也。」子墨子言曰：「雖四五國則得利焉，猶謂之非行道也。譬若醫之藥人之有病者然。今有醫於此，和合其祝藥之於天下之有病者而藥之，萬人食此，若醫四五人得利焉，猶謂之非行藥也。」（《墨子・非攻中》）

(A) 以偏概全　　　　　　(B) 損人利己

(C) 貪得無厭　　　　　　(D) 顧此失彼

13-14 爲題組

閱讀下列曲作，回答 13-14 題。

　　　俺曾見金陵玉殿鶯啼曉，秦淮水榭花開早，誰知道容易冰消！眼看他起朱樓，眼看他宴賓客，眼看他樓塌了！這青苔碧瓦堆，

俺曾睡風流覺，將五十年興亡看飽。那烏衣巷不姓王，莫愁湖鬼夜哭，鳳凰臺棲梟鳥。殘山夢最真，舊境丟難掉，不信這輿圖換稿！謅一套〈哀江南〉，放悲聲唱到老。（孔尚任《桃花扇・餘韻・哀江南》）

13. 關於上文的主旨，敘述正確的選項是：
    (A) 天下興亡，匹夫有責，誓圖光復山河
    (B) 天道循環，無往不復，不必悲傷痛哭
    (C) 作舊地之遊，悔風流之事，興奮勵之志
    (D) 話興衰之感，抒亡國之痛，訴故國之思

14. 關於上文的文句，詮釋正確的選項是：
    (A) 俺曾睡風流覺：我曾在此快活的玩樂，喻自在如昔，足堪安慰
    (B) 鳳凰臺棲梟鳥：惡鳥棲息於鳳凰臺上，喻哲人已遠，觸景傷懷
    (C) 殘山夢最真：雖然只有殘山剩水，風景卻如夢如幻，真是美麗
    (D) 不信這輿圖換稿：難以相信這故國河山，竟輕易落入他人之手

15-16 為題組

閱讀下文，回答 15-16 題。

　　能言者未必能行，能行者未必能言。觀李、杜二公，崎嶇板蕩之際，語語王霸，褒貶得失。忠孝之心，驚動千古。騷雅之妙，雙振當時。兼眾善於無今，集大成於往作。歷世之下，想見風塵。惜乎長轡未騁，奇才並屈，竹帛少色，徒列空言，嗚呼哀哉！昔謂杜之□□，李之□□，神聖之際，二公造焉。觀於海者難為水，遊李、杜之門者難為詩。斯言信哉。（辛文房《唐才子傳》）

15. 文中□□，依次填入的字詞，最恰當的選項是：
(A) 典重／飄逸　　　　　(B) 婉約／豪放
(C) 輕豔／奇詭　　　　　(D) 儒緩／清新

16. 下列關於文意的解釋，正確的選項是：
(A) 作者認為李、杜既是「能言」者，又擁有「能行」的機遇
(B) 「騷雅之妙」意指李、杜的作品，全屬〈離騷〉典雅風格
(C) 「竹帛少色」意指李、杜名垂青史，其他詩人則相形失色
(D) 「觀於海者難為水」意指李、杜詩作傑出，他人難以超越

17. 閱讀下文，選出**不符合**文意的選項：

　　書學以師古為第一義。近世書家以臆騁，動無法度，如射不掛鵠，琴不按譜，如是亦何難之有！變化從心，從心不踰，嗚呼！難之矣。近世詩與古文亦然，此可以驚河伯，不足以當海若也！崇禎十二年六月，嵩山樵者王鐸臨古，因題於末，以俟相知如何。（王鐸〈臨閣帖‧題末〉）

(A) 作者認為近世書家不受法度限制，求新求變，精神值得肯定
(B) 作者臨古之後，認為書法與詩文創作，應以學習古人為優先
(C) 「可以驚河伯，不足以當海若」，是指雖有小成，但境界不高
(D) 作者認為書法創作任意變化，卻不失法度，此一境界很難達到

二、多選題（21分）

說明：第18題至第24題，每題有5個選項，其中至少有一個是正確的選項，請將正確選項畫記在答案卡之「選擇題答案區」。各題之選項獨立判定，所有選項均答對者，得3分；答錯1個選項者，得1.8分；答錯2個選項者，得0.6分；答錯多於2個選項或所有選項均未作答者，該題以零分計算。

18. 下列各組「」內的字，前後字形**不同**的選項是：
(A) 一見「ㄓㄨㄥ」情／老態龍「ㄓㄨㄥ」
(B) 投桃「ㄅㄠˋ」李／「ㄅㄠˋ」薪救火
(C) 「ㄓㄢˇ」露才華／大有「ㄓㄢˇ」獲
(D) 糟「ㄊㄚˋ」資源／腳「ㄊㄚˋ」實地
(E) 魚「ㄍㄨㄢˋ」而出／醍醐「ㄍㄨㄢˋ」頂

19. 下列各組文句「」內的字，前後意義相同的選項是：
(A) 「弱」國入朝／天下非小「弱」也
(B) 罰加乎「姦」令／「姦」臣猶有所譎其辭
(C) 「食」以草具／「食」之，比門下之魚客
(D) 天下皆知美之「為」美／生而不有，「為」而不恃
(E) 百姓樂用，諸侯親「服」／「服」太阿之劍，乘纖離之馬

20. 下列文句「」內的詞語，使用正確的選項是：
(A) 他們欺世盜名，同是「一丘之貉」，誰也好不到那裡去
(B) 這次演講比賽，參賽者個個「口無遮攔」，很難分出勝負
(C) 老李嘆道：我「人微言輕」，雖有建言，上級也不會重視
(D) 李廠長奉獻了畢生心力，他的豐功偉績，簡直是「擢髮難數」
(E) 老早就聽聞您才高學博，本公司正「虛位以待」，請您來任職

21. 「反問」雖採問句形式，卻屬無疑而問、明知故問，意在強調預設的觀點。下列屬於反問句的選項是：
(A) 壯士，能復飲乎
(B) 誰習計會，能為文收責於薛者乎
(C) 吾師道也，夫庸知其年之先後生於吾乎
(D) 風俗頹敝如是，居位者雖不能禁，忍助之乎
(E) 況為大臣而無所不取，無所不為，則天下其有不亂，國家其有不亡者乎

22. 鄭愁予在〈錯誤〉詩中有：「我達達的馬蹄是美麗的錯誤」之句，下列合乎「美麗的錯誤」之情境的選項是：

(A) 相親不下五十次的我，始終找不到有緣人，簡直想放棄了。還好我繼續相了第五十一次親，因此認識了你，也因此有美好的人生

(B) 這是最後一次了，我約你在校門口第二棵樹下見面，你依然沒出現。如果你認為我們的相識是一場錯誤，那就讓一切隨風而逝吧

(C) 因為粗心而下錯站的我，只好在等車的空檔裡百無聊賴的閒晃。穿過鐵軌，走進一家小店，竟遇見好久不見的你！頓時，所有的懊惱都被驚喜所取代

(D) 往昔，水鳥神祕的遷徙行為以及按時南北漂泊的生活一直使我著迷。完成觀察後，看到原本要設立保育區的沼澤地繼續遭受破壞，我好像是做錯了事一樣，再也不願去涉足

(E) 因為迷戀著川端康成筆下〈伊豆舞孃〉的美麗，所以我來到了天城隧道。在寂靜的隧道中行走，我彷彿遇見了那個旅行的青年，以及熱鬧的走唱藝人，不自覺的感動起來。可是走出隧道後才發現，這原來不是天城隧道，不禁啞然失笑。但是何妨？隧道是「假」的，但我的感動都是真的啊

23. 下列詞作，藉歷史人物寄託作者情懷的選項是：

(A) 遙想公瑾當年，小喬初嫁了，雄姿英發。羽扇綸巾，談笑間，強虜灰飛煙滅

(B) 東風夜放花千樹。更吹落，星如雨。寶馬雕車香滿路。鳳簫聲動，玉壺光轉，一夜魚龍舞

(C) 試問夜如何？夜已三更，金波淡，玉繩低轉。但屈指西風幾時來，又不道，流年暗中偷換

(D) 將軍百戰身名裂。向河梁，回頭萬里，故人長絕。易水蕭蕭
西風冷，滿座衣冠似雪。正壯士，悲歌未徹

(E) 元嘉草草，封狼居胥，贏得倉皇北顧。四十三年，望中猶記，
烽火揚州路。可堪回首，佛狸祠下，一片神鴉社鼓。憑誰問，
廉頗老矣，尚能飯否

24. 閱讀下列小說，選出符合文意的選項：

　　有鸚鵡飛集他山，山中禽獸輒相愛重。鸚鵡自念：雖樂不可
久也，便去。後數月，山中大火，鸚鵡遙見，便入水沾羽，飛而
灑水。天神言：「汝雖有志意，何足云也？」對曰：「雖知不能救，
然嘗僑居是山，禽獸行善，皆為兄弟，不忍見耳。」天神感應，
即為滅火。（劉義慶《宣驗記‧鸚鵡滅火》）

(A) 「雖樂不可久也」意謂鸚鵡預知山中將有災禍

(B) 「入水沾羽，飛而灑水」歌詠鸚鵡的渴望自由

(C) 「汝雖有志意，何足云也」讚許鸚鵡的不屈不撓

(D) 「禽獸行善，皆為兄弟」呈現鸚鵡對山中禽獸的感恩

(E) 作者描述了「不忍」以及「知其不可而為之」的精神

第貳部分：非選擇題（佔 45 分）

說明：本部分共有二題，請依各題提示作答，答案必須寫在「答案
　　　卷」上，並標明題號一、二。作答務必使用筆尖較粗之黑色
　　　墨水的筆書寫，且不得使用鉛筆。

一、文章解讀（占 18 分）

　　　　閱讀框內文字後，請闡釋：（一）作者認為什麼是青年的天
德？（二）作者認為青年如何「繼天德以立人德」？（一）（二）
合計文長約 250 — 300 字（約 11 — 14 行）。

> 青年如嫩芽初發，含苞待放，代表天地之生機，人類之元氣。青年自然純潔，縱有一點灰塵，因其生力推動，終將隨風飛去。青年不怕壓力，不畏權威，嚮往的是頭上碧茫茫的太虛，要求頂天立地，所以有開拓萬古之心胸，推倒一世豪傑之氣概；青年自然富有正義感，總行走於堂堂正正的大道。凡此，皆是造物者給與青年的恩惠，並非青年努力而成，是青年之天德而非人德，青年不應在此驕傲，青年的責任在：依自覺的努力，繼天德以立人德。
>
> 青年朋友們，你可曾在自然純潔之外，時時拂拭心靈灰塵？你可曾在自然的不怕壓力，反抗權威外，真正培植一己之力量，深植根柢於歷史文化之土壤？你可曾在自然的正義感之外，細細思維何謂人間社會最高正義，並為實現此一正義而百折不回？除了憑藉一己之力，實踐抱負，迎向光明之外，你可曾發憤營求師友相勉或尚友古人，以擴大你的胸量，提高你的志氣？這些都端賴你自覺的努力，而不能只恃青年的天德。（改寫自唐君毅《青年與學問‧說青年之人生》）

二、引導寫作（占 27 分）

　　每個人心中都有著對遠方的憧憬，陶淵明為此構築了桃花源，哥倫布為此勇渡大西洋。你的心中是否也有一個遠方在召喚？也許是個神祕的國度，也許是一種嚮往的生命型態，也或許是一個人生的目標。**請以「遠方」為題**，寫一篇文章，論說、記敘、抒情皆可。

102年度指定科目考試國文科試題詳解

第壹部分：選擇題

一、單選題

1. B

【解析】(A) ㄅㄞˋ　　　(B) ㄐㄧˇ／ㄑㄧˇ
　　　　(C) ㄧㄝˋ　　　(D) ㄇㄧˊ

2. D

【解析】(D) 標題「『首位』文學院院長，是老外」與內容「『成立五十年來首位』外國籍院長」在時間描述上不一致。

3. C

【解析】由第一句「我懷想著故鄉的雷聲和雨聲」可推知後面應由「雷聲」、「雨聲」兩方面來著筆。「丁」描寫雷聲，由「戊」的「震動」、「驚醒」故知應接在「丁」後；「乙」描寫雨聲，「甲」寫受雨滋潤生長，故接在「乙」後，而「乙」的「又以」與第一句先雷後雨，故知「丁戊」在「乙甲」前。而「我心裡」幾句寫懷鄉的憂鬱情緒，故「丙」放在最後。

4. D

【解析】對仗句必須遵守「字數相同、平仄相反、詞性相同、詞義相關」等原則。判斷對仗句的簡易方法是：先看末字及偶數字平仄，再看詞性；而詞性判斷可以先掌握動詞。各選項末字皆合平仄，而各句第二字僅有第三句「海」為仄聲，比對各選項第三句第二字：苑、

草、殿、臺，則僅有 (D) 選項「臺」為平聲。再以詞
性檢驗：

題　　　目	對　　　應　　　句
「關城樹色／催（動）寒近」	「御苑砧聲／向（動）晚多」
「亂花／漸欲（動）／ 迷（動）人眼」	「淺草／纔能（動）／ 沒（動）馬蹄」
「蒼海／客歸（動） 珠迸（動）淚」	「章臺／人去（動）／ 骨遺（動）香」
「翠華想（動）像（動）／ 空山裡」	「御殿虛（動）無（動）／ 野寺中」

【語譯與出處】

(1) 李頎＜送魏萬之京＞：「關塞城牆邊的樹木變了顏色，顯現
　　出寒冷近逼；皇城裡，薄暮時分的擣衣聲也多了起來。」

(2) 白居易＜錢塘湖春行＞：「花越開越繁盛，可想見將撩亂遊
　　人雙眼了；而春草初生，才長到遮住馬蹄的高度。」

(3) 宋祁＜落花＞：「我看了花落而傷情落淚，花雖離枝而香氣
　　猶存。」（此詩以「女子」喻「花」，故以女子之香消玉殞
　　喻落花。）

(4) 杜甫＜詠懷古蹟＞五首之四：「想像皇帝的車馬駛進這空山
　　裡，而當年富麗堂皇的宮殿，如今成為荒廢無人的野寺。」

5. **B**

　【解析】　(A) 那個人。
　　　　　　(B) 屈原作＜離騷＞，故後人亦稱詩人為「騷人」。
　　　　　　(C) 當時參加修褉的人。
　　　　　　(D) 美女。

6. **D**

　【解析】　題目語譯：「在上位者學習禮樂，則能愛護百姓；在
　　　　　　下位者學習禮樂，則易於使喚。」

(A) 君子懂得義理，小人只懂得利益。

(B) 君子與人相處都親厚而不結黨偏私，小人結黨偏私而不能待人普遍親厚。

(C) 君子態度坦然自若而不驕傲，小人驕傲而不坦然自若。

(D) 在上位者敢爲而無視義理，就會犯上作亂；在下位者敢爲而無視義理，就會偷盜。(從「有勇無義」可知並非從道德上區分)。

7. **C**

【解析】(A) 劉基：元末明初人；「諮諏善道……」出自三國諸葛亮＜出師表＞。

(B) 韓愈：中唐人；「蓋文章……」出自三國曹丕＜典論論文＞。

(C) 陶淵明：東晉人；「山不在高……」出自中唐劉禹錫。

(D) 王安石：北宋人；「滄浪之水……」出自戰國屈原＜漁父＞。

8. **C**

【解析】(甲) 屈原：戰國。屈原常以「香草」喻高潔的人格。「招魂」、「九歌」爲屈原作品名。「呵壁」是屈原被放逐後，憤慨鬱結，見廟中壁畫，就壁畫內容質疑上天，而作＜天問＞的典故。「湘流」則是屈原葬身之處。

(乙) 諸葛亮：三國。從「王業不偏安」(出自＜後出師表＞：「漢賊不兩立，王業不偏安。」)、「兩表」(前、後出師表)、「盡瘁」(＜後出師表＞：「鞠躬盡瘁，死而後已。」)可知爲諸葛亮。

(丙) 孔子：春秋。由「教垂萬世」及「繼堯舜禹湯文

武周公」的道統而「作之師」可知是至聖先師
——孔子。

(丁) 李白：唐代。李白號「青蓮居士」，好飲酒。「潁
川水」之典故出自堯欲召隱者許由為官，許由聽
到這個消息覺得髒了耳朵，而以潁川水洗耳。

9. **C**

【解析】 (C) 龍應台作品多為「雜文」，兼及小說、文學評論。
沒有戲劇。

10. **D**

【解析】 由「張公」可知為父親，故 (A) (C) 刪去。「矜鑒」為居
喪的應用文中，請求對方察閱的提稱語；「鈞鑒」為一
般書信、公文中，對尊長的提稱語。

11. **B**

【解析】 由於桓公事事都交給管仲處理，而引來優人對桓公的
嘲弄，故桓公的回答應該針對此點為自己辯解。

【語譯】 齊桓公在位時，晉國的客人來，負責接待的官員幾次
詢問該以何種禮儀接待，桓公都說「去問仲父（對管
仲的尊稱）。」旁邊的優人就笑著說：「當君王真容易啊！
只要講『仲父』就行了。」桓公說：「我聽說『為君者
找人才時辛苦，用對人才就能安逸過日子了。』我好
不容易才找到管仲這個人才，找到他後，為什麼不能
安逸度日呢？」(《韓非子》)

(A) 我不刻意作為，而百姓自然會受教化。(《老子》)

(C) 用道德來治理國家，執政者便能像北極星一樣，
居於中心，受到眾星拱繞。(《論語》)

(D) 君位尊崇，則君王的命令容易推行；官位修整，
則職司分明；法制清楚，則百姓便會因畏懼刑罰
而守法重紀。(《商君書》)

12. **A**

　【解析】　墨子認為為戰爭辯解的人舉的例子只是特例，不能用
　　　　　　以解釋所有的情況。

　【語譯】　為戰爭辯解的人說：「南方像楚王、吳王，北方像齊
　　　　　　君、晉君，在他們初受封時，國土還不到方圓數百
　　　　　　里，國人還不到數十萬人。因為四處攻伐，土地擴張
　　　　　　到幾千里平方，人民多到幾百萬人。所以應該要攻
　　　　　　伐。」墨子說：「即使有四、五個國家因此得利，也
　　　　　　還不能說它是正道。就好像醫生給有病的人開藥，
　　　　　　現在有個醫生為病人調配藥劑，一萬個人吃了這帖
　　　　　　藥，有四、五個人被治好了，也還不能說這帖藥是
　　　　　　有效的。」

13-14 為題組

13. **D**
14. **D**

　【語譯】　我曾經見聞過金陵皇宮早晨鶯聲繚繞，秦淮河畔樓臺
　　　　　　上的花早早就開了的景況，誰知道這一切像冰雪般輕
　　　　　　易就消融了！親眼看他蓋華樓、宴請賓客，也親眼看
　　　　　　著樓坍塌！現在這片長滿青苔的碧瓦堆上，我曾在此
　　　　　　快活地大睡一覺，把五十年來的興衰都看盡了（形容
　　　　　　過去的一切如夢）。那烏衣巷的人家不姓王，莫愁湖
　　　　　　邊鬼夜夜啼哭，鳳凰臺上棲息著梟鳥（烏衣巷、莫愁
　　　　　　湖、鳳凰台皆在金陵）。國土殘破，像一場最真實的
　　　　　　夢，過往的情境難以忘卻，不敢相信地圖改換（改朝
　　　　　　換代）！就編造這一套＜哀江南＞曲，悲聲唱到老吧！

15-16 為題組

15. **A**

　【解析】　由「遊李、杜之門者難為詩」與文中的高度評價，可

知「李、杜」二公應指「李白、杜甫」，以此選擇符合二人詩風之詞。(C) 輕豔：輕靡華麗。(D) 儒緩：寬柔。

16. **D**

【解析】 (B)「騷雅」指的是＜離騷＞、＜大雅＞、＜小雅＞，即《楚辭》、《詩經》的詩歌傳統。

【語譯】 能立言的人未必能建立功業，能建立功業的人未必能立言。我看杜甫、李白二位，在國家動盪的時候，每句話都提到王霸之道，批評政治得失。忠君愛國之心，足以驚動千古；詩才之高，都能震動當時。能兼眾人之美，集前賢詩作之善。經過幾代，還能想像他們當時激起的影響。可惜他們卓越的才能未能發揮，兩人都懷才不遇，而使史書少了幾分色彩，只留下他們的作品，真是可惜啊！以前人說杜甫的「典雅莊重」，李白的「清新灑脫」，兩人都已到達出神入化的境界。看過大海的，很難再被一般的河水吸引；遨遊於李、杜的作品中的人，一般的詩也不能被他看重了。這話說得很確實啊！

17. **A**

【語譯】 書法之學以學習古人為第一要義。近來書法家多出於己意，書寫不遵守規範，就好像射箭卻不掛箭靶，彈琴不按曲譜，這樣做又有什麼困難！隨著心意變化而不逾越規範，唉！這才是真的困難啊！近來詩和古文寫作也是這樣，但這樣寫出來的作品格局太小，只能驚動河神，而不足以與海神相當。崇禎十二年六月，嵩山樵者王鐸臨摹古人書帖有感而發，因此題寫在卷末，以等待知音回應。

二、多選題

18. **BC(D)E**
　【解析】　(A) 鍾
　　　　　　(B) 報／抱
　　　　　　(C) 嶄／斬
　　　　　　(D) 蹋（踏）／踏（「糟蹋」亦作「糟踏」，但一般不寫「糟踏」，故此選項可選可不選。）
　　　　　　(E) 貫／灌

19. **AC**
　【解析】　(A) 弱小。
　　　　　　(B) 觸犯、違反（動詞）／狡詐的（形容詞）。
　　　　　　(C) 給對方吃。　　　(D) 是／創造。
　　　　　　(E) 服從、聽命／佩帶。

20. **ACE**
　【解析】　(A) 同樣低劣的一群人。
　　　　　　(B) 說話沒有顧忌。
　　　　　　(C) 地位低微，言論不被重視。
　　　　　　(D) （罪行）多得難以計算。
　　　　　　(E) 留著位置等候有才德者。

21. **CDE**
　【解析】　(A) 疑問。壯士，能再喝嗎？
　　　　　　(B) 疑問。誰學過會計，能為我去薛地收債？
　　　　　　(C) 激問。我學的是「道」，哪在意對方的年紀比我大還是小呢？
　　　　　　(D) 激問。社會風俗衰敗至此，在上位者即使不能禁止，難道忍心助長它嗎？

(E) 激問。何況當大臣而沒什麼不敢拿的，沒什麼不敢
做的，那麼天下哪有不亂，國家哪有不滅亡的呢？

22. **CE**

【解析】「美麗的錯誤」指某事雖是錯誤，但仍有美好之處。

(A)「相親了五十一次」並非「錯誤」。

(B) 看不出美好的部分。

(C) 粗心造成的錯誤卻驚喜地遇見好久不見你。

(D)「遭破壞」這個錯誤沒有美好的部分。

(E) 雖發現隧道是假，但感動仍是真的，仍美好。

23. **ADE**

【解析】(A) 藉「公瑾」(周瑜) 抒發情懷。出自蘇軾＜念奴嬌
赤壁懷古＞。

(B) 寫元宵夜賞燈的盛況，純寫景。出自辛棄疾＜青
玉案＞。

(C) 想像蜀主孟昶與花蕊夫人在夏夜乘涼時的對話，
沒有寄託個人情懷。出自蘇軾＜洞仙歌＞。

(D) 這是一首送別詞。前四句，用李陵送別蘇武典
故；後四句用荊軻易水送別典故，寄託自己送別
堂弟的心情。出自辛棄疾＜賀新郎＞。

(E) 藉趙王遣使探問廉頗是否尚可用的典故，表達希
望受朝廷任用的心意。出自辛棄疾＜永遇樂＞。

24. **DE**

【語譯】有隻鸚鵡棲息到另一座山，山中的禽鳥走獸都愛護看
重牠。鸚鵡自想：在這裡雖然過得快樂，但也不能久
待，便離開了。過了幾個月，山中發生大火，鸚鵡遠
遠看到了，便到水中用羽毛沾水，飛到山上灑水救火。
天神說：「你雖然有這份心意，但哪裡救得了火呢？」

鸚鵡回答：「就算明知救不了，但我暫居這座山的時
候，禽鳥走獸對我很好，就像兄弟一樣，我不忍心見
到牠們受難。」天神感動於鸚鵡的心意，立刻幫忙滅
了火。

第貳部分：非選擇題

一、文章解讀

（一）作者由幾個面向來說明青年的天德：

1. 青年生機勃發，充滿生命力；
2. 青年質樸純眞，縱有些微瑕疵，也能因生命力的推進而抖落微塵；
3. 青年不畏壓力，不懼權威，能掙脫束縛，開拓新局；
4. 青年富有正義感。

然而此皆造物者之恩惠，非青年之功，故稱「天德」。

（二）作者認爲，擁有造物者給與之「天德」尚不足以成就人的尊
　　　嚴，必須在此基礎上「繼天德以立人德」。首先要能自覺天
　　　德不足爲恃，努力以人德繼之：要有自省能力，時時拂拭心
　　　靈灰塵；要能從歷史文化的土壤中培植出自己的力量；要思
　　　索何謂人間社會的正義，並爲它的實現奔走；要能從良師益
　　　友、往哲典範中取法，開闊胸襟，恢弘志氣。

二、作文

【範文】

遠方

　　麥哲倫駛向未知的大洋，因他相信遠方的終點會回到腳下；牧羊
少年越過大海，穿過撒哈拉，只爲夢中的金字塔；玄奘相信眞知在萬
里之外的天竺，終於將一路艱險踏成蓮花──他們都相信，夢想，在
遠方。

　　對於遠方，我們總懷有浪漫的想望，我們相信遠方有我們要追尋的夢想，所以不被家園的溫馨羈絆；我們又不確知遠方到底是什麼模樣，所以更激起一探究竟的欲望。它就像在水一方的佳人，讓人即使濡濕了衣裳，即使道阻且長，也要溯游溯洄想盡辦法到達彼方。

　　我喜歡踏上遺址，感受前人曾經生活過的蛛絲馬跡；我喜歡站在玻璃櫃前，用眼光摩娑著古人玩賞過的一器一物；我喜歡在文字的導航中，跟隨往哲的人生軌跡。站在硫氣薰人、白煙氤氳的山道上，踏著郁永河三百多年前的足印，眼前的馬路變成高莽榛林，天空更藍，周圍只剩下硫穴「啵啵啵」水被燙得跳起來的聲音。環顧四周，我們看的是一樣的山嗎？而山你還記得三百多年前凝視過你的那個漢人嗎？

　　走到一號坑前，俯視著羅列成陣的兵士，二千多年前的匠人頂著棚外同一個豔陽揮汗，吸著同一塊土地揚起的塵土，你們的一生是幾尊兵俑？你們的心中是詛咒還是敬畏？還是跟我一樣對於君王異想天開的驚嘆？

　　我的遠方，是歷史的遠方，許許多多生命刻劃在時間化石上的存在證據。然而我並不想成為一名考古學家，我追尋著遠方，只為尋找單位更大的參照座標。它不是一天八節、一學期二十週、高中六學期，而是從百年、千年的時間單位，讓我省思作為人的極限與挑戰，讓我想想我該怎樣綻放僅此一次的美麗，直到我也成為別人追尋的遠方。

　　遠方，讓我跳脫了視野的逼仄。生命盡頭的遠方，是我們必然被輸往的終點；而歷史長軸上的每一個遠方，都可以是起點。我的追尋，在遠方。

102 年指考國文科非選擇題閱卷評分原則說明

閱卷召集人：謝海平（逢甲大學中文系教授）

　　本次參與指考國文科閱卷的委員，大部分爲國內各大學中文系、國文系、語文教育系或共同科之教師，亦有若干科技大學共同科教師，共 175 人，分爲 16 組。除由正、副召集人統籌所有閱卷事宜外，每組均置一位協同主持人，負責該組閱卷工作，協同主持人皆爲各大學之專任教授。

　　大學入學考試國文科自 99 年首次採用電腦螢幕閱卷，經過多次的程式測試、修訂，以及電腦操作的演練，今年的閱卷工作更爲流暢純熟。7 月 7 日，由正、副召集人與五位協同主持人，抽取 3000 份來自全省各考區的答案卷，詳加評閱、分析、討論，草擬評分原則。每題選出「A」、「B」、「C」等第之標準卷各 1 份，及試閱卷各 18 份。7 月 8 日，再由正、副召集人與 16 位協同主持人深入討論、評比所選出的標準卷及試閱卷，並審視、修訂所擬之評分原則，確定之後，製作閱卷手冊，供 7 月 9 日正式閱卷前各組協同主持人說明及全體閱卷委員參考之用，並作爲評分時之參考。

　　本次國文科考試，非選擇題共二大題，占 45 分。第一大題爲「文章解讀」，占 18 分；第二大題爲「作文」，占 27 分。

　　第一大題評量重點分爲兩部分：(一) 闡釋引文作者(唐君毅)認爲什麼是青年的「天德」。(二) 闡釋引文作者認爲青年如何「繼天德以立人德」。前者有四個重點：1. 天德是上天賦予青年的恩惠；2. 青年自然純潔；3. 青年不畏壓力、權威；4. 青年富正義感。後者有五個重點：

1. 經由自覺努力以立人德；2. 拂拭心靈，保持自然純潔；3. 植根歷史文化，以培養一己之力；4. 思維並實踐人間正義；5. 尚友古人或與師友相勉。凡「天德」與「人德」皆闡釋深入，內容完整，條理清楚，文筆流暢者，給 A 等分數（18 分～13 分）；「天德」與「人德」闡釋未臻完善，內容平實，脈絡大致清楚，文筆尚稱通順者，給 B 等（12 分～7 分）；「天德」與「人德」闡釋不全，內容貧乏，脈絡不清，文筆蕪亂者，則降入 C 等（6 分～1 分）。其次，再視標點符號使用恰當與否與錯別字之多寡，斟酌扣分；至於字數，則少於 9 行或多於 16 行者，酌扣 1 分。

　　第二大題為作文，要求考生以「遠方」為題寫一篇文章，論說、記敘、抒情皆可。評閱重點，從「題旨發揮」、「資料掌握」、「結構安排」、「字句運用」四項指標，加以評分。凡能緊扣題旨發揮，思路清晰，內容充實，論述周延，富有創意；舉例詳實貼切，材料運用恰當；結構嚴謹，脈絡清楚，條理分明；文筆流暢，修辭優美，字句妥切，用詞精當，得 A 等（27 分～19 分）。尚能照題旨發揮，思路尚稱清晰，內容平實，論述尚稱周延，略有創意；舉例平實疏略，材料運用尚稱恰當；結構大致完整，脈絡大致清楚，條理尚稱分明；文筆平順，修辭尚可，字句通順，用詞大致適當，得 B 等（18 分～10 分）。題旨不明或偏離題旨，思路不清，內容浮泛，論述不周延，缺乏創意；舉例鬆散模糊，材料運用不當；結構鬆散，脈絡不清，條理紛雜；文筆蕪蔓，修辭粗俗，字句欠通順，用詞不當，得 C 等（9 分～1 分）。

　　另外，文未終篇，至多 18 分。並視標點符號之使用與錯別字之多寡，斟酌扣分。完全文不對題或作答內容完全照抄試題者，評給零分。

大考中心公佈 102 學年度指定科目考試
國文、英文及數學甲、乙選擇（填）題答案

國文 題號	答案	英文 題號	答案	題號	答案	數學甲	題號	答案	數學乙	題號	答案
1	B	1	A	27	K		1	5		1	2
2	D	2	D	28	G		2	3		2	2
3	C	3	C	29	B		3	2		3	3,5
4	D	4	A	30	I		4	2		4	1,4,5
5	B	5	B	31	B		5	3,4,5		5	1,2,4,5
6	D	6	C	32	D		6	1,2,5		6	2
7	C	7	A	33	F		7	2,4		7	1,2,4
8	C	8	D	34	A		8	1,2		8	1
9	C	9	C	35	E		9	1,3,5	A	9	2
10	D	10	D	36	D	A	10	6		10	0
11	B	11	D	37	D		11	5	B	11	5
12	A	12	C	38	C		12	2		12	2
13	D	13	B	39	B		13	3	C	13	1
14	D	14	D	40	B	B	14	5		14	3
15	A	15	A	41	C		15	3			
16	D	16	C	42	D						
17	A	17	B	43	A						
18	BCDE (BCE)	18	A	44	C						
19	AC	19	B	45	B						
20	ACE	20	A	46	A						
21	CDE	21	C	47	D						
22	CE	22	A	48	C						
23	ADE	23	E	49	B						
24	DE	24	F	50	D						
		25	L	51	A						
		26	H								

大考中心公佈 102 學年度指定科目考試
歷史、地理、公民與社會選擇（填）題答案

歷 史				地 理				公 民 與 社 會			
題號	答案	題號	答案	題號	答案	題號	答案	題號	答案	題號	答案
1	A	27	B	1	B	27	C	1	D	27	D
2	C	28	A	2	A	28	D	2	C	28	B
3	C	29	B	3	B	29	A	3	B	29	B
4	B	30	A	4	D	30	D	4	B	30	A
5	D	31	A	5	D	31	A	5	D	31	D
6	D	32	A	6	B	32	C	6	C	32	A
7	A	33	D	7	C	33	C	7	D	33	C
8	D	34	D	8	B	34	A	8	B	34	C
9	B	35	D	9	A	35	D	9	A	35	A
10	B	36	B	10	C	36	B	10	D	36	C
11	C	37	AB	11	B	37	C	11	C	37	C
12	B	38	BDE	12	D	38	B	12	B	38	D
13	C	39	ADE	13	A			13	B	39	B
14	A	40	BDE	14	D			14	D	40	BCD
15	A			15	D			15	C	41	ACE
16	C			16	C			16	C	42	CD
17	C			17	A			17	D	43	BCE
18	D			18	D			18	C	44	AB
19	A			19	D			19	D	45	CD
20	B			20	C			20	B	46	BC
21	A			21	C			21	B	47	BD
22	C			22	A			22	A	48	CD
23	C			23	B			23	A	49	CE
24	C			24	C			24	B	50	BCD
25	D			25	A			25	D		
26	B			26	B			26	D		

大考中心公佈 102 學年度指定科目考試
物理、化學、生物選擇題答案

物 理		化 學		生		物	
題號	答案	題號	答案	題號	答案	題號	答案
1	D	1	D	1	A	25	ABD
2	A	2	A	2	C	26	ACE
3	A	3	C	3	D	27	ADE
4	B	4	C	4	A	28	DE
5	C	5	B	5	A	29	AE
6	E	6	E	6	D	30	ACE
7	A	7	D	7	D	31	BE
8	D	8	E	8	B	32	AE
9	E	9	D	9	B	33	ABE
10	D	10	B	10	C	34	BCE
11	A	11	E	11	C	35	ACE
12	E	12	C	12	B	36	ACE
13	C	13	DE	13	A	37	CDE
14	D	14	ABC	14	C	38	C
15	A	15	CE	15	A	39	B
16	D	16	CE	16	D	40	B
17	B	17	BDE	17	B	41	C
18	B	18	AB	18	C	42	D
19	C	19	AC	19	D	43	A
20	E	20	CE	20	B	44	BCD
21	BCE	21	AE	21	ABE		
22	ABD	22	CDE	22	DE		
23	BD	23	BDE	23	BD		
24	BE	24	ABE	24	ADE		

102 學年度指定科目考試
各科成績標準一覽表

科　　目	頂　標	前　標	均　標	後　標	底　標
國　　文	73	67	59	49	42
英　　文	82	73	56	38	26
數　學　甲	78	67	50	32	21
數　學　乙	84	75	58	36	21
化　　學	78	67	49	32	23
物　　理	78	67	49	32	23
生　　物	89	84	71	55	44
歷　　史	80	73	63	50	41
地　　理	76	70	62	52	44
公民與社會	82	76	67	56	49

※ 以上五項標準均取為整數（小數只捨不入），且其計算均不含缺考生之成績，
　計算方式如下：

頂標：成績位於第 88 百分位數之考生成績。
前標：成績位於第 75 百分位數之考生成績。
均標：成績位於第 50 百分位數之考生成績。
後標：成績位於第 25 百分位數之考生成績。
底標：成績位於第 12 百分位數之考生成績。

例：　某科之到考考生為 99982 人，則該科五項標準為

　　頂標：成績由低至高排序，取第 87985 名（99982×88%=87984.16，取整數，
　　　　　小數無條件進位）考生的成績，再取整數(小數只捨不入)。
　　前標：成績由低至高排序，取第 74987 名（99982×75%=74986.5，取整數，
　　　　　小數無條件進位）考生的成績，再取整數(小數只捨不入)。
　　均標：成績由低至高排序，取第 49991 名（99982×50%=49991）考生的成績，
　　　　　再取整數(小數只捨不入)。
　　後標：成績由低至高排序，取第 24996 名（99982×25%=24995.5，取整數，
　　　　　小數無條件進位）考生的成績，再取整數(小數只捨不入)。
　　底標：成績由低至高排序，取第 11998 名（99982×12%=11997.84，取整數，
　　　　　小數無條件進位）考生的成績，再取整數(小數只捨不入)。

102 年指定科目考試英文科成績人數累計表

分　　數	人　　數	百 分 比	自高分往低分累計		自低分往高分累計	
			累計人數	累計百分比	累計人數	累計百分比
100.00	0	0.00%	0	0.00%	62948	100.00%
99.00 - 99.99	3	0.00%	3	0.00%	62948	100.00%
98.00 - 98.99	11	0.02%	14	0.02%	62945	100.00%
97.00 - 97.99	39	0.06%	53	0.08%	62934	99.98%
96.00 - 96.99	74	0.12%	127	0.20%	62895	99.92%
95.00 - 95.99	117	0.19%	244	0.39%	62821	99.80%
94.00 - 94.99	179	0.28%	423	0.67%	62704	99.61%
93.00 - 93.99	251	0.40%	674	1.07%	62525	99.33%
92.00 - 92.99	342	0.54%	1016	1.61%	62274	98.93%
91.00 - 91.99	428	0.68%	1444	2.29%	61932	98.39%
90.00 - 90.99	489	0.78%	1933	3.07%	61504	97.71%
89.00 - 89.99	576	0.92%	2509	3.99%	61015	96.93%
88.00 - 88.99	652	1.04%	3161	5.02%	60439	96.01%
87.00 - 87.99	717	1.14%	3878	6.16%	59787	94.98%
86.00 - 86.99	791	1.26%	4669	7.42%	59070	93.84%
85.00 - 85.99	808	1.28%	5477	8.70%	58279	92.58%
84.00 - 84.99	886	1.41%	6363	10.11%	57471	91.30%
83.00 - 83.99	880	1.40%	7243	11.51%	56585	89.89%
82.00 - 82.99	936	1.49%	8179	12.99%	55705	88.49%
81.00 - 81.99	902	1.43%	9081	14.43%	54769	87.01%
80.00 - 80.99	949	1.51%	10030	15.93%	53867	85.57%
79.00 - 79.99	947	1.50%	10977	17.44%	52918	84.07%
78.00 - 78.99	913	1.45%	11890	18.89%	51971	82.56%
77.00 - 77.99	933	1.48%	12823	20.37%	51058	81.11%
76.00 - 76.99	971	1.54%	13794	21.91%	50125	79.63%
75.00 - 75.99	962	1.53%	14756	23.44%	49154	78.09%
74.00 - 74.99	922	1.46%	15678	24.91%	48192	76.56%
73.00 - 73.99	925	1.47%	16603	26.38%	47270	75.09%
72.00 - 72.99	925	1.47%	17528	27.85%	46345	73.62%
71.00 - 71.99	886	1.41%	18414	29.25%	45420	72.15%
70.00 - 70.99	890	1.41%	19304	30.67%	44534	70.75%
69.00 - 69.99	897	1.42%	20201	32.09%	43644	69.33%
68.00 - 68.99	925	1.47%	21126	33.56%	42747	67.91%
67.00 - 67.99	901	1.43%	22027	34.99%	41822	66.44%
66.00 - 66.99	864	1.37%	22891	36.36%	40921	65.01%
65.00 - 65.99	926	1.47%	23817	37.84%	40057	63.64%
64.00 - 64.99	829	1.32%	24646	39.15%	39131	62.16%
63.00 - 63.99	908	1.44%	25554	40.60%	38302	60.85%
62.00 - 62.99	900	1.43%	26454	42.03%	37394	59.40%
61.00 - 61.99	838	1.33%	27292	43.36%	36494	57.97%
60.00 - 60.99	922	1.46%	28214	44.82%	35656	56.64%
59.00 - 59.99	902	1.43%	29116	46.25%	34734	55.18%
58.00 - 58.99	878	1.39%	29994	47.65%	33832	53.75%
57.00 - 57.99	859	1.36%	30853	49.01%	32954	52.35%
56.00 - 56.99	899	1.43%	31752	50.44%	32095	50.99%
55.00 - 55.99	868	1.38%	32620	51.82%	31196	49.56%
54.00 - 54.99	951	1.51%	33571	53.33%	30328	48.18%
53.00 - 53.99	917	1.46%	34488	54.79%	29377	46.67%
52.00 - 52.99	886	1.41%	35374	56.20%	28460	45.21%

51.00 - 51.99	925	1.47%	36299	57.67%	27574	43.80%
50.00 - 50.99	895	1.42%	37194	59.09%	26649	42.33%
49.00 - 49.99	904	1.44%	38098	60.52%	25754	40.91%
48.00 - 48.99	914	1.45%	39012	61.97%	24850	39.48%
47.00 - 47.99	883	1.40%	39895	63.38%	23936	38.03%
46.00 - 46.99	836	1.33%	40731	64.71%	23053	36.62%
45.00 - 45.99	927	1.47%	41658	66.18%	22217	35.29%
44.00 - 44.99	864	1.37%	42522	67.55%	21290	33.82%
43.00 - 43.99	849	1.35%	43371	68.90%	20426	32.45%
42.00 - 42.99	846	1.34%	44217	70.24%	19577	31.10%
41.00 - 41.99	795	1.26%	45012	71.51%	18731	29.76%
40.00 - 40.99	817	1.30%	45829	72.80%	17936	28.49%
39.00 - 39.99	858	1.36%	46687	74.17%	17119	27.20%
38.00 - 38.99	759	1.21%	47446	75.37%	16261	25.83%
37.00 - 37.99	748	1.19%	48194	76.56%	15502	24.63%
36.00 - 36.99	765	1.22%	48959	77.78%	14754	23.44%
35.00 - 35.99	775	1.23%	49734	79.01%	13989	22.22%
34.00 - 34.99	761	1.21%	50495	80.22%	13214	20.99%
33.00 - 33.99	713	1.13%	51208	81.35%	12453	19.78%
32.00 - 32.99	696	1.11%	51904	82.46%	11740	18.65%
31.00 - 31.99	694	1.10%	52598	83.56%	11044	17.54%
30.00 - 30.99	697	1.11%	53295	84.67%	10350	16.44%
29.00 - 29.99	666	1.06%	53961	85.72%	9653	15.33%
28.00 - 28.99	653	1.04%	54614	86.76%	8987	14.28%
27.00 - 27.99	679	1.08%	55293	87.84%	8334	13.24%
26.00 - 26.99	674	1.07%	55967	88.91%	7655	12.16%
25.00 - 25.99	643	1.02%	56610	89.93%	6981	11.09%
24.00 - 24.99	613	0.97%	57223	90.91%	6338	10.07%
23.00 - 23.99	582	0.92%	57805	91.83%	5725	9.09%
22.00 - 22.99	575	0.91%	58380	92.74%	5143	8.17%
21.00 - 21.99	553	0.88%	58933	93.62%	4568	7.26%
20.00 - 20.99	545	0.87%	59478	94.49%	4015	6.38%
19.00 - 19.99	546	0.87%	60024	95.35%	3470	5.51%
18.00 - 18.99	501	0.80%	60525	96.15%	2924	4.65%
17.00 - 17.99	455	0.72%	60980	96.87%	2423	3.85%
16.00 - 16.99	431	0.68%	61411	97.56%	1968	3.13%
15.00 - 15.99	395	0.63%	61806	98.19%	1537	2.44%
14.00 - 14.99	295	0.47%	62101	98.65%	1142	1.81%
13.00 - 13.99	233	0.37%	62334	99.02%	847	1.35%
12.00 - 12.99	208	0.33%	62542	99.36%	614	0.98%
11.00 - 11.99	135	0.21%	62677	99.57%	406	0.64%
10.00 - 10.99	86	0.14%	62763	99.71%	271	0.43%
9.00 - 9.99	83	0.13%	62846	99.84%	185	0.29%
8.00 - 8.99	42	0.07%	62888	99.90%	102	0.16%
7.00 - 7.99	26	0.04%	62914	99.95%	60	0.10%
6.00 - 6.99	12	0.02%	62926	99.97%	34	0.05%
5.00 - 5.99	10	0.02%	62936	99.98%	22	0.03%
4.00 - 4.99	6	0.01%	62942	99.99%	12	0.02%
3.00 - 3.99	2	0.00%	62944	99.99%	6	0.01%
2.00 - 2.99	0	0.00%	62944	99.99%	4	0.01%
1.00 - 1.99	1	0.00%	62945	100.00%	4	0.01%
0.00 - 0.99	3	0.00%	62948	100.00%	3	0.00%
缺考	3018					

102 年指定科目考試數學科(甲)成績人數累計表

分　數	人　數	百分比	自高分往低分累計		自低分往高分累計	
			累計人數	累計百分比	累計人數	累計百分比
100.00	77	0.26%	77	0.26%	29170	100.00%
99.00 - 99.99	8	0.03%	85	0.29%	29093	99.74%
98.00 - 98.99	40	0.14%	125	0.43%	29085	99.71%
97.00 - 97.99	10	0.03%	135	0.46%	29045	99.57%
96.00 - 96.99	103	0.35%	238	0.82%	29035	99.54%
95.00 - 95.99	29	0.10%	267	0.92%	28932	99.18%
94.00 - 94.99	107	0.37%	374	1.28%	28903	99.08%
93.00 - 93.99	123	0.42%	497	1.70%	28796	98.72%
92.00 - 92.99	97	0.33%	594	2.04%	28673	98.30%
91.00 - 91.99	117	0.40%	711	2.44%	28576	97.96%
90.00 - 90.99	162	0.56%	873	2.99%	28459	97.56%
89.00 - 89.99	163	0.56%	1036	3.55%	28297	97.01%
88.00 - 88.99	189	0.65%	1225	4.20%	28134	96.45%
87.00 - 87.99	175	0.60%	1400	4.80%	27945	95.80%
86.00 - 86.99	186	0.64%	1586	5.44%	27770	95.20%
85.00 - 85.99	211	0.72%	1797	6.16%	27584	94.56%
84.00 - 84.99	215	0.74%	2012	6.90%	27373	93.84%
83.00 - 83.99	219	0.75%	2231	7.65%	27158	93.10%
82.00 - 82.99	227	0.78%	2458	8.43%	26939	92.35%
81.00 - 81.99	258	0.88%	2716	9.31%	26712	91.57%
80.00 - 80.99	278	0.95%	2994	10.26%	26454	90.69%
79.00 - 79.99	282	0.97%	3276	11.23%	26176	89.74%
78.00 - 78.99	321	1.10%	3597	12.33%	25894	88.77%
77.00 - 77.99	323	1.11%	3920	13.44%	25573	87.67%
76.00 - 76.99	328	1.12%	4248	14.56%	25250	86.56%
75.00 - 75.99	338	1.16%	4586	15.72%	24922	85.44%
74.00 - 74.99	363	1.24%	4949	16.97%	24584	84.28%
73.00 - 73.99	368	1.26%	5317	18.23%	24221	83.03%
72.00 - 72.99	375	1.29%	5692	19.51%	23853	81.77%
71.00 - 71.99	384	1.32%	6076	20.83%	23478	80.49%
70.00 - 70.99	389	1.33%	6465	22.16%	23094	79.17%
69.00 - 69.99	386	1.32%	6851	23.49%	22705	77.84%
68.00 - 68.99	369	1.26%	7220	24.75%	22319	76.51%
67.00 - 67.99	407	1.40%	7627	26.15%	21950	75.25%
66.00 - 66.99	386	1.32%	8013	27.47%	21543	73.85%
65.00 - 65.99	387	1.33%	8400	28.80%	21157	72.53%
64.00 - 64.99	411	1.41%	8811	30.21%	20770	71.20%
63.00 - 63.99	425	1.46%	9236	31.66%	20359	69.79%
62.00 - 62.99	456	1.56%	9692	33.23%	19934	68.34%
61.00 - 61.99	421	1.44%	10113	34.67%	19478	66.77%
60.00 - 60.99	459	1.57%	10572	36.24%	19057	65.33%
59.00 - 59.99	434	1.49%	11006	37.73%	18598	63.76%
58.00 - 58.99	438	1.50%	11444	39.23%	18164	62.27%
57.00 - 57.99	452	1.55%	11896	40.78%	17726	60.77%
56.00 - 56.99	418	1.43%	12314	42.21%	17274	59.22%
55.00 - 55.99	452	1.55%	12766	43.76%	16856	57.79%
54.00 - 54.99	430	1.47%	13196	45.24%	16404	56.24%
53.00 - 53.99	425	1.46%	13621	46.70%	15974	54.76%
52.00 - 52.99	456	1.56%	14077	48.26%	15549	53.30%

51.00 - 51.99	392	1.34%	14469	49.60%	15093	51.74%
50.00 - 50.99	474	1.62%	14943	51.23%	14701	50.40%
49.00 - 49.99	430	1.47%	15373	52.70%	14227	48.77%
48.00 - 48.99	454	1.56%	15827	54.26%	13797	47.30%
47.00 - 47.99	411	1.41%	16238	55.67%	13343	45.74%
46.00 - 46.99	422	1.45%	16660	57.11%	12932	44.33%
45.00 - 45.99	423	1.45%	17083	58.56%	12510	42.89%
44.00 - 44.99	434	1.49%	17517	60.05%	12087	41.44%
43.00 - 43.99	384	1.32%	17901	61.37%	11653	39.95%
42.00 - 42.99	469	1.61%	18370	62.98%	11269	38.63%
41.00 - 41.99	399	1.37%	18769	64.34%	10800	37.02%
40.00 - 40.99	419	1.44%	19188	65.78%	10401	35.66%
39.00 - 39.99	379	1.30%	19567	67.08%	9982	34.22%
38.00 - 38.99	441	1.51%	20008	68.59%	9603	32.92%
37.00 - 37.99	364	1.25%	20372	69.84%	9162	31.41%
36.00 - 36.99	360	1.23%	20732	71.07%	8798	30.16%
35.00 - 35.99	349	1.20%	21081	72.27%	8438	28.93%
34.00 - 34.99	413	1.42%	21494	73.69%	8089	27.73%
33.00 - 33.99	324	1.11%	21818	74.80%	7676	26.31%
32.00 - 32.99	422	1.45%	22240	76.24%	7352	25.20%
31.00 - 31.99	285	0.98%	22525	77.22%	6930	23.76%
30.00 - 30.99	392	1.34%	22917	78.56%	6645	22.78%
29.00 - 29.99	350	1.20%	23267	79.76%	6253	21.44%
28.00 - 28.99	367	1.26%	23634	81.02%	5903	20.24%
27.00 - 27.99	319	1.09%	23953	82.12%	5536	18.98%
26.00 - 26.99	394	1.35%	24347	83.47%	5217	17.88%
25.00 - 25.99	237	0.81%	24584	84.28%	4823	16.53%
24.00 - 24.99	375	1.29%	24959	85.56%	4586	15.72%
23.00 - 23.99	345	1.18%	25304	86.75%	4211	14.44%
22.00 - 22.99	271	0.93%	25575	87.68%	3866	13.25%
21.00 - 21.99	290	0.99%	25865	88.67%	3595	12.32%
20.00 - 20.99	381	1.31%	26246	89.98%	3305	11.33%
19.00 - 19.99	115	0.39%	26361	90.37%	2924	10.02%
18.00 - 18.99	374	1.28%	26735	91.65%	2809	9.63%
17.00 - 17.99	291	1.00%	27026	92.65%	2435	8.35%
16.00 - 16.99	209	0.72%	27235	93.37%	2144	7.35%
15.00 - 15.99	300	1.03%	27535	94.39%	1935	6.63%
14.00 - 14.99	277	0.95%	27812	95.34%	1635	5.61%
13.00 - 13.99	80	0.27%	27892	95.62%	1358	4.66%
12.00 - 12.99	265	0.91%	28157	96.53%	1278	4.38%
11.00 - 11.99	122	0.42%	28279	96.95%	1013	3.47%
10.00 - 10.99	149	0.51%	28428	97.46%	891	3.05%
9.00 - 9.99	219	0.75%	28647	98.21%	742	2.54%
8.00 - 8.99	122	0.42%	28769	98.63%	523	1.79%
7.00 - 7.99	71	0.24%	28840	98.87%	401	1.37%
6.00 - 6.99	118	0.40%	28958	99.27%	330	1.13%
5.00 - 5.99	6	0.02%	28964	99.29%	212	0.73%
4.00 - 4.99	79	0.27%	29043	99.56%	206	0.71%
3.00 - 3.99	64	0.22%	29107	99.78%	127	0.44%
2.00 - 2.99	0	0.00%	29107	99.78%	63	0.22%
1.00 - 1.99	57	0.20%	29164	99.98%	63	0.22%
0.00 - 0.99	6	0.02%	29170	100.00%	6	0.02%
缺考	1723					

102 年指定科目考試數學科(乙)成績人數累計表

分　　數	人　數	百分比	自高分往低分累計		自低分往高分累計	
			累計人數	累計百分比	累計人數	累計百分比
100.00	308	0.60%	308	0.60%	51363	100.00%
99.00 - 99.99	6	0.01%	314	0.61%	51055	99.40%
98.00 - 98.99	15	0.03%	329	0.64%	51049	99.39%
97.00 - 97.99	48	0.09%	377	0.73%	51034	99.36%
96.00 - 96.99	449	0.87%	826	1.61%	50986	99.27%
95.00 - 95.99	185	0.36%	1011	1.97%	50537	98.39%
94.00 - 94.99	30	0.06%	1041	2.03%	50352	98.03%
93.00 - 93.99	604	1.18%	1645	3.20%	50322	97.97%
92.00 - 92.99	275	0.54%	1920	3.74%	49718	96.80%
91.00 - 91.99	446	0.87%	2366	4.61%	49443	96.26%
90.00 - 90.99	456	0.89%	2822	5.49%	48997	95.39%
89.00 - 89.99	146	0.28%	2968	5.78%	48541	94.51%
88.00 - 88.99	1060	2.06%	4028	7.84%	48395	94.22%
87.00 - 87.99	503	0.98%	4531	8.82%	47335	92.16%
86.00 - 86.99	143	0.28%	4674	9.10%	46832	91.18%
85.00 - 85.99	1280	2.49%	5954	11.59%	46689	90.90%
84.00 - 84.99	328	0.64%	6282	12.23%	45409	88.41%
83.00 - 83.99	590	1.15%	6872	13.38%	45081	87.77%
82.00 - 82.99	1013	1.97%	7885	15.35%	44491	86.62%
81.00 - 81.99	221	0.43%	8106	15.78%	43478	84.65%
80.00 - 80.99	1169	2.28%	9275	18.06%	43257	84.22%
79.00 - 79.99	883	1.72%	10158	19.78%	42088	81.94%
78.00 - 78.99	294	0.57%	10452	20.35%	41205	80.22%
77.00 - 77.99	1362	2.65%	11814	23.00%	40911	79.65%
76.00 - 76.99	491	0.96%	12305	23.96%	39549	77.00%
75.00 - 75.99	629	1.22%	12934	25.18%	39058	76.04%
74.00 - 74.99	1273	2.48%	14207	27.66%	38429	74.82%
73.00 - 73.99	422	0.82%	14629	28.48%	37156	72.34%
72.00 - 72.99	1032	2.01%	15661	30.49%	36734	71.52%
71.00 - 71.99	1040	2.02%	16701	32.52%	35702	69.51%
70.00 - 70.99	403	0.78%	17104	33.30%	34662	67.48%
69.00 - 69.99	1151	2.24%	18255	35.54%	34259	66.70%
68.00 - 68.99	771	1.50%	19026	37.04%	33108	64.46%
67.00 - 67.99	565	1.10%	19591	38.14%	32337	62.96%
66.00 - 66.99	1050	2.04%	20641	40.19%	31772	61.86%
65.00 - 65.99	585	1.14%	21226	41.33%	30722	59.81%
64.00 - 64.99	791	1.54%	22017	42.87%	30137	58.67%
63.00 - 63.99	885	1.72%	22902	44.59%	29346	57.13%
62.00 - 62.99	503	0.98%	23405	45.57%	28461	55.41%
61.00 - 61.99	854	1.66%	24259	47.23%	27958	54.43%
60.00 - 60.99	734	1.43%	24993	48.66%	27104	52.77%
59.00 - 59.99	549	1.07%	25542	49.73%	26370	51.34%
58.00 - 58.99	804	1.57%	26346	51.29%	25821	50.27%
57.00 - 57.99	605	1.18%	26951	52.47%	25017	48.71%
56.00 - 56.99	606	1.18%	27557	53.65%	24412	47.53%
55.00 - 55.99	760	1.48%	28317	55.13%	23806	46.35%
54.00 - 54.99	508	0.99%	28825	56.12%	23046	44.87%
53.00 - 53.99	715	1.39%	29540	57.51%	22538	43.88%
52.00 - 52.99	633	1.23%	30173	58.74%	21823	42.49%

51.00 - 51.99	517	1.01%	30690	59.75%	21190	41.26%
50.00 - 50.99	640	1.25%	31330	61.00%	20673	40.25%
49.00 - 49.99	550	1.07%	31880	62.07%	20033	39.00%
48.00 - 48.99	526	1.02%	32406	63.09%	19483	37.93%
47.00 - 47.99	590	1.15%	32996	64.24%	18957	36.91%
46.00 - 46.99	513	1.00%	33509	65.24%	18367	35.76%
45.00 - 45.99	554	1.08%	34063	66.32%	17854	34.76%
44.00 - 44.99	541	1.05%	34604	67.37%	17300	33.68%
43.00 - 43.99	442	0.86%	35046	68.23%	16759	32.63%
42.00 - 42.99	562	1.09%	35608	69.33%	16317	31.77%
41.00 - 41.99	489	0.95%	36097	70.28%	15755	30.67%
40.00 - 40.99	464	0.90%	36561	71.18%	15266	29.72%
39.00 - 39.99	511	0.99%	37072	72.18%	14802	28.82%
38.00 - 38.99	463	0.90%	37535	73.08%	14291	27.82%
37.00 - 37.99	462	0.90%	37997	73.98%	13828	26.92%
36.00 - 36.99	560	1.09%	38557	75.07%	13366	26.02%
35.00 - 35.99	373	0.73%	38930	75.79%	12806	24.93%
34.00 - 34.99	523	1.02%	39453	76.81%	12433	24.21%
33.00 - 33.99	454	0.88%	39907	77.70%	11910	23.19%
32.00 - 32.99	444	0.86%	40351	78.56%	11456	22.30%
31.00 - 31.99	506	0.99%	40857	79.55%	11012	21.44%
30.00 - 30.99	481	0.94%	41338	80.48%	10506	20.45%
29.00 - 29.99	386	0.75%	41724	81.23%	10025	19.52%
28.00 - 28.99	571	1.11%	42295	82.35%	9639	18.77%
27.00 - 27.99	292	0.57%	42587	82.91%	9068	17.65%
26.00 - 26.99	526	1.02%	43113	83.94%	8776	17.09%
25.00 - 25.99	519	1.01%	43632	84.95%	8250	16.06%
24.00 - 24.99	413	0.80%	44045	85.75%	7731	15.05%
23.00 - 23.99	540	1.05%	44585	86.80%	7318	14.25%
22.00 - 22.99	512	1.00%	45097	87.80%	6778	13.20%
21.00 - 21.99	255	0.50%	45352	88.30%	6266	12.20%
20.00 - 20.99	694	1.35%	46046	89.65%	6011	11.70%
19.00 - 19.99	216	0.42%	46262	90.07%	5317	10.35%
18.00 - 18.99	523	1.02%	46785	91.09%	5101	9.93%
17.00 - 17.99	573	1.12%	47358	92.20%	4578	8.91%
16.00 - 16.99	312	0.61%	47670	92.81%	4005	7.80%
15.00 - 15.99	458	0.89%	48128	93.70%	3693	7.19%
14.00 - 14.99	573	1.12%	48701	94.82%	3235	6.30%
13.00 - 13.99	62	0.12%	48763	94.94%	2662	5.18%
12.00 - 12.99	528	1.03%	49291	95.97%	2600	5.06%
11.00 - 11.99	216	0.42%	49507	96.39%	2072	4.03%
10.00 - 10.99	316	0.62%	49823	97.00%	1856	3.61%
9.00 - 9.99	436	0.85%	50259	97.85%	1540	3.00%
8.00 - 8.99	204	0.40%	50463	98.25%	1104	2.15%
7.00 - 7.99	158	0.31%	50621	98.56%	900	1.75%
6.00 - 6.99	251	0.49%	50872	99.04%	742	1.44%
5.00 - 5.99	12	0.02%	50884	99.07%	491	0.96%
4.00 - 4.99	136	0.26%	51020	99.33%	479	0.93%
3.00 - 3.99	181	0.35%	51201	99.68%	343	0.67%
2.00 - 2.99	4	0.01%	51205	99.69%	162	0.32%
1.00 - 1.99	123	0.24%	51328	99.93%	158	0.31%
0.00 - 0.99	35	0.07%	51363	100.00%	35	0.07%
缺考	3054					

102 年指定科目考試地理科成績人數累計表

分　　數	人　數	百分比	自高分往低分累計		自低分往高分累計	
			累計人數	累計百分比	累計人數	累計百分比
100.00	0	0.00%	0	0.00%	38314	100.00%
99.00 - 99.99	0	0.00%	0	0.00%	38314	100.00%
98.00 - 98.99	0	0.00%	0	0.00%	38314	100.00%
97.00 - 97.99	0	0.00%	0	0.00%	38314	100.00%
96.00 - 96.99	4	0.01%	4	0.01%	38314	100.00%
95.00 - 95.99	1	0.00%	5	0.01%	38310	99.99%
94.00 - 94.99	3	0.01%	8	0.02%	38309	99.99%
93.00 - 93.99	1	0.00%	9	0.02%	38306	99.98%
92.00 - 92.99	22	0.06%	31	0.08%	38305	99.98%
91.00 - 91.99	9	0.02%	40	0.10%	38283	99.92%
90.00 - 90.99	72	0.19%	112	0.29%	38274	99.90%
89.00 - 89.99	27	0.07%	139	0.36%	38202	99.71%
88.00 - 88.99	121	0.32%	260	0.68%	38175	99.64%
87.00 - 87.99	52	0.14%	312	0.81%	38054	99.32%
86.00 - 86.99	238	0.62%	550	1.44%	38002	99.19%
85.00 - 85.99	76	0.20%	626	1.63%	37764	98.56%
84.00 - 84.99	374	0.98%	1000	2.61%	37688	98.37%
83.00 - 83.99	101	0.26%	1101	2.87%	37314	97.39%
82.00 - 82.99	531	1.39%	1632	4.26%	37213	97.13%
81.00 - 81.99	184	0.48%	1816	4.74%	36682	95.74%
80.00 - 80.99	728	1.90%	2544	6.64%	36498	95.26%
79.00 - 79.99	223	0.58%	2767	7.22%	35770	93.36%
78.00 - 78.99	955	2.49%	3722	9.71%	35547	92.78%
77.00 - 77.99	281	0.73%	4003	10.45%	34592	90.29%
76.00 - 76.99	1124	2.93%	5127	13.38%	34311	89.55%
75.00 - 75.99	350	0.91%	5477	14.30%	33187	86.62%
74.00 - 74.99	1356	3.54%	6833	17.83%	32837	85.70%
73.00 - 73.99	382	1.00%	7215	18.83%	31481	82.17%
72.00 - 72.99	1452	3.79%	8667	22.62%	31099	81.17%
71.00 - 71.99	407	1.06%	9074	23.68%	29647	77.38%
70.00 - 70.99	1598	4.17%	10672	27.85%	29240	76.32%
69.00 - 69.99	469	1.22%	11141	29.08%	27642	72.15%
68.00 - 68.99	1606	4.19%	12747	33.27%	27173	70.92%
67.00 - 67.99	432	1.13%	13179	34.40%	25567	66.73%
66.00 - 66.99	1728	4.51%	14907	38.91%	25135	65.60%
65.00 - 65.99	476	1.24%	15383	40.15%	23407	61.09%
64.00 - 64.99	1694	4.42%	17077	44.57%	22931	59.85%
63.00 - 63.99	443	1.16%	17520	45.73%	21237	55.43%
62.00 - 62.99	1760	4.59%	19280	50.32%	20794	54.27%
61.00 - 61.99	488	1.27%	19768	51.59%	19034	49.68%
60.00 - 60.99	1687	4.40%	21455	56.00%	18546	48.41%
59.00 - 59.99	409	1.07%	21864	57.07%	16859	44.00%
58.00 - 58.99	1670	4.36%	23534	61.42%	16450	42.93%
57.00 - 57.99	391	1.02%	23925	62.44%	14780	38.58%
56.00 - 56.99	1632	4.26%	25557	66.70%	14389	37.56%
55.00 - 55.99	319	0.83%	25876	67.54%	12757	33.30%
54.00 - 54.99	1456	3.80%	27332	71.34%	12438	32.46%
53.00 - 53.99	250	0.65%	27582	71.99%	10982	28.66%
52.00 - 52.99	1376	3.59%	28958	75.58%	10732	28.01%

51.00 - 51.99	236	0.62%	29194	76.20%	9356	24.42%
50.00 - 50.99	1253	3.27%	30447	79.47%	9120	23.80%
49.00 - 49.99	185	0.48%	30632	79.95%	7867	20.53%
48.00 - 48.99	1107	2.89%	31739	82.84%	7682	20.05%
47.00 - 47.99	157	0.41%	31896	83.25%	6575	17.16%
46.00 - 46.99	967	2.52%	32863	85.77%	6418	16.75%
45.00 - 45.99	106	0.28%	32969	86.05%	5451	14.23%
44.00 - 44.99	849	2.22%	33818	88.27%	5345	13.95%
43.00 - 43.99	88	0.23%	33906	88.50%	4496	11.73%
42.00 - 42.99	712	1.86%	34618	90.35%	4408	11.50%
41.00 - 41.99	69	0.18%	34687	90.53%	3696	9.65%
40.00 - 40.99	695	1.81%	35382	92.35%	3627	9.47%
39.00 - 39.99	62	0.16%	35444	92.51%	2932	7.65%
38.00 - 38.99	550	1.44%	35994	93.94%	2870	7.49%
37.00 - 37.99	35	0.09%	36029	94.04%	2320	6.06%
36.00 - 36.99	441	1.15%	36470	95.19%	2285	5.96%
35.00 - 35.99	29	0.08%	36499	95.26%	1844	4.81%
34.00 - 34.99	369	0.96%	36868	96.23%	1815	4.74%
33.00 - 33.99	22	0.06%	36890	96.28%	1446	3.77%
32.00 - 32.99	325	0.85%	37215	97.13%	1424	3.72%
31.00 - 31.99	18	0.05%	37233	97.18%	1099	2.87%
30.00 - 30.99	278	0.73%	37511	97.90%	1081	2.82%
29.00 - 29.99	13	0.03%	37524	97.94%	803	2.10%
28.00 - 28.99	229	0.60%	37753	98.54%	790	2.06%
27.00 - 27.99	13	0.03%	37766	98.57%	561	1.46%
26.00 - 26.99	161	0.42%	37927	98.99%	548	1.43%
25.00 - 25.99	9	0.02%	37936	99.01%	387	1.01%
24.00 - 24.99	125	0.33%	38061	99.34%	378	0.99%
23.00 - 23.99	3	0.01%	38064	99.35%	253	0.66%
22.00 - 22.99	79	0.21%	38143	99.55%	250	0.65%
21.00 - 21.99	1	0.00%	38144	99.56%	171	0.45%
20.00 - 20.99	60	0.16%	38204	99.71%	170	0.44%
19.00 - 19.99	0	0.00%	38204	99.71%	110	0.29%
18.00 - 18.99	51	0.13%	38255	99.85%	110	0.29%
17.00 - 17.99	0	0.00%	38255	99.85%	59	0.15%
16.00 - 16.99	31	0.08%	38286	99.93%	59	0.15%
15.00 - 15.99	0	0.00%	38286	99.93%	28	0.07%
14.00 - 14.99	13	0.03%	38299	99.96%	28	0.07%
13.00 - 13.99	0	0.00%	38299	99.96%	15	0.04%
12.00 - 12.99	5	0.01%	38304	99.97%	15	0.04%
11.00 - 11.99	0	0.00%	38304	99.97%	10	0.03%
10.00 - 10.99	5	0.01%	38309	99.99%	10	0.03%
9.00 - 9.99	0	0.00%	38309	99.99%	5	0.01%
8.00 - 8.99	0	0.00%	38309	99.99%	5	0.01%
7.00 - 7.99	0	0.00%	38309	99.99%	5	0.01%
6.00 - 6.99	2	0.01%	38311	99.99%	5	0.01%
5.00 - 5.99	0	0.00%	38311	99.99%	3	0.01%
4.00 - 4.99	0	0.00%	38311	99.99%	3	0.01%
3.00 - 3.99	0	0.00%	38311	99.99%	3	0.01%
2.00 - 2.99	0	0.00%	38311	99.99%	3	0.01%
1.00 - 1.99	0	0.00%	38311	99.99%	3	0.01%
0.00 - 0.99	3	0.01%	38314	100.00%	3	0.01%
缺考	2212					

102 年指定科目考試歷史科成績人數累計表

分　　數	人　數	百 分 比	自高分往低分累計		自低分往高分累計	
			累計人數	累計百分比	累計人數	累計百分比
100.00	0	0.00%	0	0.00%	38512	100.00%
99.00 - 99.99	0	0.00%	0	0.00%	38512	100.00%
98.00 - 98.99	4	0.01%	4	0.01%	38512	100.00%
97.00 - 97.99	7	0.02%	11	0.03%	38508	99.99%
96.00 - 96.99	13	0.03%	24	0.06%	38501	99.97%
95.00 - 95.99	20	0.05%	44	0.11%	38488	99.94%
94.00 - 94.99	23	0.06%	67	0.17%	38468	99.89%
93.00 - 93.99	62	0.16%	129	0.33%	38445	99.83%
92.00 - 92.99	79	0.21%	208	0.54%	38383	99.67%
91.00 - 91.99	115	0.30%	323	0.84%	38304	99.46%
90.00 - 90.99	135	0.35%	458	1.19%	38189	99.16%
89.00 - 89.99	232	0.60%	690	1.79%	38054	98.81%
88.00 - 88.99	185	0.48%	875	2.27%	37822	98.21%
87.00 - 87.99	333	0.86%	1208	3.14%	37637	97.73%
86.00 - 86.99	324	0.84%	1532	3.98%	37304	96.86%
85.00 - 85.99	419	1.09%	1951	5.07%	36980	96.02%
84.00 - 84.99	398	1.03%	2349	6.10%	36561	94.93%
83.00 - 83.99	583	1.51%	2932	7.61%	36163	93.90%
82.00 - 82.99	551	1.43%	3483	9.04%	35580	92.39%
81.00 - 81.99	613	1.59%	4096	10.64%	35029	90.96%
80.00 - 80.99	587	1.52%	4683	12.16%	34416	89.36%
79.00 - 79.99	820	2.13%	5503	14.29%	33829	87.84%
78.00 - 78.99	723	1.88%	6226	16.17%	33009	85.71%
77.00 - 77.99	810	2.10%	7036	18.27%	32286	83.83%
76.00 - 76.99	770	2.00%	7806	20.27%	31476	81.73%
75.00 - 75.99	871	2.26%	8677	22.53%	30706	79.73%
74.00 - 74.99	791	2.05%	9468	24.58%	29835	77.47%
73.00 - 73.99	992	2.58%	10460	27.16%	29044	75.42%
72.00 - 72.99	897	2.33%	11357	29.49%	28052	72.84%
71.00 - 71.99	945	2.45%	12302	31.94%	27155	70.51%
70.00 - 70.99	895	2.32%	13197	34.27%	26210	68.06%
69.00 - 69.99	934	2.43%	14131	36.69%	25315	65.73%
68.00 - 68.99	906	2.35%	15037	39.04%	24381	63.31%
67.00 - 67.99	960	2.49%	15997	41.54%	23475	60.96%
66.00 - 66.99	891	2.31%	16888	43.85%	22515	58.46%
65.00 - 65.99	908	2.36%	17796	46.21%	21624	56.15%
64.00 - 64.99	916	2.38%	18712	48.59%	20716	53.79%
63.00 - 63.99	932	2.42%	19644	51.01%	19800	51.41%
62.00 - 62.99	823	2.14%	20467	53.14%	18868	48.99%
61.00 - 61.99	839	2.18%	21306	55.32%	18045	46.86%
60.00 - 60.99	857	2.23%	22163	57.55%	17206	44.68%
59.00 - 59.99	846	2.20%	23009	59.75%	16349	42.45%
58.00 - 58.99	785	2.04%	23794	61.78%	15503	40.25%
57.00 - 57.99	818	2.12%	24612	63.91%	14718	38.22%
56.00 - 56.99	733	1.90%	25345	65.81%	13900	36.09%
55.00 - 55.99	719	1.87%	26064	67.68%	13167	34.19%
54.00 - 54.99	712	1.85%	26776	69.53%	12448	32.32%
53.00 - 53.99	779	2.02%	27555	71.55%	11736	30.47%
52.00 - 52.99	659	1.71%	28214	73.26%	10957	28.45%

51.00 - 51.99	645	1.67%	28859	74.94%	10298	26.74%
50.00 - 50.99	645	1.67%	29504	76.61%	9653	25.06%
49.00 - 49.99	638	1.66%	30142	78.27%	9008	23.39%
48.00 - 48.99	559	1.45%	30701	79.72%	8370	21.73%
47.00 - 47.99	567	1.47%	31268	81.19%	7811	20.28%
46.00 - 46.99	533	1.38%	31801	82.57%	7244	18.81%
45.00 - 45.99	478	1.24%	32279	83.82%	6711	17.43%
44.00 - 44.99	516	1.34%	32795	85.16%	6233	16.18%
43.00 - 43.99	454	1.18%	33249	86.33%	5717	14.84%
42.00 - 42.99	418	1.09%	33667	87.42%	5263	13.67%
41.00 - 41.99	377	0.98%	34044	88.40%	4845	12.58%
40.00 - 40.99	376	0.98%	34420	89.37%	4468	11.60%
39.00 - 39.99	312	0.81%	34732	90.18%	4092	10.63%
38.00 - 38.99	339	0.88%	35071	91.07%	3780	9.82%
37.00 - 37.99	318	0.83%	35389	91.89%	3441	8.93%
36.00 - 36.99	309	0.80%	35698	92.69%	3123	8.11%
35.00 - 35.99	266	0.69%	35964	93.38%	2814	7.31%
34.00 - 34.99	259	0.67%	36223	94.06%	2548	6.62%
33.00 - 33.99	244	0.63%	36467	94.69%	2289	5.94%
32.00 - 32.99	227	0.59%	36694	95.28%	2045	5.31%
31.00 - 31.99	186	0.48%	36880	95.76%	1818	4.72%
30.00 - 30.99	177	0.46%	37057	96.22%	1632	4.24%
29.00 - 29.99	182	0.47%	37239	96.69%	1455	3.78%
28.00 - 28.99	198	0.51%	37437	97.21%	1273	3.31%
27.00 - 27.99	129	0.33%	37566	97.54%	1075	2.79%
26.00 - 26.99	154	0.40%	37720	97.94%	946	2.46%
25.00 - 25.99	117	0.30%	37837	98.25%	792	2.06%
24.00 - 24.99	132	0.34%	37969	98.59%	675	1.75%
23.00 - 23.99	89	0.23%	38058	98.82%	543	1.41%
22.00 - 22.99	96	0.25%	38154	99.07%	454	1.18%
21.00 - 21.99	62	0.16%	38216	99.23%	358	0.93%
20.00 - 20.99	72	0.19%	38288	99.42%	296	0.77%
19.00 - 19.99	49	0.13%	38337	99.55%	224	0.58%
18.00 - 18.99	45	0.12%	38382	99.66%	175	0.45%
17.00 - 17.99	29	0.08%	38411	99.74%	130	0.34%
16.00 - 16.99	34	0.09%	38445	99.83%	101	0.26%
15.00 - 15.99	19	0.05%	38464	99.88%	67	0.17%
14.00 - 14.99	15	0.04%	38479	99.91%	48	0.12%
13.00 - 13.99	4	0.01%	38483	99.92%	33	0.09%
12.00 - 12.99	5	0.01%	38488	99.94%	29	0.08%
11.00 - 11.99	8	0.02%	38496	99.96%	24	0.06%
10.00 - 10.99	6	0.02%	38502	99.97%	16	0.04%
9.00 - 9.99	1	0.00%	38503	99.98%	10	0.03%
8.00 - 8.99	1	0.00%	38504	99.98%	9	0.02%
7.00 - 7.99	0	0.00%	38504	99.98%	8	0.02%
6.00 - 6.99	1	0.00%	38505	99.98%	8	0.02%
5.00 - 5.99	1	0.00%	38506	99.98%	7	0.02%
4.00 - 4.99	0	0.00%	38506	99.98%	6	0.02%
3.00 - 3.99	0	0.00%	38506	99.98%	6	0.02%
2.00 - 2.99	1	0.00%	38507	99.99%	6	0.02%
1.00 - 1.99	1	0.00%	38508	99.99%	5	0.01%
0.00 - 0.99	4	0.01%	38512	100.00%	4	0.01%
缺考	2249					

102 年指定科目考試公民與社會科成績人數累計表

分　　數	人　數	百分比	自高分往低分累計		自低分往高分累計	
			累計人數	累計百分比	累計人數	累計百分比
100.00	0	0.00%	0	0.00%	33052	100.00%
99.00 - 99.99	3	0.01%	3	0.01%	33052	100.00%
98.00 - 98.99	7	0.02%	10	0.03%	33049	99.99%
97.00 - 97.99	7	0.02%	17	0.05%	33042	99.97%
96.00 - 96.99	31	0.09%	48	0.15%	33035	99.95%
95.00 - 95.99	29	0.09%	77	0.23%	33004	99.85%
94.00 - 94.99	71	0.21%	148	0.45%	32975	99.77%
93.00 - 93.99	68	0.21%	216	0.65%	32904	99.55%
92.00 - 92.99	152	0.46%	368	1.11%	32836	99.35%
91.00 - 91.99	150	0.45%	518	1.57%	32684	98.89%
90.00 - 90.99	291	0.88%	809	2.45%	32534	98.43%
89.00 - 89.99	193	0.58%	1002	3.03%	32243	97.55%
88.00 - 88.99	408	1.23%	1410	4.27%	32050	96.97%
87.00 - 87.99	258	0.78%	1668	5.05%	31642	95.73%
86.00 - 86.99	537	1.62%	2205	6.67%	31384	94.95%
85.00 - 85.99	387	1.17%	2592	7.84%	30847	93.33%
84.00 - 84.99	664	2.01%	3256	9.85%	30460	92.16%
83.00 - 83.99	451	1.36%	3707	11.22%	29796	90.15%
82.00 - 82.99	760	2.30%	4467	13.52%	29345	88.78%
81.00 - 81.99	508	1.54%	4975	15.05%	28585	86.48%
80.00 - 80.99	837	2.53%	5812	17.58%	28077	84.95%
79.00 - 79.99	559	1.69%	6371	19.28%	27240	82.42%
78.00 - 78.99	929	2.81%	7300	22.09%	26681	80.72%
77.00 - 77.99	638	1.93%	7938	24.02%	25752	77.91%
76.00 - 76.99	958	2.90%	8896	26.92%	25114	75.98%
75.00 - 75.99	676	2.05%	9572	28.96%	24156	73.08%
74.00 - 74.99	1039	3.14%	10611	32.10%	23480	71.04%
73.00 - 73.99	730	2.21%	11341	34.31%	22441	67.90%
72.00 - 72.99	1046	3.16%	12387	37.48%	21711	65.69%
71.00 - 71.99	711	2.15%	13098	39.63%	20665	62.52%
70.00 - 70.99	1093	3.31%	14191	42.94%	19954	60.37%
69.00 - 69.99	729	2.21%	14920	45.14%	18861	57.06%
68.00 - 68.99	1046	3.16%	15966	48.31%	18132	54.86%
67.00 - 67.99	729	2.21%	16695	50.51%	17086	51.69%
66.00 - 66.99	1111	3.36%	17806	53.87%	16357	49.49%
65.00 - 65.99	689	2.08%	18495	55.96%	15246	46.13%
64.00 - 64.99	1019	3.08%	19514	59.04%	14557	44.04%
63.00 - 63.99	707	2.14%	20221	61.18%	13538	40.96%
62.00 - 62.99	1048	3.17%	21269	64.35%	12831	38.82%
61.00 - 61.99	618	1.87%	21887	66.22%	11783	35.65%
60.00 - 60.99	893	2.70%	22780	68.92%	11165	33.78%
59.00 - 59.99	583	1.76%	23363	70.69%	10272	31.08%
58.00 - 58.99	884	2.67%	24247	73.36%	9689	29.31%
57.00 - 57.99	474	1.43%	24721	74.79%	8805	26.64%
56.00 - 56.99	797	2.41%	25518	77.21%	8331	25.21%
55.00 - 55.99	517	1.56%	26035	78.77%	7534	22.79%
54.00 - 54.99	717	2.17%	26752	80.94%	7017	21.23%
53.00 - 53.99	449	1.36%	27201	82.30%	6300	19.06%
52.00 - 52.99	643	1.95%	27844	84.24%	5851	17.70%

51.00 - 51.99	377	1.14%	28221	85.38%	5208	15.76%
50.00 - 50.99	546	1.65%	28767	87.04%	4831	14.62%
49.00 - 49.99	363	1.10%	29130	88.13%	4285	12.96%
48.00 - 48.99	482	1.46%	29612	89.59%	3922	11.87%
47.00 - 47.99	271	0.82%	29883	90.41%	3440	10.41%
46.00 - 46.99	378	1.14%	30261	91.56%	3169	9.59%
45.00 - 45.99	249	0.75%	30510	92.31%	2791	8.44%
44.00 - 44.99	333	1.01%	30843	93.32%	2542	7.69%
43.00 - 43.99	228	0.69%	31071	94.01%	2209	6.68%
42.00 - 42.99	292	0.88%	31363	94.89%	1981	5.99%
41.00 - 41.99	191	0.58%	31554	95.47%	1689	5.11%
40.00 - 40.99	211	0.64%	31765	96.11%	1498	4.53%
39.00 - 39.99	119	0.36%	31884	96.47%	1287	3.89%
38.00 - 38.99	206	0.62%	32090	97.09%	1168	3.53%
37.00 - 37.99	107	0.32%	32197	97.41%	962	2.91%
36.00 - 36.99	155	0.47%	32352	97.88%	855	2.59%
35.00 - 35.99	105	0.32%	32457	98.20%	700	2.12%
34.00 - 34.99	113	0.34%	32570	98.54%	595	1.80%
33.00 - 33.99	69	0.21%	32639	98.75%	482	1.46%
32.00 - 32.99	82	0.25%	32721	99.00%	413	1.25%
31.00 - 31.99	36	0.11%	32757	99.11%	331	1.00%
30.00 - 30.99	61	0.18%	32818	99.29%	295	0.89%
29.00 - 29.99	39	0.12%	32857	99.41%	234	0.71%
28.00 - 28.99	36	0.11%	32893	99.52%	195	0.59%
27.00 - 27.99	23	0.07%	32916	99.59%	159	0.48%
26.00 - 26.99	31	0.09%	32947	99.68%	136	0.41%
25.00 - 25.99	14	0.04%	32961	99.72%	105	0.32%
24.00 - 24.99	18	0.05%	32979	99.78%	91	0.28%
23.00 - 23.99	13	0.04%	32992	99.82%	73	0.22%
22.00 - 22.99	20	0.06%	33012	99.88%	60	0.18%
21.00 - 21.99	9	0.03%	33021	99.91%	40	0.12%
20.00 - 20.99	6	0.02%	33027	99.92%	31	0.09%
19.00 - 19.99	2	0.01%	33029	99.93%	25	0.08%
18.00 - 18.99	6	0.02%	33035	99.95%	23	0.07%
17.00 - 17.99	1	0.00%	33036	99.95%	17	0.05%
16.00 - 16.99	2	0.01%	33038	99.96%	16	0.05%
15.00 - 15.99	1	0.00%	33039	99.96%	14	0.04%
14.00 - 14.99	2	0.01%	33041	99.97%	13	0.04%
13.00 - 13.99	2	0.01%	33043	99.97%	11	0.03%
12.00 - 12.99	2	0.01%	33045	99.98%	9	0.03%
11.00 - 11.99	1	0.00%	33046	99.98%	7	0.02%
10.00 - 10.99	2	0.01%	33048	99.99%	6	0.02%
9.00 - 9.99	0	0.00%	33048	99.99%	4	0.01%
8.00 - 8.99	1	0.00%	33049	99.99%	4	0.01%
7.00 - 7.99	0	0.00%	33049	99.99%	3	0.01%
6.00 - 6.99	0	0.00%	33049	99.99%	3	0.01%
5.00 - 5.99	0	0.00%	33049	99.99%	3	0.01%
4.00 - 4.99	0	0.00%	33049	99.99%	3	0.01%
3.00 - 3.99	0	0.00%	33049	99.99%	3	0.01%
2.00 - 2.99	0	0.00%	33049	99.99%	3	0.01%
1.00 - 1.99	1	0.00%	33050	99.99%	3	0.01%
0.00 - 0.99	2	0.01%	33052	100.00%	2	0.01%
缺考	2293				

102 年指定科目考試物理科成績人數累計表

分　　數	人　　數	百 分 比	自高分往低分累計		自低分往高分累計	
			累計人數	累計百分比	累計人數	累計百分比
100.00	7	0.03%	7	0.03%	26710	100.00%
99.00 - 99.99	12	0.04%	19	0.07%	26703	99.97%
98.00 - 98.99	15	0.06%	34	0.13%	26691	99.93%
97.00 - 97.99	35	0.13%	69	0.26%	26676	99.87%
96.00 - 96.99	38	0.14%	107	0.40%	26641	99.74%
95.00 - 95.99	46	0.17%	153	0.57%	26603	99.60%
94.00 - 94.99	71	0.27%	224	0.84%	26557	99.43%
93.00 - 93.99	76	0.28%	300	1.12%	26486	99.16%
92.00 - 92.99	88	0.33%	388	1.45%	26410	98.88%
91.00 - 91.99	111	0.42%	499	1.87%	26322	98.55%
90.00 - 90.99	117	0.44%	616	2.31%	26211	98.13%
89.00 - 89.99	139	0.52%	755	2.83%	26094	97.69%
88.00 - 88.99	156	0.58%	911	3.41%	25955	97.17%
87.00 - 87.99	199	0.75%	1110	4.16%	25799	96.59%
86.00 - 86.99	189	0.71%	1299	4.86%	25600	95.84%
85.00 - 85.99	204	0.76%	1503	5.63%	25411	95.14%
84.00 - 84.99	228	0.85%	1731	6.48%	25207	94.37%
83.00 - 83.99	238	0.89%	1969	7.37%	24979	93.52%
82.00 - 82.99	288	1.08%	2257	8.45%	24741	92.63%
81.00 - 81.99	271	1.01%	2528	9.46%	24453	91.55%
80.00 - 80.99	281	1.05%	2809	10.52%	24182	90.54%
79.00 - 79.99	283	1.06%	3092	11.58%	23901	89.48%
78.00 - 78.99	320	1.20%	3412	12.77%	23618	88.42%
77.00 - 77.99	281	1.05%	3693	13.83%	23298	87.23%
76.00 - 76.99	287	1.07%	3980	14.90%	23017	86.17%
75.00 - 75.99	313	1.17%	4293	16.07%	22730	85.10%
74.00 - 74.99	332	1.24%	4625	17.32%	22417	83.93%
73.00 - 73.99	294	1.10%	4919	18.42%	22085	82.68%
72.00 - 72.99	317	1.19%	5236	19.60%	21791	81.58%
71.00 - 71.99	301	1.13%	5537	20.73%	21474	80.40%
70.00 - 70.99	358	1.34%	5895	22.07%	21173	79.27%
69.00 - 69.99	350	1.31%	6245	23.38%	20815	77.93%
68.00 - 68.99	335	1.25%	6580	24.63%	20465	76.62%
67.00 - 67.99	345	1.29%	6925	25.93%	20130	75.37%
66.00 - 66.99	355	1.33%	7280	27.26%	19785	74.07%
65.00 - 65.99	341	1.28%	7621	28.53%	19430	72.74%
64.00 - 64.99	373	1.40%	7994	29.93%	19089	71.47%
63.00 - 63.99	365	1.37%	8359	31.30%	18716	70.07%
62.00 - 62.99	343	1.28%	8702	32.58%	18351	68.70%
61.00 - 61.99	331	1.24%	9033	33.82%	18008	67.42%
60.00 - 60.99	344	1.29%	9377	35.11%	17677	66.18%
59.00 - 59.99	349	1.31%	9726	36.41%	17333	64.89%
58.00 - 58.99	341	1.28%	10067	37.69%	16984	63.59%
57.00 - 57.99	427	1.60%	10494	39.29%	16643	62.31%
56.00 - 56.99	372	1.39%	10866	40.68%	16216	60.71%
55.00 - 55.99	343	1.28%	11209	41.97%	15844	59.32%
54.00 - 54.99	305	1.14%	11514	43.11%	15501	58.03%
53.00 - 53.99	400	1.50%	11914	44.61%	15196	56.89%
52.00 - 52.99	387	1.45%	12301	46.05%	14796	55.39%

51.00 - 51.99	365	1.37%	12666	47.42%	14409	53.95%
50.00 - 50.99	347	1.30%	13013	48.72%	14044	52.58%
49.00 - 49.99	361	1.35%	13374	50.07%	13697	51.28%
48.00 - 48.99	355	1.33%	13729	51.40%	13336	49.93%
47.00 - 47.99	378	1.42%	14107	52.82%	12981	48.60%
46.00 - 46.99	351	1.31%	14458	54.13%	12603	47.18%
45.00 - 45.99	377	1.41%	14835	55.54%	12252	45.87%
44.00 - 44.99	368	1.38%	15203	56.92%	11875	44.46%
43.00 - 43.99	386	1.45%	15589	58.36%	11507	43.08%
42.00 - 42.99	405	1.52%	15994	59.88%	11121	41.64%
41.00 - 41.99	381	1.43%	16375	61.31%	10716	40.12%
40.00 - 40.99	456	1.71%	16831	63.01%	10335	38.69%
39.00 - 39.99	418	1.56%	17249	64.58%	9879	36.99%
38.00 - 38.99	430	1.61%	17679	66.19%	9461	35.42%
37.00 - 37.99	412	1.54%	18091	67.73%	9031	33.81%
36.00 - 36.99	439	1.64%	18530	69.37%	8619	32.27%
35.00 - 35.99	386	1.45%	18916	70.82%	8180	30.63%
34.00 - 34.99	419	1.57%	19335	72.39%	7794	29.18%
33.00 - 33.99	416	1.56%	19751	73.95%	7375	27.61%
32.00 - 32.99	460	1.72%	20211	75.67%	6959	26.05%
31.00 - 31.99	401	1.50%	20612	77.17%	6499	24.33%
30.00 - 30.99	412	1.54%	21024	78.71%	6098	22.83%
29.00 - 29.99	425	1.59%	21449	80.30%	5686	21.29%
28.00 - 28.99	400	1.50%	21849	81.80%	5261	19.70%
27.00 - 27.99	391	1.46%	22240	83.26%	4861	18.20%
26.00 - 26.99	386	1.45%	22626	84.71%	4470	16.74%
25.00 - 25.99	390	1.46%	23016	86.17%	4084	15.29%
24.00 - 24.99	368	1.38%	23384	87.55%	3694	13.83%
23.00 - 23.99	348	1.30%	23732	88.85%	3326	12.45%
22.00 - 22.99	357	1.34%	24089	90.19%	2978	11.15%
21.00 - 21.99	334	1.25%	24423	91.44%	2621	9.81%
20.00 - 20.99	288	1.08%	24711	92.52%	2287	8.56%
19.00 - 19.99	282	1.06%	24993	93.57%	1999	7.48%
18.00 - 18.99	233	0.87%	25226	94.44%	1717	6.43%
17.00 - 17.99	229	0.86%	25455	95.30%	1484	5.56%
16.00 - 16.99	222	0.83%	25677	96.13%	1255	4.70%
15.00 - 15.99	163	0.61%	25840	96.74%	1033	3.87%
14.00 - 14.99	176	0.66%	26016	97.40%	870	3.26%
13.00 - 13.99	165	0.62%	26181	98.02%	694	2.60%
12.00 - 12.99	137	0.51%	26318	98.53%	529	1.98%
11.00 - 11.99	96	0.36%	26414	98.89%	392	1.47%
10.00 - 10.99	85	0.32%	26499	99.21%	296	1.11%
9.00 - 9.99	62	0.23%	26561	99.44%	211	0.79%
8.00 - 8.99	41	0.15%	26602	99.60%	149	0.56%
7.00 - 7.99	56	0.21%	26658	99.81%	108	0.40%
6.00 - 6.99	20	0.07%	26678	99.88%	52	0.19%
5.00 - 5.99	11	0.04%	26689	99.92%	32	0.12%
4.00 - 4.99	11	0.04%	26700	99.96%	21	0.08%
3.00 - 3.99	3	0.01%	26703	99.97%	10	0.04%
2.00 - 2.99	1	0.00%	26704	99.98%	7	0.03%
1.00 - 1.99	1	0.00%	26705	99.98%	6	0.02%
0.00 - 0.99	5	0.02%	26710	100.00%	5	0.02%
缺考	1336					

102 年指定科目考試化學科成績人數累計表

分　　數	人　數	百分比	自高分往低分累計		自低分往高分累計	
			累計人數	累計百分比	累計人數	累計百分比
100.00	8	0.03%	8	0.03%	27234	100.00%
99.00 - 99.99	3	0.01%	11	0.04%	27226	99.97%
98.00 - 98.99	14	0.05%	25	0.09%	27223	99.96%
97.00 - 97.99	21	0.08%	46	0.17%	27209	99.91%
96.00 - 96.99	30	0.11%	76	0.28%	27188	99.83%
95.00 - 95.99	45	0.17%	121	0.44%	27158	99.72%
94.00 - 94.99	60	0.22%	181	0.66%	27113	99.56%
93.00 - 93.99	96	0.35%	277	1.02%	27053	99.34%
92.00 - 92.99	82	0.30%	359	1.32%	26957	98.98%
91.00 - 91.99	109	0.40%	468	1.72%	26875	98.68%
90.00 - 90.99	129	0.47%	597	2.19%	26766	98.28%
89.00 - 89.99	156	0.57%	753	2.76%	26637	97.81%
88.00 - 88.99	171	0.63%	924	3.39%	26481	97.24%
87.00 - 87.99	171	0.63%	1095	4.02%	26310	96.61%
86.00 - 86.99	214	0.79%	1309	4.81%	26139	95.98%
85.00 - 85.99	214	0.79%	1523	5.59%	25925	95.19%
84.00 - 84.99	230	0.84%	1753	6.44%	25711	94.41%
83.00 - 83.99	251	0.92%	2004	7.36%	25481	93.56%
82.00 - 82.99	265	0.97%	2269	8.33%	25230	92.64%
81.00 - 81.99	272	1.00%	2541	9.33%	24965	91.67%
80.00 - 80.99	295	1.08%	2836	10.41%	24693	90.67%
79.00 - 79.99	300	1.10%	3136	11.52%	24398	89.59%
78.00 - 78.99	325	1.19%	3461	12.71%	24098	88.48%
77.00 - 77.99	291	1.07%	3752	13.78%	23773	87.29%
76.00 - 76.99	329	1.21%	4081	14.98%	23482	86.22%
75.00 - 75.99	313	1.15%	4394	16.13%	23153	85.02%
74.00 - 74.99	323	1.19%	4717	17.32%	22840	83.87%
73.00 - 73.99	321	1.18%	5038	18.50%	22517	82.68%
72.00 - 72.99	352	1.29%	5390	19.79%	22196	81.50%
71.00 - 71.99	339	1.24%	5729	21.04%	21844	80.21%
70.00 - 70.99	350	1.29%	6079	22.32%	21505	78.96%
69.00 - 69.99	330	1.21%	6409	23.53%	21155	77.68%
68.00 - 68.99	358	1.31%	6767	24.85%	20825	76.47%
67.00 - 67.99	335	1.23%	7102	26.08%	20467	75.15%
66.00 - 66.99	377	1.38%	7479	27.46%	20132	73.92%
65.00 - 65.99	394	1.45%	7873	28.91%	19755	72.54%
64.00 - 64.99	359	1.32%	8232	30.23%	19361	71.09%
63.00 - 63.99	321	1.18%	8553	31.41%	19002	69.77%
62.00 - 62.99	333	1.22%	8886	32.63%	18681	68.59%
61.00 - 61.99	368	1.35%	9254	33.98%	18348	67.37%
60.00 - 60.99	376	1.38%	9630	35.36%	17980	66.02%
59.00 - 59.99	328	1.20%	9958	36.56%	17604	64.64%
58.00 - 58.99	355	1.30%	10313	37.87%	17276	63.44%
57.00 - 57.99	330	1.21%	10643	39.08%	16921	62.13%
56.00 - 56.99	365	1.34%	11008	40.42%	16591	60.92%
55.00 - 55.99	368	1.35%	11376	41.77%	16226	59.58%
54.00 - 54.99	394	1.45%	11770	43.22%	15858	58.23%
53.00 - 53.99	361	1.33%	12131	44.54%	15464	56.78%
52.00 - 52.99	359	1.32%	12490	45.86%	15103	55.46%

51.00 - 51.99	387	1.42%	12877	47.28%	14744	54.14%
50.00 - 50.99	390	1.43%	13267	48.71%	14357	52.72%
49.00 - 49.99	409	1.50%	13676	50.22%	13967	51.29%
48.00 - 48.99	330	1.21%	14006	51.43%	13558	49.78%
47.00 - 47.99	340	1.25%	14346	52.68%	13228	48.57%
46.00 - 46.99	364	1.34%	14710	54.01%	12888	47.32%
45.00 - 45.99	384	1.41%	15094	55.42%	12524	45.99%
44.00 - 44.99	414	1.52%	15508	56.94%	12140	44.58%
43.00 - 43.99	382	1.40%	15890	58.35%	11726	43.06%
42.00 - 42.99	388	1.42%	16278	59.77%	11344	41.65%
41.00 - 41.99	436	1.60%	16714	61.37%	10956	40.23%
40.00 - 40.99	378	1.39%	17092	62.76%	10520	38.63%
39.00 - 39.99	434	1.59%	17526	64.35%	10142	37.24%
38.00 - 38.99	401	1.47%	17927	65.83%	9708	35.65%
37.00 - 37.99	409	1.50%	18336	67.33%	9307	34.17%
36.00 - 36.99	396	1.45%	18732	68.78%	8898	32.67%
35.00 - 35.99	421	1.55%	19153	70.33%	8502	31.22%
34.00 - 34.99	422	1.55%	19575	71.88%	8081	29.67%
33.00 - 33.99	450	1.65%	20025	73.53%	7659	28.12%
32.00 - 32.99	422	1.55%	20447	75.08%	7209	26.47%
31.00 - 31.99	430	1.58%	20877	76.66%	6787	24.92%
30.00 - 30.99	465	1.71%	21342	78.37%	6357	23.34%
29.00 - 29.99	435	1.60%	21777	79.96%	5892	21.63%
28.00 - 28.99	441	1.62%	22218	81.58%	5457	20.04%
27.00 - 27.99	473	1.74%	22691	83.32%	5016	18.42%
26.00 - 26.99	374	1.37%	23065	84.69%	4543	16.68%
25.00 - 25.99	417	1.53%	23482	86.22%	4169	15.31%
24.00 - 24.99	408	1.50%	23890	87.72%	3752	13.78%
23.00 - 23.99	365	1.34%	24255	89.06%	3344	12.28%
22.00 - 22.99	367	1.35%	24622	90.41%	2979	10.94%
21.00 - 21.99	396	1.45%	25018	91.86%	2612	9.59%
20.00 - 20.99	340	1.25%	25358	93.11%	2216	8.14%
19.00 - 19.99	309	1.13%	25667	94.25%	1876	6.89%
18.00 - 18.99	281	1.03%	25948	95.28%	1567	5.75%
17.00 - 17.99	282	1.04%	26230	96.31%	1286	4.72%
16.00 - 16.99	183	0.67%	26413	96.99%	1004	3.69%
15.00 - 15.99	191	0.70%	26604	97.69%	821	3.01%
14.00 - 14.99	187	0.69%	26791	98.37%	630	2.31%
13.00 - 13.99	111	0.41%	26902	98.78%	443	1.63%
12.00 - 12.99	82	0.30%	26984	99.08%	332	1.22%
11.00 - 11.99	88	0.32%	27072	99.41%	250	0.92%
10.00 - 10.99	64	0.24%	27136	99.64%	162	0.59%
9.00 - 9.99	32	0.12%	27168	99.76%	98	0.36%
8.00 - 8.99	24	0.09%	27192	99.85%	66	0.24%
7.00 - 7.99	18	0.07%	27210	99.91%	42	0.15%
6.00 - 6.99	10	0.04%	27220	99.95%	24	0.09%
5.00 - 5.99	9	0.03%	27229	99.98%	14	0.05%
4.00 - 4.99	1	0.00%	27230	99.99%	5	0.02%
3.00 - 3.99	2	0.01%	27232	99.99%	4	0.01%
2.00 - 2.99	1	0.00%	27233	100.00%	2	0.01%
1.00 - 1.99	0	0.00%	27233	100.00%	1	0.00%
0.00 - 0.99	1	0.00%	27234	100.00%	1	0.00%
缺考	1386					

102 年指定科目考試生物科成績人數累計表

分　　　數	人　　數	百 分 比	自高分往低分累計		自低分往高分累計	
			累計人數	累計百分比	累計人數	累計百分比
100.00	2	0.01%	2	0.01%	18363	100.00%
99.00 - 99.99	4	0.02%	6	0.03%	18361	99.99%
98.00 - 98.99	16	0.09%	22	0.12%	18357	99.97%
97.00 - 97.99	57	0.31%	79	0.43%	18341	99.88%
96.00 - 96.99	92	0.50%	171	0.93%	18284	99.57%
95.00 - 95.99	193	1.05%	364	1.98%	18192	99.07%
94.00 - 94.99	285	1.55%	649	3.53%	17999	98.02%
93.00 - 93.99	338	1.84%	987	5.37%	17714	96.47%
92.00 - 92.99	375	2.04%	1362	7.42%	17376	94.63%
91.00 - 91.99	395	2.15%	1757	9.57%	17001	92.58%
90.00 - 90.99	419	2.28%	2176	11.85%	16606	90.43%
89.00 - 89.99	397	2.16%	2573	14.01%	16187	88.15%
88.00 - 88.99	447	2.43%	3020	16.45%	15790	85.99%
87.00 - 87.99	423	2.30%	3443	18.75%	15343	83.55%
86.00 - 86.99	426	2.32%	3869	21.07%	14920	81.25%
85.00 - 85.99	452	2.46%	4321	23.53%	14494	78.93%
84.00 - 84.99	426	2.32%	4747	25.85%	14042	76.47%
83.00 - 83.99	411	2.24%	5158	28.09%	13616	74.15%
82.00 - 82.99	431	2.35%	5589	30.44%	13205	71.91%
81.00 - 81.99	414	2.25%	6003	32.69%	12774	69.56%
80.00 - 80.99	393	2.14%	6396	34.83%	12360	67.31%
79.00 - 79.99	381	2.07%	6777	36.91%	11967	65.17%
78.00 - 78.99	336	1.83%	7113	38.74%	11586	63.09%
77.00 - 77.99	366	1.99%	7479	40.73%	11250	61.26%
76.00 - 76.99	342	1.86%	7821	42.59%	10884	59.27%
75.00 - 75.99	364	1.98%	8185	44.57%	10542	57.41%
74.00 - 74.99	338	1.84%	8523	46.41%	10178	55.43%
73.00 - 73.99	316	1.72%	8839	48.13%	9840	53.59%
72.00 - 72.99	335	1.82%	9174	49.96%	9524	51.87%
71.00 - 71.99	306	1.67%	9480	51.63%	9189	50.04%
70.00 - 70.99	307	1.67%	9787	53.30%	8883	48.37%
69.00 - 69.99	338	1.84%	10125	55.14%	8576	46.70%
68.00 - 68.99	314	1.71%	10439	56.85%	8238	44.86%
67.00 - 67.99	307	1.67%	10746	58.52%	7924	43.15%
66.00 - 66.99	272	1.48%	11018	60.00%	7617	41.48%
65.00 - 65.99	292	1.59%	11310	61.59%	7345	40.00%
64.00 - 64.99	257	1.40%	11567	62.99%	7053	38.41%
63.00 - 63.99	274	1.49%	11841	64.48%	6796	37.01%
62.00 - 62.99	287	1.56%	12128	66.05%	6522	35.52%
61.00 - 61.99	272	1.48%	12400	67.53%	6235	33.95%
60.00 - 60.99	272	1.48%	12672	69.01%	5963	32.47%
59.00 - 59.99	250	1.36%	12922	70.37%	5691	30.99%
58.00 - 58.99	263	1.43%	13185	71.80%	5441	29.63%
57.00 - 57.99	255	1.39%	13440	73.19%	5178	28.20%
56.00 - 56.99	249	1.36%	13689	74.55%	4923	26.81%
55.00 - 55.99	257	1.40%	13946	75.95%	4674	25.45%
54.00 - 54.99	251	1.37%	14197	77.31%	4417	24.05%
53.00 - 53.99	221	1.20%	14418	78.52%	4166	22.69%
52.00 - 52.99	226	1.23%	14644	79.75%	3945	21.48%

51.00 - 51.99	230	1.25%	14874	81.00%	3719	20.25%
50.00 - 50.99	213	1.16%	15087	82.16%	3489	19.00%
49.00 - 49.99	213	1.16%	15300	83.32%	3276	17.84%
48.00 - 48.99	197	1.07%	15497	84.39%	3063	16.68%
47.00 - 47.99	198	1.08%	15695	85.47%	2866	15.61%
46.00 - 46.99	155	0.84%	15850	86.31%	2668	14.53%
45.00 - 45.99	182	0.99%	16032	87.31%	2513	13.69%
44.00 - 44.99	155	0.84%	16187	88.15%	2331	12.69%
43.00 - 43.99	129	0.70%	16316	88.85%	2176	11.85%
42.00 - 42.99	153	0.83%	16469	89.69%	2047	11.15%
41.00 - 41.99	133	0.72%	16602	90.41%	1894	10.31%
40.00 - 40.99	132	0.72%	16734	91.13%	1761	9.59%
39.00 - 39.99	117	0.64%	16851	91.77%	1629	8.87%
38.00 - 38.99	132	0.72%	16983	92.48%	1512	8.23%
37.00 - 37.99	117	0.64%	17100	93.12%	1380	7.52%
36.00 - 36.99	120	0.65%	17220	93.78%	1263	6.88%
35.00 - 35.99	85	0.46%	17305	94.24%	1143	6.22%
34.00 - 34.99	93	0.51%	17398	94.74%	1058	5.76%
33.00 - 33.99	66	0.36%	17464	95.10%	965	5.26%
32.00 - 32.99	78	0.42%	17542	95.53%	899	4.90%
31.00 - 31.99	74	0.40%	17616	95.93%	821	4.47%
30.00 - 30.99	59	0.32%	17675	96.25%	747	4.07%
29.00 - 29.99	69	0.38%	17744	96.63%	688	3.75%
28.00 - 28.99	57	0.31%	17801	96.94%	619	3.37%
27.00 - 27.99	63	0.34%	17864	97.28%	562	3.06%
26.00 - 26.99	51	0.28%	17915	97.56%	499	2.72%
25.00 - 25.99	55	0.30%	17970	97.86%	448	2.44%
24.00 - 24.99	66	0.36%	18036	98.22%	393	2.14%
23.00 - 23.99	35	0.19%	18071	98.41%	327	1.78%
22.00 - 22.99	41	0.22%	18112	98.63%	292	1.59%
21.00 - 21.99	24	0.13%	18136	98.76%	251	1.37%
20.00 - 20.99	44	0.24%	18180	99.00%	227	1.24%
19.00 - 19.99	34	0.19%	18214	99.19%	183	1.00%
18.00 - 18.99	25	0.14%	18239	99.32%	149	0.81%
17.00 - 17.99	26	0.14%	18265	99.47%	124	0.68%
16.00 - 16.99	28	0.15%	18293	99.62%	98	0.53%
15.00 - 15.99	16	0.09%	18309	99.71%	70	0.38%
14.00 - 14.99	14	0.08%	18323	99.78%	54	0.29%
13.00 - 13.99	8	0.04%	18331	99.83%	40	0.22%
12.00 - 12.99	14	0.08%	18345	99.90%	32	0.17%
11.00 - 11.99	9	0.05%	18354	99.95%	18	0.10%
10.00 - 10.99	4	0.02%	18358	99.97%	9	0.05%
9.00 - 9.99	1	0.01%	18359	99.98%	5	0.03%
8.00 - 8.99	2	0.01%	18361	99.99%	4	0.02%
7.00 - 7.99	1	0.01%	18362	99.99%	2	0.01%
6.00 - 6.99	1	0.01%	18363	100.00%	1	0.01%
5.00 - 5.99	0	0.00%	18363	100.00%	0	0.00%
4.00 - 4.99	0	0.00%	18363	100.00%	0	0.00%
3.00 - 3.99	0	0.00%	18363	100.00%	0	0.00%
2.00 - 2.99	0	0.00%	18363	100.00%	0	0.00%
1.00 - 1.99	0	0.00%	18363	100.00%	0	0.00%
0.00 - 0.99	0	0.00%	18363	100.00%	0	0.00%
缺考	1280					

102 年指定科目考試國文科成績人數累計表

分　　數	人　　數	百分比	自高分往低分累計		自低分往高分累計	
			累計人數	累計百分比	累計人數	累計百分比
100.00	0	0.00%	0	0.00%	62967	100.00%
99.00 - 99.99	0	0.00%	0	0.00%	62967	100.00%
98.00 - 98.99	0	0.00%	0	0.00%	62967	100.00%
97.00 - 97.99	0	0.00%	0	0.00%	62967	100.00%
96.00 - 96.99	0	0.00%	0	0.00%	62967	100.00%
95.00 - 95.99	0	0.00%	0	0.00%	62967	100.00%
94.00 - 94.99	1	0.00%	1	0.00%	62967	100.00%
93.00 - 93.99	1	0.00%	2	0.00%	62966	100.00%
92.00 - 92.99	2	0.00%	4	0.01%	62965	100.00%
91.00 - 91.99	13	0.02%	17	0.03%	62963	99.99%
90.00 - 90.99	16	0.03%	33	0.05%	62950	99.97%
89.00 - 89.99	23	0.04%	56	0.09%	62934	99.95%
88.00 - 88.99	38	0.06%	94	0.15%	62911	99.91%
87.00 - 87.99	53	0.08%	147	0.23%	62873	99.85%
86.00 - 86.99	89	0.14%	236	0.37%	62820	99.77%
85.00 - 85.99	108	0.17%	344	0.55%	62731	99.63%
84.00 - 84.99	152	0.24%	496	0.79%	62623	99.45%
83.00 - 83.99	179	0.28%	675	1.07%	62471	99.21%
82.00 - 82.99	257	0.41%	932	1.48%	62292	98.93%
81.00 - 81.99	343	0.54%	1275	2.02%	62035	98.52%
80.00 - 80.99	441	0.70%	1716	2.73%	61692	97.98%
79.00 - 79.99	535	0.85%	2251	3.57%	61251	97.27%
78.00 - 78.99	651	1.03%	2902	4.61%	60716	96.43%
77.00 - 77.99	794	1.26%	3696	5.87%	60065	95.39%
76.00 - 76.99	868	1.38%	4564	7.25%	59271	94.13%
75.00 - 75.99	962	1.53%	5526	8.78%	58403	92.75%
74.00 - 74.99	1105	1.75%	6631	10.53%	57441	91.22%
73.00 - 73.99	1175	1.87%	7806	12.40%	56336	89.47%
72.00 - 72.99	1329	2.11%	9135	14.51%	55161	87.60%
71.00 - 71.99	1478	2.35%	10613	16.85%	53832	85.49%
70.00 - 70.99	1463	2.32%	12076	19.18%	52354	83.15%
69.00 - 69.99	1621	2.57%	13697	21.75%	50891	80.82%
68.00 - 68.99	1613	2.56%	15310	24.31%	49270	78.25%
67.00 - 67.99	1737	2.76%	17047	27.07%	47657	75.69%
66.00 - 66.99	1780	2.83%	18827	29.90%	45920	72.93%
65.00 - 65.99	1810	2.87%	20637	32.77%	44140	70.10%
64.00 - 64.99	1843	2.93%	22480	35.70%	42330	67.23%
63.00 - 63.99	1838	2.92%	24318	38.62%	40487	64.30%
62.00 - 62.99	1904	3.02%	26222	41.64%	38649	61.38%
61.00 - 61.99	1871	2.97%	28093	44.62%	36745	58.36%
60.00 - 60.99	1891	3.00%	29984	47.62%	34874	55.38%
59.00 - 59.99	1881	2.99%	31865	50.61%	32983	52.38%
58.00 - 58.99	1867	2.97%	33732	53.57%	31102	49.39%
57.00 - 57.99	1838	2.92%	35570	56.49%	29235	46.43%
56.00 - 56.99	1743	2.77%	37313	59.26%	27397	43.51%
55.00 - 55.99	1744	2.77%	39057	62.03%	25654	40.74%
54.00 - 54.99	1657	2.63%	40714	64.66%	23910	37.97%
53.00 - 53.99	1662	2.64%	42376	67.30%	22253	35.34%
52.00 - 52.99	1554	2.47%	43930	69.77%	20591	32.70%

51.00 - 51.99	1510	2.40%	45440	72.16%	19037	30.23%
50.00 - 50.99	1490	2.37%	46930	74.53%	17527	27.84%
49.00 - 49.99	1369	2.17%	48299	76.71%	16037	25.47%
48.00 - 48.99	1212	1.92%	49511	78.63%	14668	23.29%
47.00 - 47.99	1256	1.99%	50767	80.62%	13456	21.37%
46.00 - 46.99	1176	1.87%	51943	82.49%	12200	19.38%
45.00 - 45.99	1064	1.69%	53007	84.18%	11024	17.51%
44.00 - 44.99	972	1.54%	53979	85.73%	9960	15.82%
43.00 - 43.99	895	1.42%	54874	87.15%	8988	14.27%
42.00 - 42.99	842	1.34%	55716	88.48%	8093	12.85%
41.00 - 41.99	783	1.24%	56499	89.73%	7251	11.52%
40.00 - 40.99	685	1.09%	57184	90.82%	6468	10.27%
39.00 - 39.99	624	0.99%	57808	91.81%	5783	9.18%
38.00 - 38.99	562	0.89%	58370	92.70%	5159	8.19%
37.00 - 37.99	487	0.77%	58857	93.47%	4597	7.30%
36.00 - 36.99	485	0.77%	59342	94.24%	4110	6.53%
35.00 - 35.99	466	0.74%	59808	94.98%	3625	5.76%
34.00 - 34.99	389	0.62%	60197	95.60%	3159	5.02%
33.00 - 33.99	340	0.54%	60537	96.14%	2770	4.40%
32.00 - 32.99	318	0.51%	60855	96.65%	2430	3.86%
31.00 - 31.99	292	0.46%	61147	97.11%	2112	3.35%
30.00 - 30.99	222	0.35%	61369	97.46%	1820	2.89%
29.00 - 29.99	199	0.32%	61568	97.78%	1598	2.54%
28.00 - 28.99	183	0.29%	61751	98.07%	1399	2.22%
27.00 - 27.99	163	0.26%	61914	98.33%	1216	1.93%
26.00 - 26.99	150	0.24%	62064	98.57%	1053	1.67%
25.00 - 25.99	132	0.21%	62196	98.78%	903	1.43%
24.00 - 24.99	112	0.18%	62308	98.95%	771	1.22%
23.00 - 23.99	93	0.15%	62401	99.10%	659	1.05%
22.00 - 22.99	72	0.11%	62473	99.22%	566	0.90%
21.00 - 21.99	78	0.12%	62551	99.34%	494	0.78%
20.00 - 20.99	68	0.11%	62619	99.45%	416	0.66%
19.00 - 19.99	58	0.09%	62677	99.54%	348	0.55%
18.00 - 18.99	50	0.08%	62727	99.62%	290	0.46%
17.00 - 17.99	42	0.07%	62769	99.69%	240	0.38%
16.00 - 16.99	45	0.07%	62814	99.76%	198	0.31%
15.00 - 15.99	30	0.05%	62844	99.80%	153	0.24%
14.00 - 14.99	28	0.04%	62872	99.85%	123	0.20%
13.00 - 13.99	16	0.03%	62888	99.87%	95	0.15%
12.00 - 12.99	15	0.02%	62903	99.90%	79	0.13%
11.00 - 11.99	20	0.03%	62923	99.93%	64	0.10%
10.00 - 10.99	13	0.02%	62936	99.95%	44	0.07%
9.00 - 9.99	9	0.01%	62945	99.97%	31	0.05%
8.00 - 8.99	4	0.01%	62949	99.97%	22	0.03%
7.00 - 7.99	5	0.01%	62954	99.98%	18	0.03%
6.00 - 6.99	3	0.00%	62957	99.98%	13	0.02%
5.00 - 5.99	1	0.00%	62958	99.99%	10	0.02%
4.00 - 4.99	2	0.00%	62960	99.99%	9	0.01%
3.00 - 3.99	1	0.00%	62961	99.99%	7	0.01%
2.00 - 2.99	2	0.00%	62963	99.99%	6	0.01%
1.00 - 1.99	1	0.00%	62964	100.00%	4	0.01%
0.00 - 0.99	3	0.00%	62967	100.00%	3	0.00%
缺考	2970